Studia Fennica
Folkloristica 11

THE FINNISH LITERATURE SOCIETY (SKS) was founded in 1831 and has, from the very beginning, engaged in publishing operations. It nowadays publishes literature in the fields of ethnology and folkloristics, linguistics, literary research and cultural history.

The first volume of the Studia Fennica series appeared in 1933. Since 1992, the series has been divided into three thematic subseries: Ethnologica, Folkloristica and Linguistica. Two additional subseries were formed in 2002, Historica and Litteraria. The subseries Anthropologica was formed in 2007.

In addition to its publishing activities, the Finnish Literature Society maintains research activities and infrastructures, an archive containing folklore and literary collections, a research library and promotes Finnish literature abroad.

Laura Stark

Peasants, Pilgrims, and Sacred Promises

Ritual and the Supernatural in Orthodox Karelian Folk Religion

Finnish Literature Society • Helsinki

Studia Fennica Folkloristica 11

The publication has undergone a peer review.

VERTAISARVIOITU
KOLLEGIALT GRANSKAD
PEER-REVIEWED
www.tsv.fi/tunnus

The open access publication of this volume has received part funding via
Helsinki University Library.

A digital edition of a printed book first published in 2002 by the Finnish Literature Society.
Cover Design: Timo Numminen
EPUB: eLibris Media Oy

ISBN 978-951-746-366-9 (Print)
ISBN 978-951-746-578-6 (PDF)
ISBN 978-952-222-766-9 (EPUB)

ISSN 0085-6835 (Studia Fennica)
ISSN 1235-1946 (Studia Fennica Folkloristica)

DOI: http://dx.doi.org/10.21435/sff.11

A free open access version of the book is available at http://dx.doi.
org/10.21435/sff.11 or by scanning this QR code with your mobile device.

Contents

Preface and acknowledgments   7

Notes on translation and referencing of texts   9

Introduction   11
    Background of this study   11
    Source materials and themes   12
    Syncretism in Orthodox Karelian folk religion   14
    Comparing different modes of ritual activity   15
    Structure, agency and voice   16
    Remarks on the demarcation of the research focus   17

Folk religion and the sacred   20
    The concept of the sacred   20
    The nature of ritual   24
    Folk religion – some defining characteristics   28

Folk religion in Orthodox Karelia 34
    Prior research and historical overview   34
    Reciprocity and exchange in Orthodox Karelian folk religion   39
    Pre-Christian beliefs: other worlds and *väki*-force   42
    Sacred agents   50
    Pilgrimage and monasteries   54
    Types of ritual examined in this study   60
    The problem of folk religion's fuzzy taxonomies   62
    Two ritual complexes: sacred boundaries and sacred centers   70

I. SACRED BOUNDARIES – NATURE SPIRITS, SAINTS AND
THE DEAD IN THE MAINTENANCE OF CULTURAL ORDER

Boundaries against disorder   75

Illness: disorder in the human body   77
    Nenä illness and *proškenja* rites   77
    Moral orientations and the *tietäjä's* authority: aggressive versus
    conciliatory healing rites   81
    Divination: the role of the ritual specialist in the production of
    knowledge   88
    Proškenja rituals and the 'open' body   99
    Falling down and "standing up straight"   102
    The role of 'thinking' in *nenä* infection   105

Farm versus forest: disorder in the resource zone shared by humans and the forest   111
    Cattle and the forest spirit   111
    Offerings to saints in the village chapel   117
    Summer: a time of temporary truce with the forest   119
    Christianized nature spirits and forest saints in boundary maintenance   124
    The complex society of the "other side": forest as mirror for the human community   133

The poor and the dead: communal cohesion and disorder in the margins   138
    Incorporating the dead into the community of the living   138
    Memorial rites and the maintenance of socio-economic equilibrium   142

The nature/culture dichotomy in communal self-definition   147

II. SACRED CENTERS – CULTURAL IDEALS AND PILGRIMAGE TO MONASTERIES

The pilgrimage vow and sacred ideals   157
    A cult of traces   167
    Magnificent wealth versus ascetic poverty   169

III. THE DUAL SACRED – COMPARING THE TWO SACRED COMPLEXES

Competition, renunciation and territoriality: two complexes, different ethics   175
    Icons, illness and healing   177
    Sacred agents and access to strategic information   183
    Sacred time, place, and bodily movement   186

Conclusion: the sacred divided   192
    Appendix 1: Calendar of most common *praasniekka* festivals in traditional Orthodox Karelia   199
    Appendix 2: Map of Historical Comprising Orthodox Karelia 200

Notes   201

Abbreviations for archival source materials   218

Literature cited   218

Index   227

Preface and acknowledgments

This study is the outcome of an ongoing interest in ritual, magic, folk religion, and pilgrimage, and in it I bring together the topics of previous articles (Stark 1994, 1995, 1996; Stark-Arola 1997, 1998c, 1999a, 1999b) within the same framework of analysis. Because I feel that the material dealt with in this book deserves future attention and further study, I have sought to present it in a structured form that may lend itself more fruitfully to further analysis – that is, as a synchronic overview of cultural thought. Any study of the textual materials housed in the Finnish Literature Society Folklore Archives can only account for a small part of the phenomena and concepts depicted therein, no matter how strictly one delimits one's corpus of source texts. In fact, a single study can only begin to scratch the surface of the possible interpretations and theoretical approaches which can be applied to these materials. The present book is the result of an effort to approach a body of source materials which caught my interest some years ago but which for a long time was difficult to come to grips with analytically. The more closely I looked at this material, the more I became convinced that to separate pilgrimage from ritual activities surrounding the dead or nature spirits, or to consider Christian saints separately from nature spirits was to draw an artificial boundary where, at the lowest social levels of the semi-literate rural populace, the existence of such a boundary was questionable.

Bringing all of these spheres of belief and ritual together and looking more closely at their role in social categorization and cultural order was the logical next step, partly because the source materials themselves, as a product of the collection paradigm under which they were recorded, lend themselves more fruitfully to an investigation of social order and consensus than to an analysis of contestation and fragmentation or a diachronic analysis historical process and change. The notion of tradition inherent in the 19th- and early 20th-century collector's task presupposed an interest in collectively-held concepts and values, not to mention continuity and stability through time: collectors and informants tended to focus on the types of information that most people could recognize and agree upon easily, which had been transmitted from generation to generation within the community. Second, the uneven and unsystematic way in which the material was collected, with some periods and localities being over-represented and some not represented at all, makes it difficult if not impossible to trace out processes of change taking place in social behavior and cultural thought over time. My aim has therefore been to organize the material examined here within a framework which highlights its function and meaning from the folk or emic perspective, while at the same time suggesting its potential for the future application of other, possibly more dynamic, process- or practice-oriented theories; these are already touched upon in my discussions of body concepts, agency, the role of the ritual specialist, the interplay between narrative and ritual movement in pilgrimage, and the cognitive aspects involved in seeing objects and supranormal entities as anthro-pomorphic agents.

A number of persons have assisted me in the writing of this book. I wish to thank Irma-Riitta Järvinen for fruitful discussions on the topic of folk religion, Lauri Harvilahti and Elina Rahimova for their help in the translation of terms in Orthodox Karelian incantations, and Ilkka Pyysiäinen, Jyrki Pöysä, and Anna-Leena Siikala, each of whom read through earlier drafts of this manuscript and offered valuable criticism and advice. Teuvo Laitila and Senni Timonen have provided useful comments to earlier papers on the topics of this study; Senni Timonen also assisted in the translation of difficult terms. My thanks go to Eija Stark for compiling the Index, and I am grateful to the staff at the libraries and Folklore Archives of the Finnish Literature Society, and the Karelian Language Archives of the Research Institute for the Languages of Finland for their assistance in finding source materials. My early interest in pilgrimage was given encouragement at a meeting held by the Valamo research group led by Hannu Kilpeläinen, and my work in progress benefitted greatly from two conferences on folk religion organized by Prof. Ülo Valk and the Department of Estonian and Comparative Folklore at the University of Tartu. Satu Apo's work on dynamistic *väki* forces and Veikko Anttonen's work on the nature of the sacred and their support of my research interests have also been instrumental in the completion of this study. The research for this book was funded by the University of Helsinki research project *Ethnic Traditions and Societal Change: Minority Cultures in Northeastern Europe and Siberia* led by Anna-Leena Siikala.

Most anthropologists and folklorists working on the topic of folk religion can express their debt of thanks to living persons, those with whom they have lived in the field, who inspired them in their research or who provided useful information. As a researcher relying on archival material, my gratitude must be expressed, far too late in most cases, to the men and women who believed in the value of Karelian folk culture and dedicated their time and energy to collecting and recording it, often from their own neighbors and family, or even from their own memories. Starting in the latter half of the 19th century and continuing today, literally thousands of tradition enthusiasts in Finland and Karelia from all walks of life participated in one of the greatest folklore collection efforts in history, believing that someday the information they gathered on past lifeways would be of use to researchers. While I do not presume that my own study is worthy of their faith and foresight, I am grateful for their voices speaking across the decades, because what they have to say is far more evocative of a lost world of ritual knowledge than any model a researcher could construct.

Notes on translation and referencing of texts

All translations from the Finnish are mine unless otherwise stated. In the course of translating I have received linguistic assistance from several experts on Finnish language, Finnish and Karelian dialects, and Kalevala metre poetry at the University of Helsinki, the Finnish Literature Society and the Research Institute for the Languages of Finland. All mistakes are naturally my own.

Principles of translation

The translation of the folklore texts cited as examples in this study represents a compromise between preserving as closely as possible the original meaning of the text and making it comprehensible to English-language readers not necessarily familiar with the Finnish or Karelian languages. Grammatical and stylistic structures peculiar to Finnish and Karelian oral speech (mixed tenses, non-standard verbal forms, gaps and 'missing' information to be supplied by the listener from context, etc.) have been modified so as to be comprehensible to the English-language reader while still retaining as much of the original meaning as possible.

Referencing of folklore texts

The folklore texts presented as numbered examples in the main text are translations of original texts housed in the collections of either the (1) Finnish Literature Society Folklore Archives or the (2) Karelian Language Archives of the Research Institute for the Languages of Finland (KKTK– KKA). The references following the numbered examples contain the following information: first, the parish or locality in which the folklore item was collected; second, the year the folklore item was received by the Folklore Archives or the time period in which the item was recorded. The third item of information shown is the collector's or sender's name, sometimes followed by the collection series (KT, VK, KRK), as well as the number under which the folklore item is housed in manuscript form. The final entry, preceded by a dash (–), is the name of the informant, if different from the collector and if known, followed by other relevant information concerning the informant (occupation, marital status, year of birth, etc.). A key to abbreviations for collections is provided at the end of this book in the section *Literature Cited*.

Notes on pronunciation for terms from the original texts

The examples given below are rough approximations of corresponding sounds in English, and do not strive for precise phonetic accuracy.

Vowels
ä like a in cat
ö like German ö or French eu; like English e but with more strongly rounded lips
y like German ü or French u; like English i but with tightly rounded lips
u like oo in ooze (but lips more pursed)
o like ow in slow
e resembles e in set
a like a in father
i like ee in see

Consonants
š like sh in fish
h like h in hen
j like y in yes
g like g in gold
r like Spanish r (slightly rolled)

Dipthongs
ai like ai in aisle
ei like ey in hey
oi like oi in voice
ui like uy in Spanish muy
yi resembles ui in French suis
äi ä followed by a short i in the same syllable
öi ö followed by a short i in the same syllable
au resembles ow in cow
eu e followed by short u in the same syllable
iu i followed by short u in the same syllable
ou like o in so but more rounded
äy ä followed by a short y in the same syllable
öy ö followed by a short y in the same syllable
ie like ie in Spanish bien
uo like uo in Italian buona
yö y followed by a short ö in the same syllable

Word stress is always on the first syllable. Double vowels and double consonants indicate sounds of greater length. The sounds written kk or pp, for example, can be approximated in English by pronouncing the word pairs "black cat" or "top part" (note the pause before the release of breath). Long vowels are enunciated for slightly longer than short vowels, as in the English words (whose spelling does not reflect vowel length): bee (long) versus beetle (short).

Introduction

Background of this study

Orthodox Karelia lies across an important boundary running down the middle of Europe, which has historically divided the continent into two different cultural and religious zones. On one side lies Western Europe, with its history of Roman Catholic influence and legacy of Roman legal, administrative, and cultural influence. On the other side lies the cultures of Eastern or Orthodox Europe, heirs to the Byzantine Empire. This lengthy border, which extends from the Barents Sea in the North to the Balkans and Greece in the South, has been the site of intense cultural exchange and development, but also of social and religious tension. The culture and language of the Karelian people, whose area of settlement people straddles this boundary, are no exception, having been shaped by influences from all points of the compass. So too has the folklore scholarship surrounding Karelia been subject to conflicting interpretations regarding the region's significance for Finnish and Russian culture and heritage, and for the Karelians themselves (see Anttonen & Kuusi 1999:256; Anttonen 2000:262). Finnish folklorists have long seen Orthodox Karelia as one of the regions in which Finnic folk traditions were preserved the longest, the place from which answers to questions concerning the prehistory of the Finnish people could be sought. A significant portion of the folklore material that went into the compilation of the Finnish national epic, the *Kalevala*, was collected by Elias Lönnrot from Archangel Karelia. And in the early decades of the 20th century, many of the tradition bearers whose repertoires were seen to represent Finnish traditional song and folk poetry hailed from either Archangel or Ladoga Karelia (Haavio 1943). Particularly Ladoga Karelian singers toured and exhibited their talents at Finnish song festivals and folklore celebrations (e.g. Knuuttila 1986, Asplund 1994).

Yet at the same time that 19th- and early 20th-century Finnish collectors sought to harvest the rich tradition of Kalevala meter[1] folk poetry from Orthodox Karelia, they could not help noticing the presence of traditions and customs which they rightly recognized as influenced by both the Orthodox religion and Russian culture thus distinct from those practiced in

Lutheran Finland. These ritual practices centered on the village chapel and graveyard, and were directed at saints and the dead. Customs and rites directed at supernatural beings, especially nature spirits (forest spirit, water spirit, earth spirit, etc.), also showed strong influences from Orthodox Christianity. Finnish scholars recorded and analyzed these customs and rites because they found them to contain elements of older Finnic pre-Christian beliefs, but in many cases the syncretic nature of this material presented them with problems. In order to make Orthodox Karelian ritual beliefs and practices relevant for research paradigms of the late 19th- and early 20th-centuries, paradigms which included a focus on the origins and development of folklore and folk belief and the reconstruction of a unified Finnish or Balto-Finnic heritage, it was necessary to reduce them to units of ancient Finnic tradition which could be analyzed within the Historic-Geographic framework of the period. This meant first extracting the apparently ancient Balto-Finnic customs from the Orthodox shape and context in which they appeared, and teasing apart the different syncretic strands in order to trace out pre-Christian Finnish thought and its genetic linkages to the folk beliefs and practices of other Finnic and Finno-Ugric groups.

Such a separation of syncretically interwoven elements was not an easy task. Because belief proved easier than ritual to distill from its Orthodox influences, most holistic, systematic and theoretical approaches to popular religious phenomena tended to focus on *folk beliefs* (regarding the dead, nature spirits, etc.) rather than on ritual performances or ritual customs – although descriptive articles on individual rites (such as sacrificial festivals) did appear in the Finnish folkloristic literature from the 1890s onwards.

It is the aim of this book to attempt to supplement our knowledge of Orthodox Karelian rituals by focusing on popular religious ritual in the regions of Archangel (*Viena*) Karelia, Olonets (*Aunus*) Karelia, and Ladoga Karelia. This topic is approached through a holistic, systematic and meaning-oriented perspective, utilizing the linguistic expressions of cultural concepts recorded in textual descriptions of ritual activity from the late 19th- and early 20th-centuries.

Source materials and themes

The data for this study comes from over 1,000 texts covering a wide range of ritual-related themes, a lengthy time span of 140 years, and a broad regional perspective, encompassing material recorded from Ladoga Karelia, Olonets Karelia, and Archangel Karelia (see Map). These texts were recorded by Finnish and Karelian folklore collectors as well as 'writing folk informants'[2] during the period 1825–1966, and are currently housed in the Folklore Archives of the Finnish Literature Society, located in Helsinki. They represent a world view linked to rituals practiced over a broad geographical area during the 19th century and, to some extent (particularly in outlying areas), into the early decades of the 20th century as well. For this study I have brought together folklore materials hitherto considered to represent separate, even unrelated genres, and have analyzed them as a single corpus. The geographic breakdown of the texts is as follows: 518 texts from Ladoga Karelia, 301 from Archangel Karelia, and 249 from Olonets Karelia. In order to provide the reader with an overview of the topics addressed in this study, these texts have been loosely divided into thirteen categories on the basis of ritual purpose and the identity of the supernatural agent involved. As will be seen later on, however, a strict taxonomy of supranormal agents and ritual types is not possible nor even desirable when the aim of the study is to uncover the function and meaning of ritual activity, as is the case in this book.

The thirteen categories are as follows: rituals performed when letting cattle out to pasture in spring (287 texts); water-*nenä* and *proškenja* rituals directed at the water or water spirit(s) (148 texts); forest-*nenä* and *proškenja* rituals directed at the forest or forest spirit(s) (105 texts); Christian saints (95 texts); pilgrimage and monasteries (86 texts); ritual communication with the dead (61 texts); the forest-cover (*metsänpeitto*) and rituals to release farm animals trapped in it (56 texts); *cemetery-nenä* and *proškenja* rituals directed at the dead, graves or the cemetery (51 texts); divination and dreams (44 texts); specific references to vows using the term (*jeäksie/jeäksitteä*) (35 texts); earth-*nenä* and *proškenja* rituals directed at the earth or earth spirit(s) (35 texts); wind-*nenä* and *proškenja* rituals directed at the wind or wind spirit(s) (20 texts); and other *nenä*-illnesses, including those caused by holy icons (13), trees (3) and churches/chapels (9). These materials were selected because they all share a common denominator: they depict ritual relationships between humans and supranormal beings which were based on *reciprocity* and a *shared moral orientation*. The present book thus represents the first comprehensive study of traditional Orthodox Karelian materials dealing with exchange relations between humans and supranormal agents.

These categories of source materials give a superficial indication of the highly diverse spectrum of religious rites encompassed by the material in this book. While previously addressed as separate issues in Finnish studies of folk belief, folk medicine, calendrical rituals, etc., the comprehensive treatment of this corpus was delayed due to its tendency to fall through a number of epistemological gaps. First, the Kalevala meter incantations in this material do not speak to subjects which have traditionally been of interest to scholars on Kalevalaic epic, namely mythological and heroic themes and motifs. Second, the fact that this material encompasses a wide range of different rites for the healing of indeterminate illnesses has rendered it cumbersome for use in folk medicine research; and finally, the fact that many of its themes can be traced back to Russian Orthodox culture and religion has reduced its usefulness for Finnish scholars seeking to uncover the essence and roots of older *Finnic* thought from Karelian beliefs and rites. Moreover, the rituals dealt with here are characterized by seemingly random syncretic fusions, combinations of elements and influences deriving from official Orthodoxy, pre-Christian ethnic religion, and popular innovations and interpretations of Orthodox doctrine.

13

Syncretism in Orthodox Karelian folk religion

In the late 19th and early 20th centuries when these ritual descriptions were collected, the traditional cultures of Archangel, Olonets and Ladoga Karelia had, for nearly a millennium, been in a symbiotic relationship with Russian Orthodox Christianity. The Karelian culture left its mark on religious customs and art, and the legacy of Orthodoxy in turn deeply influenced Karelian traditions.[3] It is therefore not surprising that the rituals discussed in this book display numerous syncretic elements, fusions of official Christian teachings and pre-Christian ethnic folk belief.[4] Following the anthropological tradition of distinguishing between official and unofficial forms of religious belief and practice, I have designated both the religious rituals carried out by ordinary Karelian peasants[5] and the folk beliefs underlying them *folk religion*. Historically, Orthodox Karelian folk religious customs were seen by observers to be either misconstruals of official religious dogma based on ignorance within the lower stratum of agrarian society, or the 'corruption' of a purer form of ancient Finnic-Karelian ethnic belief following the introduction of Christianity to the area. The present study, on the other hand, approaches these syncretic fusions as functional adaptations to the needs of everyday life and social continuity. Admittedly, the seemingly unsystematic nature of these syncretisms does not make it easy for the researcher to identify formal patterns and regularities within it. Using as my basis the cross-cultural observations gleaned by anthropologists over the past decades regarding the ways in which folk or popular religion differs from official religion, I have sought to identify the common denominators which situate varied and seemingly unrelated religious phenomena within the same theoretical framework. These common denominators include: (1) the fact that both involved an ethic of exchange and reciprocity and (2) both were aimed at maintaining the integrity of body, farm, and community rather than seeking the salvation of the individual soul. The recognition of these common denominators shifts the focus away from the forms themselves, in all their colorful and seemingly chaotic variety, and towards the *function* of syncretic forms in social life. I strive to show that within Orthodox Karelian folk religion, Christian and pre-Christian forms of belief and practice were selectively adopted and moulded by social actors to produce a culturally intelligible and, to some degree, systematic whole. The questions raised by this study include: what elements were appropriated from Christianity to this folk religious system, and for what purpose? What social and cultural concerns were dealt with through folk religion at the level of everyday practice? What were the cultural schemas to which forms adopted into this syncretic system were made to conform? And finally, what were the motivating factors or catalysts in the system of reciprocity which maintained the ritual communication between humans and supernatural agents, and drove the system of exchange?

Comparing different modes of ritual activity

The primary aim of this book is the construction of a theoretical framework within which it is possible to analyze the folklore regarding two modes of ritual activity in Orthodox Karelia which have not yet been examined together as parts of a single phenomenon. These two modes of ritual activity are (1) communicative rites directed at nature spirits, the dead and local saints, and (2) pilgrimage to monasteries. Before I enter into a comparison between these two modes of ritual activity, an explanation of why I consider communicative rites directed at nature spirits, the dead and local saints to constitute a single mode of ritual activity in the first place may be in order. Rituals associated with the dead, nature spirits, and the saints represented in the holy icons of local village chapels all shared characteristics in common. Among these was the fact that in certain situations, humans engaged in two-way communication with these supranormal beings. Humans communicated to the dead, saints and nature spirits through symbolic gestures, offerings of gifts and verbal formulas, and these supranormal beings communicated to humans in turn through *dreams*. The most striking shared characteristic, however, was the belief that these entities could become easily "angered" and could cause supernatural illness through the infection of *väki*-force in the human body. Ritual communication was addressed to all of these entities, and gifts were given to them, in order to cure the illness.

It is perhaps not surprising that Orthodox Karelian rites directed at nature spirits, the dead, and local saints have never been examined within the same framework of analysis as pilgrimage to monasteries. At first glance, the two spheres of activity would seem to have little to do with each other. The two types of ritual activity were carried out in entirely different milieus, they were undertaken for different reasons, and they involved different types of activities – the former involved prayer and journeys on foot, while the latter utilized the offering of concrete gifts and use of Kalevala meter incantations. It is only when we delve deeper into the accounts of these ritual activities given by Orthodox Karelian informants, and begin from the 'lowest common denominators' shared by these two types of ritual activity that we begin to discern a pattern.

For example, both types of ritual activity (1) involved communication with sentient supernatural agents, and (2) were based on reciprocal relations of exchange with these agents. (3) This exchange was guided by collectively shared ethics and moral 'contracts', and (4) both types of ritual activity were responses to 'crisis' or 'disorder' in the life of the individual and/or community.

The recognition of these similarities in my research has led me to a consideration of the *differences* between the two modes of ritual activity, which could be expressed in the form of questions such as: what types of crisis or disorder were addressed within local rites versus pilgrimage? Why were nature spirits, the dead, and saints seen to infect humans with a supernatural illness while the holy men associated with monasteries were not? Similarly, why were holy icons *in local village chapels* seen to be able to infect with illness while holy icons *in monasteries* were not? Why did the *village chapels themselves* infect with supernatural illness? What does the fact that persons could be infected with this illness by just 'thinking' about it tell us about the cultural function of this explanatory illness schema? Why did Christian holy figures such as St. George and the Virgin Mary sometimes play the same role of as nature spirits in annual rites? Why were the spirits of the forest and water referred to as 'Christians' in ritual incantations? Why were the poor of the community given food during rituals intended to commemorate the dead? Why were the holy men associated with monasteries seen to be able to look into pilgrims' hearts and know their innermost secrets while nature spirits and the dead could not? These are just some of the questions that will be explored in the pages of this book.

Structure, agency and voice

In the pages which follow I undertake a structural mapping of two ritual complexes, their functions in social life and the way in which time, space, and cultural ideals were organized and perceived through them. I describe this structure as constituted through the motivated ritual and narrative behavior of individuals actors in everyday life, that is, I pay attention to individual choice in action while striving to explain how its result worked towards sustaining the social order. The present study therefore strives for a theoretical balance between agent and society. Unlike theorists of social structure such as Marcel Mauss and Claude Lévi-Strauss, whose theories saw individual interests and beliefs as largely determined by social forms and human agency thus reduced to a minor role, I argue that knowledgeable individuals acted strategically to serve their own interests (to alleviate disorder), and in doing so were aware of the importance of society's continuity for their own well-being.

Balancing between a structural model and the experiences of individual agents means that while this study traces out an analytic, etic model constructed by myself, I strive to give equal weight to the emic interpretations of informants, to their 'situated knowledges' grounded in experience (Haraway 1992:313) which are much closer to the subject matter at hand than is my own. In the interests of intellectual accountability, I provide numerous examples in order to let the 'voices' of the performers and narrators be heard, and to open up my own analysis to the scrutiny of the reader by supplying my source texts in English translation.

The voices of the informants in this study have gone through many levels of decontextualization, from the memory of the narrator, to written notes, a text in an archive, and finally as an example appearing in the context of the present study. The folklore texts used in this study are not, therefore, a direct reflection of cultural or traditional categories, beliefs, or attitudes. The material used in this study has already gone through one stage of 'interpretation' and 'filtering' by folk informants who selectively 'remembered' ritual knowledge, often adding their own commentary and evaluation to this knowledge. Informants chose to mention those ritual elements that they considered to be significant, not only within the emic cultural framework of their community, but also within the context of the informant's interests at the moment of recording, the questions asked by the collector, and the informant's relationship with the collecting archive.

And yet it is precisely because of this complex process of filtering that such texts are valuable clues to understanding older forms of knowledge and practice. For both the narrator and the collector in many cases, the social contexts of the incantations, ritual descriptions, narratives, and folk beliefs were so familiar and taken for granted that it was not considered necessary to verbalize them in the recorded descriptions. On the other hand, because of the cultural gap separating informant from collector, or collector from archive, some informants did not always assume shared knowledge with their imagined 'audience', but instead explained or provided vital background information. They anticipated questions and provided both emic classifications *and* etic explanations of those classifications when they consciously directed their texts at the collector, researcher, or archive as the primary audience. In reflecting on their own cultural knowledge and crafting a text that would be comprehensible to someone outside the folk tradition, informants thus actively and intentionally initiated a dialogue with 'outsiders' in order to work towards a jointly agreed-upon interpretation. I conceive of these descriptions as *key texts*, because they provide a means to decipher the codes used by informants and collectors alike in referring to a past, vanished world view. In the present study I have tried, where possible, to defer to the folk interpretation made in these key texts by using them as points of departure for my analysis.

Remarks on the demarcation of the research focus

The broad scope of this study carries with it certain shortcomings, most obviously that it gives a misleading impression of cultural and social uniformity across regions and even villages. Although my material consists of texts recorded in various Karelian languages (and their dialects), I do not wish to suggest that the villages in question were homogeneous in terms of language and ethnicity, or that speakers were necessarily monolingual. The high level of abstraction and generalization of my model is inevitable given the fact that my sources do not suffice over long stretches of space and time to study each region or village in detail and depth.

On the other hand, there are compensating advantages to this approach. In the study of Karelian folk religion, there exist a number of issues which are perhaps more fruitfully discussed at a level more general than that of village or region. These include activities such as pilgrimage, *proškenja* rituals and customs for honoring the dead, folk models of illness and supernatural sources of infection, the function of divination and dreams in everyday life and ideas concerning supernatural agents and their relations with humans. In Orthodox Karelia, such practices and beliefs display surprising similarities over large distances. A broad scope allows the researcher to discern patterns and schemas from a vantage point not accessible to individual members of the culture in question.

Several comments regarding my selection and interpretation of source materials must be stated at the outset. First, my corpus deals with beliefs, rites and practices associated with activities belonging to *farming and pastoralism* rather than *hunting and fishing*, activities which had their own ritual modes characterized by a different orientation to forest nature (cf. Ilomäki 1989; Tarkka 1994, 1998). These types of livelihood were not mutually exclusive: households in Orthodox Karelian rural communities were almost always engaged in both farming/animal husbandry *and* hunting/fishing/trapping modes of subsistence. In the context of both modes of subsistence, the boundary between forest nature and the human sphere (=farm, village) was addressed through ritual means (Tarkka 1994), and these rituals were in both cases characterized by communication and gift-giving between human and forest, and guided by moral codes of behavior. Beyond this, however, rituals performed in the context of hunting show distinct differences from those performed in cattle husbandry. Because hunters regularly undertook journeys deep into the forest from which they then returned home, they were engaged in particular rites of passage and ritual purification which were not undertaken by those occupied in farming or herding (cf. ibid:60). Persons engaged in cattle husbandry appear to have utilized incantation rites adopting a more hostile or cautious attitude toward the forest than did the hunter hoping for a good catch. Lotte Tarkka (1994, 1998) has shown that in Archangel Karelia the hunter's view of the forest as expressed through magic incantations was positive, even erotically charged, while for peasant-pastoralists the forest represented the threatening Other.

Second, my study does not address the content of funerary laments, sacred religious legends or epic folk poems on Marian themes, even though these genres can be said to fall within the domain of folk or popular religion. Because the function of these oral traditions was different from that of rituals used to communicate with supernatural agents, they illuminate concepts of the sacred from a different perspective than that of the rituals studied here.[6] Also, it must be pointed out that my source data do not include materials on Karelian folklore and folk life housed at the archives of the Institute of Linguistics, Literature and History, Karelian Research Center, Russian Academy of Sciences, in Petrozavodsk. While I enthusiastically acknowledge the value of these archives, to have undertaken such an examination of their materials would have prolonged this study unduly.

Finally, the present study does not explicitly address the culture of the Russian Orthodox sect of Old Believers or their influence on Orthodox Karelian folk religion. While the influence of Old Believers upon the local culture of Orthodox Karelia, especially Archangel Karelia, was in some places considerable (see Pentikäinen 1999), explicit references to their beliefs and practices do not show up in the material examined here. This is perhaps not surprising if we consider the fact that in Archangel Karelia, most of the folk poetry and folklore collected by Finnish collectors in the 19th century came from the so-called "rune-singing" villages in which Kalevala meter folk poetry was still performed, and Old Believers from the stricter sects did not, for the most part, live in these villages (see Virtanen 1942:392–393). The Karelian informants whose ritual descriptions, incantations and folk beliefs are the topic of this study resided in communities which had frequent contact with Finland, and displayed a much more lenient attitude toward outsiders and their religious customs than did villages further to the east (ibid.).

Another reason for the lack of explicit reference to the Old Belief in my material may be that the Old Believer culture was remarkable for its conservation of archaic ritual details and its strict adherence to a standard of authenticity in its customs (Pentikäinen 1999). The ritual material examined here, on the other hand, deals primarily with *communication* between humans and supernatural beings in which *simplicity, economy,* and *clarity of expression* were paramount. This material is therefore conspicuously lacking in conservative tendencies. It is my view that the avoidance of archaic elements was deliberate: the purpose of these rituals was to communicate, in a straightforward fashion, simple symbols and moral principles that would be understood not only by the healer/performer but also by the patient and the supernatural being addressed in the ritual. For example, many of the archaisms and mythical elements found in the verbal formulas and ritual performances of the *tietäjä*[7] institution were not utilized in Orthodox Karelian folk religious ritual as it is defined here. Such archaisms include shamanism-derived models of helper-spirits, animal spirits, and the topography of the other world which were part of the expertise of the *tietäjä* (cf. Siikala 1992). Just as folk religious ritual made less use of those forms deriving from earlier cultural periods which are common to the tradition of magic rites (cf. ibid.), it similarly tended to avoid references to the mystic or antiquated elements in Russian Orthodoxy which were a vital part of Old Believer ritualism.

Folk religion and the sacred

The concept of the sacred

This study, which maps out a hypothetical model of reciprocity between humans and supranormal beings, takes its inspiration from the theory of social exchange introduced by Marcel Mauss (1872–1950) in his work *Essai sur le don* (*The Gift: The Form and Functions of Exchange in Archaic Societies*). In *The Gift*, Mauss traces out the idea that mutual gift giving and exchange in social relations, and particularly the *deferred* nature of such reciprocity, can be seen as the basis for all social life and relations (ibid., see also Bourdieu 1990:112). As later scholars have made clear, exchange relations do not only create the ties that bind, they are also tactical moves in a game, consensus on a loose code of 'rules'. It is this consensus which allows social actors to participate in meaningful and mutually beneficial schemes of action (cf. Mayol 1998:15–26) and jostle for social advantage, thus creating the hierarchical relations that make a human aggregation a society. The way in which exchange gives rise to social ranking and symbolic surplus is summed up by Helmuth Berking (1999:40):

> The game of giving, like the game of honour, is not at all a zero sum game operating through reciprocity cycles; it is the modus operandi of social differentiation. In particular, the modulation of time structures, the free shaping of the time between gift and return gift, offers opportunities for the realization of a symbolic surplus; at the same time, it is the decisive gateway for the transformation of relations centred on reciprocity into ones of personal dependency.

Mauss argued that reciprocity in archaic societies was a total social fact which organized not only all manner of relations among human groups and their members, but also relations with the supernatural and divine as well: "[g]ifts to humans and to the gods also serve the purpose of buying peace between them both" (1990:17). Emile Durkheim and Marcel Mauss had already argued in their *Primitive Classification* (1903) that relationships between humans and the supernatural were modelled on relationships among persons, specifically that between the individual and the community.[8] This observation still has currency for cultural researchers today. Berking (1999:34), for example, stresses the importance of reciprocity as the basis for relationships between humans and supranormal entities on several levels:

> As the organizational principle of social cohesion par excellence, gift-exchange cannot simply be equated with the reproduction cycle of the social community. Rather, it encompasses both the living and the dead, the nature that gives everything and to which one owes so much, the supernatural forces and gods to which one sacrifices a little in order to obtain a lot.

This topic has been illuminated from another vantage point by theorists in comparative religion taking a cognitive approach. Pascal Boyer (forthcoming), for example, argues that humans have inherited, through selective evolutionary pressures (predation and social interaction), mental systems adapted for seeing agents which do not empirically exist, and for interacting with those agents as if they conducted themselves according to the same social strategies as do humans (see also Lawson & McCauley 1990; Guthrie 1993; Barrett 2000). My study takes these observations one step further and argues that when human beings apply moral templates to supranormal agents, the resulting moral actions and their arenas become *sacralized*. In other words, when mutual agreement on rules in human social life are extended to participants from the 'other world', these relations *simultaneously construct the level of the 'sacred'*. The aim of this book is thus the explication of a *moral system* shared by humans and supranormal beings in Orthodox Karelia. By virtue of their participation in this moral system, the supranormal beings involved became *sacred agents*.

In the context of the present discussion, I provide a dual definition for the concept of **sacred** in traditional and popular forms of religion. In both parts of this definition, the sacred is seen as a process or a 'doing' which promotes cultural images of social continuity and coherence. It does this by organizing 1) internal social relationships, 2) society's relationship to other, 'external' entities, 3) socially-relevant space and time, and 4) socially-relevant values and ideals. This, then, is what the concept of the sacred *does*, its function. But what, more specifically, *is* the sacred? How does it arise?

First of all, the sacred can be seen as the product of drawing cultural boundaries between things considered 'pure' and things considered 'impure'. Mary Douglas (1966, 1975) was the first to explicitly theorize the importance of purity and pollution for systems and rules of classification and the threat of social disturbance or breakdown. For Douglas, concepts of purity and impurity are relative, since pollution ideas depend on cultural classifications which are of course themselves relative: what may be polluting in one case may not be in another. In the present book, the terms 'pure' and 'impure' refer more specifically to, on the one hand, the value of potential growth, life, and reproduction for both society and the individual, versus disorder, depletion, danger, anomaly, those things threatening social integrity and continuity on the other. In his study of symbolic concepts connected to the sacred, Veikko Anttonen clarifies how the positive or 'right-hand' aspect of the sacred (purity) is associated with growth and augmentation of things socially important, and how the negative, or left-hand aspect of the sacred (impurity) is associated with degeneration and exhaustion of such growth potential. In a given culture, the function of ideas associated with the sacred is to keep these two separate (Anttonen 1996:77–78, 95):

> The social concept of the sacred, and the religious concept which derives from it, are based on the segregation of those cultural elements whose 'value, growth and productivity' have been depleted and whose disintegration and proximity would pollute, weaken, hinder or at least threaten the social value, purity and integrity of those categories producing growth (1996:78).

The concept of the **sacred** as used in this study thus refers to the process of isolating 'purity' from 'impurity' in social and cultural thought and practice. At a metaphoric level this depleted growth value corresponds to Mary Douglas' concept of 'dirt', meaning those elements which cannot be located or situated within the cultural system of classification and are therefore unable to be utilized by society. In this study, however, 'growth-value' versus 'lack of growth value' can also refer more literally to concrete biological needs and conditions such as food on the one hand, as opposed to death and disease on the other. Whether seen as vital to cultural classification or vital to biological survival, 'purity' is in both senses directly related to the continuation of society.

On the one hand, the sacred can be seen to stand for all that society considers worth preserving of itself – including the mechanisms and arrangements which allow it to perpetuate itself. The notion that things considered sacred in any society ultimately refer back to society's concept of itself is not a new observation. The classic formulation made by Durkheim and Mauss (1903) that persons order the supernatural world and the social world according to similar principles, and their conclusion that the sacred is ultimately "society writ large", are still departure points for many anthropological investigations of religious belief and practice, even if most scholars today tend to view the sacred as representing not society itself, but its more epiphenomenal values and ideals (e.g. Morinis 1992:6).

At the same time, the sacred can also be seen as the product of extending the moral contract, that is, the moral rules and conventions which characterize relations between human individuals and society, to cover supernatural agents. Just as the sacred represents society's idealized conceptions of itself, sacred agents and their interactions with humans are in most cases modelled from human social life. Scholars interested in the cognitive foundations of religion have advanced interesting hypotheses concerning why it is that religious concepts most often take the form of beings that are not only human-like, but are also agents which operate in human-like ways.[9] Because of selective evolutionary pressures arising from the fact that we are a species who has, throughout our history, been in the simultaneous position of both predator and prey, our survival is dependent on our ability to recognize other living creatures as agents. These built-in mental systems that humans are equipped with have been referred to as "Hyper-active Agent Detection" (Barrett 2000), meaning that human minds tend to postulate agents without much evidence, that we see agents in our surroundings where there may be none (Guthrie 1993; Boyer, forthcoming).

Yet even if this explains the human tendency to believe in the empirical existence of gods and spirits, humans do not necessarily see or experience gods and spirits firsthand. As Boyer (2000, forthcoming) argues, information regarding these supernatural agents generally comes from other people, and the way in which gods and spirits are understood to act is informed by mental systems geared to describing and managing interaction with other human agents. We are not only endowed with "Hyper-Active Agent Detection" systems, but also with mental systems which seek access to strategic information, and this means making informed inferences about what is going on inside another agent's mind: what he, she or it knows of some strategic information, and what he/she/it thinks that I know. Because of this need to keep the other agent's mind 'in mind', human moral intuitions allow for an "empty place-holder", for the position of "some agent who has access to my information" about a given situation (Boyer, forthcoming). A concept of god or spirit who shares human agency and the capacity for social strategizing is very likely to be activated as the most relevant way of filling in the empty place-holder in moral behavior, and thus gods and spirits become interested parties in human moral contracts and abide, to a greater or lesser degree, by human mores of conduct. If symbolic capital or surplus is created through the exchange of goods and services, and particularly by the time lapse between the act of giving and the reciprocal response (cf. Bourdieu 1990; Mayol 1998:22–23), then supernatural agents, like human agents, must be cognizant of this surplus and behave in a fashion which maximizes it.

Orthodox Karelian folk religion provides a case in point. The supranormal beings occupying the 'other side' were perceived to be sentient beings with desires, emotions, and moral awareness, all of which were necessary in order for them to 'function' within the extended system of reciprocity.

The two definitions of the sacred given above actually help to explain each other, in so far as extending moral rules and interests to supernatural agents is a useful way of drawing cultural boundaries between 'purity' and 'impurity', and conversely, notions of 'purity' and 'impurity' provide guidelines for conducting and renewing moral relationships with supernatural agents.

I now turn to the *mechanisms* by which the sacred comes into effect in cultural life, in other words, the means by which cultural boundaries between 'pure' and 'impure' are drawn, and the means by which norms of morality are extended to cover to supernatural agents. For this, we must look beyond symbolic classifications to the cultural practices which give them concrete shape and form, since the cultural Order cannot be said to exist at all if not in the minds and actions of real, embodied persons. The researcher must therefore posit mediating factors between social classification and individual practice. In the present study, those factors are *ritual* and *language*.

The nature of ritual

Language, of course, lies at the heart of the folkloristic endeavor. It is axiomatic in folklore studies that a folk belief is something not simply 'believed' but also transmitted from person to person through language. Folklore texts are indicators of communicative events having taken place within the folk culture, as well as indexes of the informants' thought processes and mental models underlying those communicative events. Because the focus of the present study is ritual, however, I forgo a more detailed discussion of the role of language and proceed directly to the main topic at hand.

To understand the role of ritual as a mediating mechanism between social practice on the one hand and social categories of 'pure' and 'impure' on the other, we must first explore the question of what ritual is and what distinguishes it from other cultural behavior. In this study I use the terms *ritual* and *rite* interchangeably, to denote distinctive and, in a loose sense, meaningful cultural behavior expressed primarily through bodily position, posture and movement. In reacting against the concept of ritual as merely the enactment of symbols and myths, anthropologists and ethnologists adopting post-structuralist and post-symbolic approaches to ritual have sought to identify some sort of lowest common denominators shared by all ritual activity (see Lewis 1980; Gerholm 1988; Parkin 1992; Bell 1990, 1992). For them, one of the primary criteria of ritual is the fact that its participants and observers hold the ritual to be a formal occasion which should be conducted in some particular way, that is, follow some sort of blueprint or set of rules, even if persons have differing ideas as to what those rules might be. In his illuminating treatment of anthropological approaches to ritual (1980), ethnographer Gilbert Lewis calls this the ritual 'ruling':

> Without this acknowledged formality, neither performers nor observers could identify *a* ritual, or speak of its performance as the enactment of *the* ritual, or identify the same ritual repeated on another occasion (Lewis 1980:22. Emphasis in original).

The idea of the ritual 'ruling' has been adopted and elaborated by other scholars, particularly anthropologists Tomas Gerholm (1988) and David Parkin (1992):

> A key notion in this development is what Lewis calls the 'ruling'. Participants in a ritual may well contest the proper conduct of the ceremony or may acknowledge their ignorance and ask others what to do or what some kind of action or object means. But that the ritual *is* a ritual and is supposed to follow some time-hallowed precedent in order to be effective or simply to be a proper performance is not in question (...) The emphasis on 'ruling', then, is an invitation to us as outside observers not to record or decipher precisely sequenced rules but rather to acknowledge that people expect there to be rules as a condition of public ritual (Parkin 1992:15. Emphasis in original).

The ritual 'ruling' is important for the present study because it is this aspect of ritual which ensures that private rituals are just as collective as public ones. Many of the rituals discussed in this study are *private* in the sense that they were performed in secret and were usually witnessed by only small numbers of persons. However, even these rituals, for example divination, *proškenja*, *pominominen*, and 'binding the forest', were clearly performed according to some traditional, collectively-held schema or framework of action. They could be categorized (and were categorized by the informants themselves) as such because they tended to be performed in similar ways and with similar aims again and again, both by different performers and over time. In other words, these private rituals were collective in that they were determined by a formal blueprint for action, the ritual 'ruling' discussed above. Lewis (1980:21) makes this same point when he says:

> We cannot say that every ritual performance has an audience. But we can say there is a public aspect to performance in the sense that the ritual (which anthropologists study) is ruled and taught and learned. The rules require recognition and transmission by some community, whether or not a restricted one within the society. Not all have equal access to the creed or dogma which may go with the ritual, not all have equal access to its performance. But as there are rules recognized by a community, so there is a public social aspect to ritual which exists independently of the particular individual in a particular situation who performs it.

According to Gerholm (1988:195), it is the ritual 'ruling', the formal quality of the activity, which serves to make the ritual distinctive and call attention to it as a special kind of act:

> [The ritual ruling] functions as a strong focusing of attention without for that reason prescribing what is to follow in terms of individual experience or private meaning. It is as if the ruling said: "This is important" —but stopped short of adding precisely why and how.

This is the second defining criteria of ritual: that it is made *distinctive* from other practices, made the center of attention in ways which mask the human agency at work. According to Lewis, rituals contain elements which catch people's attention and make the rituals peculiar, including sights, sounds, smells, stiffness or strangeness of gesture, secrecy, (we could also add strange speech modes such as Kalevala meter and strange combinations of objects such as those used in divination devices) which say 'look and listen', not simply 'see and hear'. It is through these signals that persons sense the peculiar alerting aspect of ritual (Lewis 1980: 20).

Ritual theorist Catherine Bell seems to agree with Gerholm and Lewis here. Although she does not explicitly refer to the ritual 'ruling' in her study *Ritual Theory, Ritual Practice* (1992:92), she argues, in essence, that the 'ruling' is not a universal or prerequisite of ritual but is a "strategic act" by which ritual calls attention to itself:

> Yet if ritual is interpreted in terms of practice, it becomes clear that that formality, fixity, and repetition are not intrinsic qualities of ritual so much as they are a frequent, but not universal strategy for producing ritualized acts.

For Bell as for Lewis, what is primary is the way in which ritual makes itself special, or different, in human consciousness. Because this feature of ritual lies at the core of Bell's theoretical formulation, I quote her in full below:

> Ritual practices certainly appear to be distinctive social practices simply insofar as they deliberately work to contrast themselves with other forms of practice. In this perspective ritual is not a set of distinct acts, but a *way of acting* that draws a privileged contrast between what is being done and other activities aped or mimed by the contrast. It is thus probably more appropriate to speak of "ritualization" when referring to a way of doing certain activities that differentiates those activities from other more conventional ones. Such differentiations may be drawn in a variety of ways that are culturally specific, but always in ways that the ritualized activities expect to dominate, which means that insofar as ritualized activities can effectively establish this type of contrast they gain a special status (1990:302).

Sometimes the distinctive elements which set ritual apart from other acts are collectively coded and understood symbols which express what cannot be expressed otherwise and thereby evoke a powerful set of associations. For instance, in order to get their message across as economically and as unambiguously as possible, Orthodox Karelian folk religious rituals used symbolic verbalizations and bodily gestures such as bowing down, standing up straight, offering food, giving gifts, and deferential titles in Kalevala meter, to name a few. All of these symbols referred metonymically to a broader field of social meaning. For instance, 'bowing down' was a gesture used more generally in social life when one person wished to express respect or subordination to another, or wished to ask forgiveness (see pp. 27, 82, 84). The economy and clarity of expression afforded by the use of such symbols was important, since the recipients of this ritual communication, although viewed as sentient agents, were not human and did not occupy the same "air" as humans: they were supernatural beings inhabiting the "other world" or "other air", and the aim was to avoid miscommunication with them if at all possible.

This is not to say, however, that ritual is nothing more than the performance of symbols – that its message operates at the level of the mind while the body functions simply as an instrument of expression. The corporeal element of ritual is much more complicated than this, as a number of scholars have pointed out. Embodied knowledge is not merely something abstracted or esoteric, it is connected to the social universe of the bodily participant in a very immediate and practical sense. Rituals work to alter individuals' perceptions. They are, according to Bell, a powerful ideological arena in which symbolic images and gestures exercise a particularly persuasive effect on the participants' sense of identity and social reality (1990:299). And rituals

Bowing or *prostitus* was performed not only to sacred agents, but to other persons in many everyday life situations. Here a daughter-in-law bows respectfully to her mother-in-law. Kiestinki. 1894. Photo: I.K. Inha. Finnish Literature Society.

impress information upon participants by requiring their *bodies* to incorporate this information through movement and gesture. To conform to the bodily customs of some institution or ideology is to embody, if not believe in, its doctrines: "People express allegiances with their bodies" (Sklar 1994:13). Roy Rappaport, for example, describes how the act of kneeling does not merely communicate subordination to the kneeling person but restructures the body, that is, produces a subordinated kneeler (1979:200; Bell 1992:99–100). As the physical body acts and is acted upon in ritualized activities, so too do the positions, symbols and resolutions of the ritual become messages which are imprinted on the individual at a more concrete and subconscious level than that of explicit discourse. Thus the notion of ritualization is crucial to the idea of the social body, since it is the way in which social bodies are constructed. Through ritualization, "the psychosocial entity is socialized and thereby empowered as a social presence and actor" (Bell 1990:300–301).

Yet, because we can rarely engage bodily in the same rituals as those persons we study, the analysis of how ritual creates an inner awareness through bodily movement and sensation is generally limited to what our informants can tell us, directly or indirectly, regarding that awareness. For this reason I approach the sacred not from the perspective of an inner sense of awe, ecstasy or *numen*, which is nearly impossible to document, quantify, or categorize when working with archival texts, but from the perspective of language as indexical of cultural classification and thought, thus opening the way for more culturally-sensitive studies of emic experiences of religious belief and practice. This language-centered approach is moreover appropriate because anthropologists and other social scientists have noted that unlike official religious dogma and behavior which focus on internal, spiritual transformation, popular religion tends to be defined by its participants in terms of more outwardly expressed phenomena: through sight, sound and bodily movement. As Jill Dubisch (1990:129) points out, "...in general, popular religion (...) is more outward than inward looking, more concerned with external images, with the public and communal than with the interior or mystic".

A focus on outwardly expressed language and ritual behavior rather than inwardly experienced religious awareness also allows the researcher to focus on the very forms of everyday practice and interaction which legitimize the consensual basis for social life, the 'social contract' (cf. Mayol 1998:23), both among persons and between humans and sacred agents. Vernacular language and speech events are an important part of this. Not only can lexical semantics be seen as a route to the culturally-specific logic or 'grammar' underlying the division and classification of the world using the categories of pure and impure (e.g. Anttonen 1996), but ritual behavior is closely interwoven with the 'informational field' of narratives, memorates and belief legends which reproduce and reinforce it (Morinis 1992). This is what makes *folklore* especially useful to the study of popular religion: the folklore text is a record of a series of communicative acts which have already taken place within a given culture, it is an indexical trace of a folk belief *as event*, that is, not simply 'believed' but also transmitted from person to person through language. In the same way as people display their commitment to classificatory and belief systems by acting them out through ritual, they also reveal their investment in these systems by communicating them to others through language. In this study, therefore, I am not proposing a dichotomy between ritual as 'real action' and narrative genres as mere signifiers of belief content: the two are inextricably linked parts of a systemic whole.

Folk religion – some defining characteristics

The 1980s and 1990s saw a clear upsurge of interest in traditional Finnish and Karelian religion as practiced by the 'folk',[10] a trend which reflected the increasing attention paid to European popular religion more generally.[11] The term used here, *folk religion*, follows the anthropological designation 'popular religion', denoting 'religion as practiced' as opposed to 'religion as prescribed', 'non-orthodox' as opposed to 'orthodox' forms of religion, or, historically, 'little' as opposed to 'great' religious traditions (Christian 1981:178). It refers to forms of Christianity which may derive from and are practiced at the level of 'the people' but which are nonetheless *in a dialogue with the Church* and which are linked to it in subtle ways. More specifically, it refers to the syncretic fusion of Christian and pre-Christian forms in the context of interaction with divine or supranormal entities (see Järvinen 1993; Stark 1996; Laitila 1998). Popular religion signals a fundamental difference between the people and the Church in how they conceive of Christianity's ultimate goals. It also points to a dispute concerning the right of the Church to exercise its power in social, political and economic spheres.

By virtue of its having historically been for many people in rural Europe a 'total social fact' in the Durkheimian sense (encompassing social, economic, political and cultural aspects of everyday life) institutionalized religion and the resources it possesses have been instruments of power, status and identity. However, the Church needs the consent and cooperation of its followers in order to lay claim to this power, and it is this which has produced a centuries-old dialogue between Church authorities and the people. Brettell (1990) sees this relationship between popular and priestly forms of religion as a kind of contract or accommodation, in which both sides must make compromises, at least in the short term. For this reason, any understanding of religion in European cultures needs to take into account both the popular and official faces of religion as components of a dialectic process.

The contrast between European popular and official forms of religion has been most actively studied in Southern Europe, an area in which it has a centuries-long documented history (e.g. Christian 1981). The 'divide' between popular and official forms of Christianity in Europe, most evident in Roman Catholicism but also visible in Orthodox Christianity and Protestantism may have originated in part from a difference in the way religious concepts are handled cognitively, as either intuitive basic-level concepts or more abstract theological concepts (e.g. Barrett 1999), but if so, they have evolved over the centuries into much more than this: divergent cultural and ideological stances arising from different social, political and economic experiences and needs. Similar conclusions have been reached by scholars of pilgrimage, who now recognize the *cultural* distinction between 'popular' and 'official' forms of devotional journeys (Eade and Sallnow 1991:15). This can be clearly seen in Orthodox Karelia, where the stories told by the 'folk' represent, on the whole, a different tradition, with a different set of ideological concerns, than the one transmitted by the monastery and church officials (Stark 1995, 1999).

The 'divide' between official and popular religion may represent a difference of opinion regarding what is proper behavior in 'religious' contexts, the role of church symbols and personalities such as saints, and the goal of 'religious' activity itself: whether for individual salvation on the one hand, or for maintenance of community relations and local, class and gender identities on the other. There can even exist differences between the Church and the laity regarding such fundamental religious concepts as body, soul, afterlife, and relations between the living and the dead (cf. Pardo 1989).

In addition, popular religion often mixes what the Church defines as 'true religiosity' with 'superstition' or 'magic'. At the popular level the division between these two areas tends to be blurred, as indeed it has been historically within the Catholic Church itself. [12] The relationship between popular and official religion naturally assumes different forms in Roman Catholicism and in Greek and Russian Orthodoxy. In Orthodoxy, church doctrine has tended to be more 'other-worldly' oriented, confining its authority largely to the realm of the spiritual whereas both Catholicism and Protestantism have focused their mission on 'this world', extending their influence into law and politics and emphasizing and debating the importance of deeds and 'works' for individual salvation (Badone 1990a; Bowman 1991). Popular concepts and practices dealing with 'this world' have thus met with fewer opposing models in Orthodoxy, which has more fully integrated popular religion into its institutionalized frameworks. A less pronounced social distance between priests and laity has also contributed to the integration of 'popular' and 'official' aspects of Orthodoxy (cf. Badone 1990:11).

Popular religion can be different things in different times and places. It may represent those activities and beliefs which the Church has not been able to incorporate into itself (Antes 1994), for example worship at pre-Christian sacred sites or traditional magic. It may, on the other hand, represent the survival of earlier prescribed or permitted practices which have outlived their official approval when the Church has undertaken widespread reforms. Christian (1981:178) speaks to this latter possibility when he says that the "so-called 'little tradition' is often merely a 'great tradition' that has taken root in a particular place and lasted longer than its time". As treated in this study, folk religion represents neither Christianity's 'contamination' of ethnic folk belief nor the 'misinterpretation' of Christianity by the non-literate rural populace, but a functional system in which the most useful elements of each belief system are adopted and fashioned into a syncretic whole.

While the term *popular religion* can and often does refer to the religious practices and beliefs of individuals from varied class and social backgrounds in a network of diverse and complex relationships, I have chosen the term *folk religion* to specifically denote the religious practices and beliefs of pre-modern and early modern peasants in rural agricultural areas. **My definition of the term folk religion has two primary elements**: first, folk religion refers to practices and beliefs in which the sacred is defined by *the local community* rather than by a religious institution. Second, folk religion is characterized by an emphasis on reciprocity and exchange between humans and divine or sacred agents.

These elements follow directly from the two definitions given above for the concept of the sacred. First of all, as discussed in the foregoing, the sacred is an important tool utilized by the community for cultural classification. Many anthropologists see the main function of popular religious expression to be the demarcation of important social categories and relationships such as communal and inter-communal identity and solidarity, and culturally relevant boundaries (see Douglas 1966, 1975; Riegelhaupt 1984; Stark 1994). For this reason, a phenomenological approach to the sacred as a universally recognizable 'numen' type of experience (ála Rudolf Otto and Mircea Eliade) does little to help us understand the *cultural* function of popular religion. According to ethnographer David Parkin in his discussion of the Giriama of Kenya, "People do not need to feel 'awe', 'ecstasy' or the like in order to believe religious claims" (1991:222). He goes on to argue that the emphasis on numen as a precondition of religious belief is an imposition of our views, deriving from official religion in the West upon on those we study (ibid). In discussing another aspect of religion, Mary Douglas (1975:58) states that pollution taboos, which are manifestations of the 'left-hand' aspect of the sacred, do not derive from, nor are necessarily even associated with, emotions such as terror and anxiety. They are about cultural classification, deviation, and conformity, all of which are part of the cognitive organization of the human universe necessary for everyday life.

Because of its usefulness in the construction of the social Order, the sacred has been a resource over which different groups have historically competed for control. Anthropologists and historians have noted that in the case of the institutionally-defined sacred, the Church may try to monopolize the sacred by elaborating it into a rational world view, universalizing it, fixing it, naming it, and placing distance between it and the people. The official Church here is namely concerned with the construction and maintenance of social Order through cultural classification occurring at a more abstract, universal and/or philosophical level than that with which ordinary people are concerned in their everyday lives. The sacred becomes something over which the Church has hegemony, and individuals can be banished from the sphere of purity and relegated to impurity *if they do not follow institutional rules*, and if they do not perform individual, inner, or spiritual self-examination. The priest is the mediator between ordinary persons and the sacred, and Church officialdom defines the norms of how to relate to the sacred through Church teachings. Yet the concept of the sacred has also been useful for members of agrarian communities in ordering their own local, communal systems of rules and classification in a context in which most social relations were face to face, and in which individual loyalties were focused on home, kin group, village and parish.

Real people in complicated situations find themselves in need of concepts for divine agents which promote rapid generation of inferences and predictions rather than abstract reflection (Barrett 1999). Because of this, the popularly-defined sacred is characterized by expansion, fluidity, and plurality, as well as a close, personal, and unmediated interaction with the supernatural and divine. Researchers have explored the tendency within popular or folk religion for the sacred symbols and personalities of Christianity to become less unitary, universal and abstract, and more fragmented, individualized, localized and concrete, in other words, rendered more intimate and 'everyday' than the Church is often comfortable with (cf. Di Nola 1976; Moreno 1994; Nesti 1994). In Orthodox Karelia, many of the 'abstract' Christian concepts inherent in objects, times or places were reinterpreted in folk religion to provide concrete utility: holy icons for example, which according to Church doctrine were supposed to provide models for the Christian life, became powerful supernatural agents in and of themselves. In many cultures, subjecthood and objecthood can become fragmented and interchangeable within folk religious beliefs. In rural Italy, for example, the figure of the Virgin Mary has splintered off into dozens of different female saints named Mary, each belonging to a different district or village and with a different sphere of patronage, sometimes related to each other through kinship, as 'sisters' for example (Di Nola 1976; Binde 1999:117–118). These distinct Mary figures serve the community's need to distinguish itself from neighboring villages, to bolster communal identity, something that a universal figure of the Virgin Mary could not provide. In other words, in popular religion it is the fact that (1) individuals are involved in real-time problem solving (Barrett 1999) and (2) cultural identification and classification take place at the level of *the community* (see Brettel 1990) which defines the functions and definitions of the sacred.

As discussed in the foregoing, the sacred also arises whenever the moral contract between individual and society is extended to supernatural agents. The form taken by moral contracts between human agents in a given culture, therefore, will determine in large part the type of relationship between humans and the divine.[13] In traditional agrarian cultures, one of the most important features of social relations has been an emphasis on exchange and reciprocity.[14] Ritual mechanisms to minimize envy, equalize the distribution of resources and reinforce mutual obligations, often through practical and symbolic exchange mechanisms, are all recognizable features of a 'peasant mentality'. It should therefore come as no surprise that one of the hallmarks of folk religion in traditional agrarian cultures is the fact that relations between humans and supernatural agents are characterized first and foremost by *exchange*.

George Foster was one of the first scholars to bring together diverse anthropological observations concerning this model of traditional peasant behavior in his classic essay "Peasant Society and the Image of Limited Good" (1965). In it, he identifies the image of 'limited good' as a cognitive orientation shared by persons in peasant communities, in which desirable things, those relating to both economic prosperity and social and cultural values, exist in finite quantity and are always in short supply. If 'good' exists in limited amounts which cannot be expanded, and if the peasant perceives the system to be 'closed', then according to this model "an individual or family can improve their position only at the expense of others" (1965:297). Even before Foster's essay, this image of 'limited good' was identified in Finnish and Karelian folk belief by Toivo Vuorela (1960).[15] This cognitive orientation was expressed in the Finnish-Karelian culture area through the concept of 'luck' (*onni*), which was thought to exist in finite quantity, and the 'stealing', 'spoiling', or 'breaking' of such luck. According to Foster, *the model of 'limited good' is closely related to reciprocal relations of exchange* because in peasant societies great pressure is applied to the person whose 'good' has increased to restore the balance by giving something in return, either to the community or to supernatural benefactors (p. 305–306).[16]

In Orthodox Karelia, one form of reciprocity that levelled differences in wealth through the redistribution of resources was the accommodation of relatives and other guests during village festivals or *praasniekkas*. Each household fed and housed a number of guests when the festival was held in its home village, and in turn, the members of this household stayed in the homes of other relatives and friends when festivals were held in other villages (Sarmela 1969, Sauhke 1971). Other forms wealth redistribution included the alms and food given to beggars and the itinerant poor whose ranks had swelled during the many famine years in the last half of the 19th century. Gifts were also given to impoverished brides who went from farm to farm collecting such aid prior to the wedding. Not all of the alms given to the poor were given directly – many were given to village chapels which then redistributed the gifts to the poor, or in conjunction with various rites of remembrance for the dead (see pages 142–146).

In early modern peasant communities of Europe, an "equity-conscious" world view and exchange-oriented behavior were not limited to human relations, but were often extended to relationships with the supernatural as well (Badone 1990:12). This means that in folk religion, relations with God, the saints and other divine figures were often extensions of communal interpersonal relations governed above all by mutual obligations and exchange (Foster 1965, Di Tota 1981; Schneider 1990, Badone 1990). On the basis of Archangel Karelian incantations and folk beliefs, Lotte Tarkka (1994:76) has pointed out that in the pastoralist context, competition between neighboring farms expressed most vehemently through harmful sorcery (see Stark 1998) provided a model for the antagonistic and competitive relationship between the human community and nature spirits seen to dwell in the forest. The paying of various annual taxes and tithes to authorities such as the State, Church and manor lords equally provided a model for both the "taxes" (vero) or food given to the dead of the kin group, and the yearly devotional offerings of agricultural products to the saints represented in the icons of the village chapel.

Folk religion in Orthodox Karelia

Prior research and historical overview

Historically, Orthodox Karelia has occupied an intermediate position on the borders between eastern and western Christendom. The dialects of Orthodox Karelia, which are closely related to Finnish, have distinguished it from neighboring parts of Russia to the south and east, while religion has served as the salient cultural boundary between Orthodox Karelia and Finland (the latter has been almost entirely Lutheran since the Reformation). In Orthodox Karelia, elements of indigenous pre-Christian belief and practices were preserved even into the 20th century. While Finland was incorporated into the Roman Catholic Church during the 12th and 13th centuries, Karelia came under the cultural influence of the Orthodox Church and Russia from the 12th century onward, and many cultural influences from Russian and Byzantine Orthodoxy were transmitted to the rural populace through the institution of monasticism as it spread northward (Kirkinen 1970/1963; Kilpeläinen 2000).

The system of folk religion in Orthodox Karelia, which survived to a surprisingly late date, was the product of a centuries-long dialogue with an Orthodox church that gave local communities the space and freedom to interpret and appropriate Christian teachings as best suited their everyday ritual needs. Because this vigorous tradition survived into the beginning of this century, and because the prodigious collecting efforts of both 'educated' and 'folk' collectors in the 19th and early 20th centuries produced a sizeable body of documentation concerning this tradition, there are few areas in Europe which can rival Orthodox Karelia in terms of the depth and richness of its folk religious source materials.

During the last decades of the 19th and first decades of the 20th centuries, Orthodox Karelian folk belief and folk religion were enthusiastically observed, documented and described in, for example, Arvid Genetz' "Kuvaelmia kansan elämästä Salmin kihlakunnassa (Depictions of folk life in Salmi, 1870)" Julius Ailio's article "Uhritavoista Mantsin- ja Lunkulansaarella Salmissa (Sacrificial customs on the islands of Mantsinsaari and

Lunkulansaari in Salmi", 1897), Eino Leskinen's article "Lunkulan pässi-
uhri (The sacrificial ram of Lunkula, 1934)" Viljo Jääskeläinen's article
"Bokin päivillä Salmin Lunkulassa (During the days of the *bokki*-ram in
Lunkula village, Salmi, 1912)", and Samuli Paulaharju's *Syntymä, lapsuus
ja kuolema: Vienan Karjalan tapoja ja uskomuksia (Birth, Childhood and
Death: Customs and Beliefs of Archangel Karelia,* 1924). A new era of
scientific interest in explaining the origins and development of Finnish and
Karelian folk religious customs and beliefs was marked by the works of
Julius Krohn *(Suomen suvun pakanallinen jumalanpalvelus/The Pagan
Worship of Deities among the Finnic peoples,* 1894), his son Kaarle Krohn's
Suomalaisten runojen uskonto (The Religion of Finnish Folk Poems, 1915),
and Matti Varonen's *Vainajainpalvelus muinaisilla suomalaisilla (The
Veneration of the Dead among the Ancient Finns,* 1898). In the 1920s, this
interest continued with Ilmari Manninen's *Die Dämonistischen Krankheiten
im Finnischen Volksaberglauben* (1922), which dealt with human illnesses
caused by the animated and personified environment, as well as Uno
Holmberg's (later Harva's) "Metsän peitossa (In the forest cover, 1923)"
and V.J. Mansikka's "Eräs inkeriläis-itäkarjalainen vainajainjuhla (An
Ingrian-Karelian festival for the dead, 1923)", among others. The 1930s
saw the appearance of articles on sacred legends linked to monasteries
(Haavio 1936), as well as on death-cult practices, including memorial meals
to honor the dead (Haavio 1934, 1937; Harva 1932; and Lehmusto 1937).
Interest in memorial rites, cults surrounding Christian saints and domestic
spirits, and other ethnic communal celebrations continued into the 1940s,
when V.J. Mansikka published two articles on practices surrounding saints'
cults in Finland and Karelia (1941, 1943). Harva addressed traditions
pertaining to forest spirits and the cult of the dead in his book *Suomalaisten
muinaisusko* (Ancient Religion of the Finns, 1948) and various works by
Martti Haavio dealt with cultural place spirits (1942) and sacrificial feasts
(1949).

Subsequent decades saw the continuation of comparative research on
Karelian folk religion (e.g. Kemppinen 1967), as well as a new emphasis on
ritual theory and folk models of illness (i.e. Honko 1959, 1960, 1979). The
1960s and 1970s also saw a new generation of researchers pose a different
set of questions, with an new emphasis on magic, folk belief and folk religion
as elements of individual and cultural cosmologies (e.g. Köngäs-Maranda
1967; Pentikäinen 1969, 1971). In the 1990s, scholars turned their attention
to the broader questions of folk religious world view, this time drawing on
comparative materials from archeology and linguistics and utilizing
theoretical frameworks from cognitive and semantic research (e.g. Siikala
1992; Tarkka 1994, 1998; Anttonen 1996), as well as working from their
own field data (e.g. Jetsu 1999; Järvinen 1996, 1998, 1999; Järvinen & Timonen 1992; Utriainen 1998b).

The corpus of source materials examined in this book includes folk belief
and ritual descriptions, belief legends, Kalevala-meter incantations and the
lexical entries of linguistic researchers from the Finnish Literature Society
Folklore Archives and the Karelian Lexical Archives of the Research Insti-

tute of the Languages of Finland. These texts were recorded between 1825 and 1966 from informants familiar with the culture and traditions of Archangel Karelia, Ladoga Karelia and Olonets Karelia, the three historical areas comprising Orthodox Karelia.

Olonets and Archangel Karelia have always been part of Russia, while Ladoga Karelia came under the sphere of the Swedish empire and Lutheran church in 1617 but was ceded, along with Finland, back to Orthodox Russia in 1809. During the period 1809–1917, the border between Ladoga Karelia and neighboring Russian Karelia was open, and for all practical purposes non-existent. After Finnish independence in 1917, however, the border between the two closed, but Ladoga Karelia remaining part of Finland. The Orthodox religion became a second national religion in Finland alongside the Evangelical Lutheran Church, but while the religious freedoms of the Orthodox population of Ladoga Karelian were thus secured until World War II, ties with Orthodoxy in Russia, now persecuted and suppressed by the Soviet regime, were cut off entirely. In 1944, Ladoga Karelia was ceded to the Soviet Union. Its population, however, was evacuated to Finland and resettled within its new borders, and Ladoga Karelian evacuees have continued to provide Finnish folklore collectors and religious studies scholars with information regarding Orthodox Karelian folk religion.

The persistence of pre-Christian ethnic beliefs in 19th- and early 20th-century Orthodox Karelia is best explained by the region's peripheral location, since neither government nor church authorities were able to monitor this remote region effectively. In addition, the liturgical language in most areas of Karelia was Church Slavonic until the late 19th century. Priests, many of whom spoke no Karelian and had only a low-level education, might visit outlying villages only occasionally (Lavonen and Stepanova 1999:29; Laitila 1999:394). In Archangel Karelia in particular, there were very few churches until the end of the 19th century. Statistics from 1865 show that in an area comprising approximately ten parishes, each containing dozens of villages each, only five churches existed. In addition to these were 27 village chapels or *tsasounas* in which services were held when travelling priests visited. Karelians also visited the *tsasounas* and conducted rites in the absence of priests as well (Lavonen and Stepanova 1999:29–30), as described in the following recollected narrative:

> There was nonetheless not a single literate person in the village and on Sunday when visiting the village chapel, people mumbled to themselves the prayers learned from priests and monks and brought offerings of butter and wool. This was so that they would have good cattle-luck in the summer and that the cattle would thrive in other ways as well. After the people had said their prayers for a while and burned the tapers in front of the holy icons, the chapel elder (*starosta*) told them: "Go, everyone, and eat supper." (Salmi. 1962. Eino Toiviainen a) 1759).

All of these factors allowed a strong religious complex to develop at the popular level, a complex which represented a selective fusion of pre-Christian folk beliefs and the centuries-long influence of official Orthodox ritualism. This influence had become deeply ingrained in the daily lives of Karelians in the form of ritual prayer, fasting, the keeping of holy icons in the home, the baptism of newborns, and the wearing of cross pendants.[17] Religious teachings, particularly those originating from monasteries, made a significant impact on general concepts of morality and ethics, as can be seen most clearly from sacred legends (Järvinen 1981). Mercy and hospitality toward the less fortunate, submission to a fate ordained by God, the eventual exposure of hidden guilt or wrongdoing, and the value of humility over arrogance and pride were all virtues emphasized in the Orthodox Karelian sacred legend tradition (ibid).

The impact of official Christian doctrine concerning Biblical narratives and the identity of holy personages, on the other hand, remained surprisingly superficial even into the 19th century. For example, Jacob Fellman, a folk poetry collector travelling in Archangel Karelia in 1829, encountered the persistence of a pre-Christian cosmology in a version of the Creation story told by some elderly men, as recounted by Leea Virtanen (1968:47):

> Christianity's influence on folk concepts in Karelia long remained superficial, producing merely outwardly habits. Fellman tells of having asked several elderly men in Vuokkiniemi what they believed concerning the creation of the world, and of receiving the answer: "Kah, holy brother, we have the same belief as you. The eagle flew from the north, laid an egg on Väinämöinen's knėe and from that created the world. Thus do you also believe."[18]

Nearly a century later, Orthodox Karelia was still being portrayed as a backwoods in which 'pagan' beliefs and practices existed long after they had died out in many other parts of Europe. On the one hand, certain nationalist-minded writers romanticized Orthodox Karelia as the cradle of Kalevala meter folk poetry and lauded folk religious customs and references to pre-Christian divinities as survivals of a purer form of Finnic cultural heritage. Ethnologist J. Lukkarinen (1918:67), for instance, commented on the customs he observed in Archangel Karelia as follows:

> The true archenemies of the Karelian people, the Russian bugbears, have been happy to call Karelians "pure Orthodox Russians". But such idle talk is rarely heard. For any unbiased observer can easily notice that Karelians are as just as impure devotees of the Orthodox faith as the Russians themselves.
> And that is definitely in their favor.

Other educated observers, however, disapproved of what they considered to be evidence of the ignorant and irrational beliefs held by the Karelian populace. Finnish observers, both Lutheran and Orthodox alike, were critical of what they saw as superstition and lack of modern enlightenment in Karelian folk customs and devotional practices. Much of the interest in describing and documenting these practices arose in part from the desire to eradicate them and educate the Karelian populace toward a more 'civilized', modern world view, as is revealed in comments made by collector and photographer I.K. Inha on the basis of a visit to Archangel Karelia in 1894, and those by an anonymous Finnish Orthodox priest (1907) concerning the parish of Salmi in Ladoga Karelia:

> Religious concepts are, in this land where the people do not receive instruction in their own language, naturally in a most primitive state. What the folk lack in terms of civilized enlightenment, they try to make up for by faithfully preserving their ancient traditional knowledge, and this is primarily what has kept it alive. But in addition to more pure and decent concepts, they have also preserved an astonishing amount of superstition. It was truly difficult at first for this traveller to become accustomed to the idea that in our day and age there is still an entire people, although small in number, who are, at the threshold of civilization, so thoroughly devoted to the old magic, that it hardly ever occurs to them to doubt it. Lönnrot told many examples of this, nor have things greatly changed since then. Such groups as the so-called Old Believers, who adhere most strictly to the old Christianity of Russia, live in all naivety in the deepest pagan superstitions. At Karelian weddings this belief in magic is more publicly rampant, but it dominates all areas of life. The scant schooling that the folk receive in Russian-language grammar schools is not in itself much use in popular enlightenment, for it is in a foreign language.[19]

> This parish is undoubtedly the most obscure and most ignorant in our country. The most obscure and most ignorant even of its own religion amongst the Finnish Orthodox population. In this parish, members of the Orthodox church live in the lowest kind of ignorance and magic belief. The godly truths of the Orthodox church here are hidden from the ordinary people by a thick blanket of ignorance and superstition.
> ...In a word, the people outwardly perform all that the church requires, but without knowing its real significance, not knowing, for example, such a thing as the meaning of making the sign of the cross, not to mention other outward customs.
> ...One encounters crudity and superstition wherever one looks.[20]

The existence of magic and pre-Christian beliefs in Karelia was also noted by Russian writers. In 1892, a writer in Olonets going by the initials N. Tš. pointed out in an article published in the newspaper *Olonetškije gubernskije vedomosti* that the Karelian people still knew incantations, ritual laments and mysterious rites, and believed in the spirits of home and forest as well as other kinds of place spirits, which he considered "vestiges of pre-Christian belief". In the writer's opinion, this state of affairs was due to the complete lack of education among both the Karelians and their Orthodox priests (Lavonen & Stepanova 1999:29). In a book published on Karelia in 1917, Russian researcher I.V. Olenev also discussed superstition among the Karelians and the pre-Christian beliefs which were part of their religious outlook (ibid:34).

The pre-Christian aspects of Karelian popular religion were already deplored as the basest form of ignorance and superstition as early as the 1550s, when Lutheran Bishop Mikael Agricola condemned the "false gods and spirits" worshipped by Finns and Karelians. In the Preface to his Finnish-language *Psalter*, Agricola mentions such practices as ritual lamentation and the bringing of food to the graves of the dead, as well as the leaving of offerings and sacrifices on large stones and in selected sacred groves. He also mentions the names and functions of several forest and water spirits revered by the Karelians. [21] These sacred practices and the belief in nature spirits noted by Agricola in the 16th-century survived well into the 20th-century in Orthodox Karelia.

Who were these Karelian 'folk' viewed so ambivalently by educated Finnish observers? They were small-scale peasant farmers who nonetheless relied heavily on other forms of livelihood such as livestock husbandry, hunting, fishing, trapping, peddling, logging, and seasonal wage labour. Orthodox Karelia was characterized by a lack of "permanent and traditional class differences" (Sarmela 1969:263), but it was not socially homogeneous, representing instead "a mixture of official Russian social organization, Russian village culture and Finnish backwoods culture in its social structure" (Sarmela ibid.). Settlement patterns reflected a sparsely-distributed population. In 1860, only 190,000 persons lived in Olonets and Archangel Karelia combined, 90% of which were peasants (Hämynen 1998:162). Olonets Karelia was far more populated than Archangel Karelia, which according to church records had less than 17,000 residents in the 1860s (Nieminen 1998:280). Throughout Orthodox Karelia, the vast majority of persons lived in the countryside. Particularly in northern Ladoga Karelia and Archangel Karelia, peasants engaged in multiple forms of economy year-round (Hämynen 1998:168, 171). In the poorest areas, namely Archangel Karelia and Border Karelia, farms could only produce on average enough crops to feed themselves for 4–6 months out of the year (ibid).

The vast majority of Orthodox Karelians lived in poverty and had little formal education: in 1883, for example, only slightly more than half of all Orthodox persons in Border Karelia (comprising the parishes of Salmi, Impilahti, Korpiselkä, Soanlahti, Suistamo and Suojärvi) could read, but not necessarily write (Kirkinen et. al. 1995: 266). For those in many villages, contact with Orthodox church officials appears to have been limited to infrequent visits by priests as well as meeting monks in the course of pilgrimage to monasteries. While priests often officiated at popular ritual events (sacrificial feasts, village festivals, memorial rituals for the deceased and ritual 'feeding' of the dead), and both monks and priests taught the people ritual practices and prayers in Church Slavonic, their religious outlook, if it in fact differed significantly from that held by the laity, does not appear to have made much impact on popular practices. Archival folk descriptions often mention the presence of *a* priest at a given ritual event, but the priest's name, distinguishing characteristics, attitudes or actions are conspicuously absent in these accounts, and the same is true for monks at monasteries.

Reciprocity and exchange in Orthodox Karelian folk religion

Because sacred agents were expected to share the moral code of the human community, a close reading of the ritual descriptions can reveal the moral guidelines which organized people's conceptions of themselves as social and cultural beings. In other words, it can tell us something not only about the ethical aspect of the sacred, but also about human social relationships as well.

Orthodox Karelian folk religious ritual comprised a system of obligations between Karelian peasants/pastoralists and sacred agents, a system whose *modus operandi* was reciprocity and exchange. This exchange ethic was also an integral part of interpersonal relations within the community, and the two levels, social and supernatural, served to reinforce each other. Ritually-organized relations between humans and supernatural or divine beings, therefore, did not only regulate the balance between 'this world' and 'the other side', they also facilitated the processes connected to the model of social equilibrium and 'limited good' *within the peasant community itself.*

In Orthodox Karelia, for example, the reciprocal relationship between humans and supranormal beings tended to restrict the accumulation of individual resources by favoring economic balance within the community. The strict annual cycle of normative practices attached to saints' days, in which economic endeavors (plowing, hunting, letting the cows out to graze) were started and finished by everyone in the community on the same day, helped to ensure that all fared equally well or poorly. This was important, since within the world view which acknowledged the limited nature of 'good', "[t]he individual or family that acquires more than its share of a 'good', and particularly an economic "good", is (…) viewed as a threat to the community at large" (Foster 1965:302).

Numerous stories tell of persons who were punished for trying to 'get ahead' by working on saints' days which others considered holy:[22] on St. Elijah's Day, for example, lightning struck persons working in the fields or burned down their barn full of newly-harvested hay.[23] Anni Levantyttö Pappini, interviewed in 1968, had not yet moved to Jyvöälahti village when the following event took place, but she had been told of it:

> 1)
> Over there the farm has burned – "it was burned down during the war" – from which people went on St. Elijah's Day to harvest hay. The man had said: "If one tries to observe all of these St. Elijah Days then he'll end up starving!" He worked in the hay meadow all the day long, and got many loads of hay into the hay rick. But what happened next? "A thunder storm arose and lightning struck and burned down the entire hay rick, there it went!" But the hay belonging to those who had not laboured on St. Elijah's Day turned out well: "On the next day, the others harvested their hay which was dry" (Virtaranta 1978:170–171).

Yet another mechanism for the alleviation of social inequality and the restoration of economic balance can be found in the sacrifices and offerings made to saints in the local chapel, offerings of food given at *piirut* celebrations, and food brought to the cemetery for the dead. These offerings were often redistributed to the poor who had gathered in anticipation in large groups in the cemetery or near the house where the memorial rituals were held.[24]

In folk religious ritual, reciprocity between humans and sacred agents operated according to a code of ethical principles acknowledged by both parties. Agreement upon shared 'rules of the game' and submission to a system of mutual moral obligations were expressed through *collective symbols*. Such symbols included various verbalizations and bodily gestures/postures: bowing down, standing up straight, giving food, making a vow, addressing or greeting the other party using deferential titles, the presence of a 'witness' at the ritual performance, and gift-giving – such gifts were sometimes referred to as "taxes" (*vero*),[25] highlighting the fact that they were given in submission to a higher authority (see also Pentikäinen 1969:95).

Moral responsibility was shared equally between humans and sacred agents: if either party failed to meet its obligations, that party could be punished. For example, humans could be punished for neglecting their duties to the sacred agent, or for failure to fulfill a promise made to that agent:

2a)
...Pešši Alvoitu got into trouble on Lake Ladoga, and he promised to light a taper costing a whole ruble in honor of St. Nicholas (*Miikkula*) if the saint would rescue him. After surviving, however, he forgot about his promise, but fell ill because of it. A gypsy woman who read his palm told him the reason for his illness, and Pešši took the taper to St. Nicholas.
(Salmi. 1935. Martta Pelkonen 247. –Natalju Hilipäntytär Ryögy, 61 years).

2b)
On the mainland there was an old woman who promised, when she had walked past the village chapel and cemetery without making the sign of the cross, "You'll get a piece of cloth, I'll bring it to the cemetery". But the woman most likely never took it and she never saw another day of health after that. She wasted away and died.
(Tulomajärvi. 1943. Helmi Helminen 2385. –Solomanida Petrov, b. 1862).

On the other hand, if the sacred agent failed to fulfill its part of the bargain, it too could be punished.[26] In one narrative from Ladoga Karelia, an old man in Suojärvi prayed to Saint Elijah (*Ilja*) while burning candles beneath the icon, offered pasties and alcohol and said to him, "Saint Ilja, watch over my cows so that bears don't get them". But when a bear happened to kill the best cow, the old man became furious, took an axe to the icon and destroyed it, saying, "I fed you my best pies and gave you my best liquor and this is the miracle you gave me".[27]

In Orthodox Karelia, reciprocal relations between humans and divine beings were formalized in the notion of a 'promise': informants described explicit promises being made to nature spirits, saints represented in the village chapel, and holy men associated with monasteries. Indeed, it is the formalized notion of the promise or vow (*jeäksintä*) which links local rites carried out on farms and in communities on the one hand, and pilgrimage to distant monasteries on the other. *Jeäksintä* referred to (1) holy vows made to visit a monastery in exchange for the curing of a long-term illness, but it also referred

41

to (2) the act of bringing to a local or more distant village chapel gifts promised to a saint in return for the alleviation of sudden pain (toothache, headache, leg pain), or in return for a good catch of fish or protection from storms when on the open water. Such gifts included livestock, butter, cabbages, flax, wool, tapers and money.[28] (3) Offerings were also given as part a *jeäksintä* vow to *nature spirits* either to increase the giver's prosperity or to be healed from illness.

The scale of Orthodox Karelian folk religious activity can thus be seen as a continuum, from local rites directed at nature spirits, the dead, and saints in local village chapels, to pilgrimages to monasteries. Distinct as they were, these two levels of religious ritual activity were linked to each other by the fact that *jeäksintä* promises to visit a site occupied by a sacred agent were directed at holy persons thought to exist both in one's home village and in distant shrines (see pages 61–62, 68–69).

Pre-Christian beliefs: other worlds and väki-*force*

The rituals discussed in this study represent a syncretic fusion of concepts derived from Orthodox Christianity and the older strata of pre-Christian Karelian ethnic belief. Two of the most fundamental elements of the older belief, which can most likely be traced back to a shamanistic world view (Siikala 1992), are 1) the division between 'this world' (the world of living humans) and the 'other world' (the world of the supernatural, divine beings and spirits); and 2) the belief that numerous entities in the world possessed a dynamistic quality, that is, they contained a supranormal, 'mana'-like force known as *väki*.

These cultural sub-models of belief are just two of a large number of such models comprising a magico-mythical world view. Other sub-models include belief in the evil eye, and various mechanisms of magical harm such as curses and 'spoiling'. Some of this knowledge was general knowledge possessed by most ordinary persons, while some of it was the province of a ritual specialist with the abilities of a seer, healer and sorcerer, known in the vernacular as the *tietäjä*, lit. "one who knows". In the realm of the *tietäjä's* expertise we find knowledge of the magical power of the word, as well as of shamanic-derived models of helper-spirits, animal spirits, and the topography of the other world. All of these should be treated as analytically separate from dynamistic *väki*-force, although in actual belief and practice these cultural sub-models and their component schemata tended to overlap.

For instance, the model of magical harm due to the 'evil eye' (*paha silmä*) or 'mouthings' (*suutelus*) (see Vuorela 1960), should not, in my view, be considered an example of dynamistic *väki*-force, since the two types of supernatural harm operated according to different rules of logic. For example, women were at higher risk from *väki* forces in the environment solely due to their gender, but not from the evil eye (Apo 1998:81–82; Stark-Arola 1998:234–238), and there is no evidence that persons who were dynamistically more powerful (possessed stronger *luonto*) were thereby more capable than other persons of exerting the evil eye. However, being part of the same magico-mythical worldview, the two models could in some cases be seen to interact with each other (for example the use of female *väki* to ward off 'eyeings' or 'mouthings', see Stark-Arola 1998a).

Likewise, I posit that *väki* force was different from the 'power of the word' in incantations – these represent two separate categories of power or force. Incantations were communication used to persuade *väki*-filled entities to transfer their force either to the healer (in the case of *luonto*-force), or away from the patient (in asking the entity to remove its *vihat*, for example). Folk informants never spoke of incantations as having *väki*. It was the ritual specialist (*tietäjä*), not the spoken incantations, who could be more *väki*-filled, if for instance the *tietäjä* possessed powerful *luonto* force, or carried with him objects which contained *väki*-force (bear's claws, dirt from the cemetery, etc.).

I have divided part of the broader magico-mythical world view of Finnish-Karelian traditional thought into cultural sub-models, and have plotted them schematically in Figure 1. Although the diagram is not meant to be comprehensive, it brings together a number of Finnish-Karelian beliefs, traditional rites and modes of thought oriented toward the magical and supernatural which are discussed in this and other studies (e.g. Hautala 1960; Vuorela 1960; Siikala 1980, 1992; Apo 1993, 1995, 1998; Stark-Arola 1993, 1998a, 1998b, forthcoming). This is so that the reader can see how the topics of this study fit into a larger framework of supernaturally-oriented folk belief. The arrows in the diagram are intended to indicate which elements of knowledge were necessary for which ritual activities.

On the right side of the diagram are shown beliefs in magical harm by human agents and the rites used to counter this harm. These include beliefs in "spoiling", curses and the evil eye (see Vuorela 1960; Stark-Arola 1998a), everyday self-protective magic (see Siikala 1992:239–250), *lempi*-raising (see Stark-Arola 1998a), rites of magical revenge or counter-sorcery, and sending the illness-agent or "dog" back to its "master" (Stark, forthcoming).

On the left side of the diagram are the types of ritual knowledge which figure most prominently in this book: "Knowledge of supernatural beings", "Proškenja rites, apologies and offerings to nature spirits and the dead", and "Binding the forest or water spirit". The aim of the diagram, which should be viewed as merely indicative, is to situate the rituals which are the focus of this study in the context of other types of rites and thinking concerning the supernatural, and to show which types of knowledge and activities, broadly speaking, were the domain of the *tietäjä* and which belonged to more general everyday knowledge shared more widely among community members.

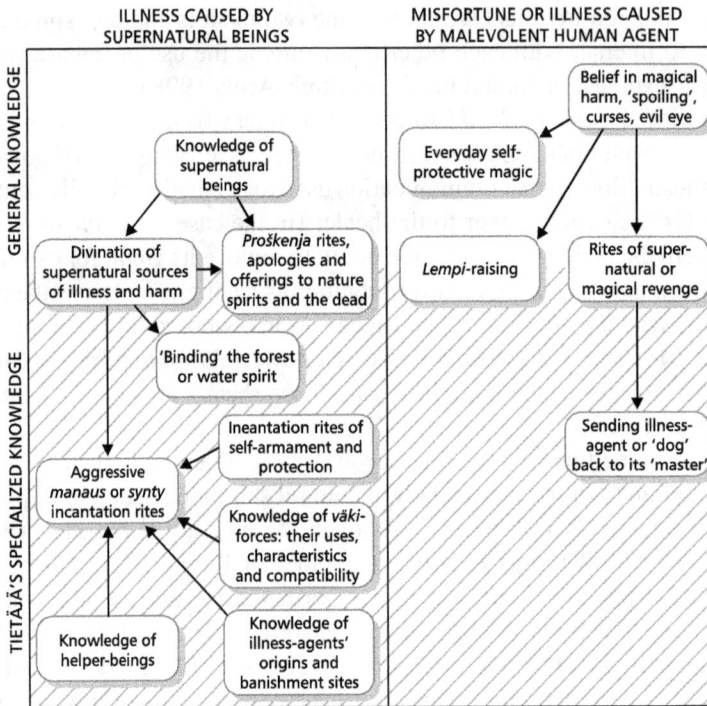

Figure 1. Sub-models of Finnish-Karelian traditional knowledge regarding supernatural harm.

In the figure above, belief in *väki*-forces is given its own domain represented by an oval bubble. Belief in the dichotomy between this world and the other, however, is not represented in Figure 1 as a separate domain because it in fact pervaded the entire magico-mythical worldview. While belief in *väki*-forces and knowledge of the mechanisms by which they operated was a specialized area of competence, generalized knowledge of the other world underlay all forms of belief in the supernatural – this is because magical harm was seen to come from the other world, even if summoned and 'sent' by a human enemy, and supernatural agents such as place spirits, divine protectors and the dead were seen to reside in the other world. It should be pointed out, however, that the specific mythical sites in the other world to which illness-agents were banished by the *tietäjä* represent a more specialized area of ritual knowledge, and are therefore shown separately in the figure above.

The fundamental duality of 'this world' (*tämänpuoli*) versus the 'other side' (*tuonpuoli*) was thus a core component of Finnish-Karelian folk belief, which was manifested in a rich array of concepts representing different historical layers of tradition (see Siikala 1992). Older Finno-Ugric conceptions of this world versus other worlds took the form of a cosmos with three, seven or nine layers or levels in which the world of living humans was located in the middle, that of the dead in the lower worlds, and powerful spirit beings in the upper worlds (Siikala 1992:52). Such an ancient cosmology is no longer apparent in the rituals examined in this study. Another feature of the older Finno-Ugric and shamanistic world view is the concept of a distant land of the dead, *Tuonela* or *Manala*, located beyond a body of water, or *Pohjola* as a land of the dead in the North (cf. Siikala 1992:104–149). Such places and their denizens are still mentioned in late 19th- and 20th- century healing incantations used by the *tietäjä* to protect himself. Additional sites in the other world mentioned in healing incantations included "heaven", wherein Ukko, the supreme god, dwelled; and various places of banishment in a mythical, far-flung wilderness, such as a "landlocked lake" (*umpilampi*), and "copper mountain" (*vaskivuori*, see Siikala 1992). On the other hand, the Orthodox Karelian rituals for the dead dealt with here emphasize the concept of a local 'land of the dead', that is, the village cemetery in which the dead dwelled in their graves (cf. Konkka 1985:54; Siikala 1992:115–117).

The Orthodox Karelian ritual descriptions and underlying beliefs recorded in the latter half of the 19th and first half of the 20th centuries do not offer a single coherent model for the 'other world' or 'other side'. Generally, living humans were represented as occupying 'this world' or 'this air', and all other supranormal and sacred agents (the dead, place spirits, God, saints and holy men, etc.) were seen to be residents of some 'other world' or 'other air'. It is often not clear whether these sacred agents were conceived of as occupying a single 'other world' together, or some succeeding series of 'other worlds'. Individual informants could refer to several interconnected 'other worlds' in their descriptions or verbal formulas: for instance Anni Lehtonen from Archangel Karelia mentioned a number of different "other worlds" connected to the dead in her interviews with folklore collector Samuli Paulaharju (Utriainen 1992). For Lehtonen, *Tuonela* was the dwelling place of dead, which, like *Manala*, could be thought of as the underground world of the grave, but it also possessed its own topography such as a river, fiery river or watchdog (ibid:87), images familiar from Karelian epic poetry (see Siikala 1992). In *Tuonela*, the dead lived in the manner of the living to some extent, even holding weddings for those who had died young (Utriainen ibid:88). *Manala*, which was in many ways seen to be similar to *Tuonela* in Lehtonen's descriptions, nonetheless did not reflect the everyday world of the living in the same way that *Tuonela* did. Those who ended up in *Manala* did so through no fault of their own – they were described as victims of irrational circumstances or sorcery and were generally seen to exist in a more passive state. The third type of world for the dead, or the *tuonilmainen* ("other air") was a place associated with sanctions, rewards or punishments in the afterlife. In the manner of the Christian Purgatory, whatever sins or taboo violations one had committed in life, one was forced to suffer corresponding punishments in the *tuonilmainen*. Terhi Utriainen (1992:92–93) characterizes the *tuonilmainen* as a moralized representation of the space associated with death, one reflecting cultural restrictions, norms and ideals in the individual's relationship with society. Even more nebulous were Anni Lehtonen's concepts of *taivas* ("heaven") and *helvetti* ("hell"), which were seen in positive versus negative terms respectively. Reaching *taivas*, however, did not depend on fulfilling moral conditions, rather, certain circumstances beyond the deceased's control, such as where one died, or the time of year, could result in being taken to *taivas* (Utriainen ibid:93–94).

In another case, Simana Sissonen, a *tietäjä* from Mekrijärvi in Orthodox Eastern Finland, used healing incantations which contained images of both a celestial other world, that is, "heaven"(*taivonen*) which contained divine helpers such as the Virgin Mary, and a distant other world located in the dark realm of the North (*Pohjola*), "beyond nine seas", which contained a different set of supernatural agents, including Väinämöinen, the ancient hero of Kalevalaic epic (Piela 2001).

The concept of the 'other world' or 'other side' glossed a number of divisions: that between the living and the dead, that between the forest wilderness and the human realm, and that between humans and divine figures such as God and saints. Each of the 'other worlds' also had its representative space in 'this world': that is, physical places or objects seen to be the locus of supranormal agency containing otherworldly force. These included: the cemetery, the village chapel, the forest, bodies of water or wells, icons and sarcophagi in monasteries, and the holy icons which hung in icon corners of homes, in chapels and churches. Each type of sacred agent was represented as inhabiting a different sort of 'other side'. The other world occupied by nature spirits, for example, was not a supernatural world per se, meaning above and beyond the natural physical world, but a world which was *extra societatem*, 'outside' society, as first proposed by Elli Köngäs-Maranda in connection with Finnish magic incantations (1967:91, see also Tarkka 1998). According to Köngäs-Maranda, 'other worlds' were sociomorphic realms which were substituted for the 'unknown' parts of the present reality, chiefly the wilderness.

The dead, on the other hand, were usually seen to carry on a vague otherworldly existence in the local cemetery. But even in the grave the deceased person was not seen to be tied only to the underground world of the cemetery: according to Harva (1932:480), Karelian laments speak occasionally of "the paths of the dead" which were the narrow trails along which the dead might wander the world from their cemetery residences. *Kalma*, on the other hand, which was the contagious, contaminating force of death, could extend beyond the boundaries of the cemetery: to riverbanks on which corpses had been washed, for example. And because cemeteries were sometimes situated far from the village itself (Harva 1932:476), in the midst of the forest, *kalma* also appears to have been closely identified with the natural wilderness.

The notion of the other world occupied by Christian saints is even more vague, and in many cases, saints were simply seen to be physically present in the holy icons which depicted them. These icons hung in all Orthodox homes, chapels and churches, occupying important places of honor. One tale which tells of holy icons destroyed in a monastery fire makes explicit the concrete equation between saints and the icons representing them. The informant reports that according to beliefs held by Orthodox Karelians, the holy icons were no longer to be found after the fire because the *jumalas* (= saints, holy icons) "had fled the fire on their own":

3)
…And when it had not been possible to save all of the holy icons, so the Russians said to the monks searching for them: the great *jumalas* escaped and the little *jumalas* got trampled underfoot. Namely in the great rush to stamp out the fire.
(Sortavala. 1938. Juho Hyvärinen. –Jaakko Kiukkonen, farmer, b. 1878)

Monastery figures, too, were manifested in the holy icons displayed in monasteries and churches. But unlike saints displayed in local village chapels, the holy men who founded the monasteries were believed to have physically lived and walked in the regions surrounding the monasteries, having left behind concrete traces such as footprints in stone.

The complexity and ambiguous nature of conceptual 'other worlds' can be seen from deeply-rooted concepts of supranormal contagion: the otherworldly 'essences' of the dead, wilderness, and even holy icons did not stay in their own realm but infected or attacked humans in 'this world' (see pages 77–110, 177–182). This cultural concept of contagion was reinforced by actual physical manifestations of disorder which were caused by, or seen to be caused by, agents and forces from the 'other worlds' (cattle attacked by forest predators, cattle lost in forest, mysterious human illness).

The second highly pervasive element of Finnish magical world view was therefore the belief in the existence of a dynamistic component to the entities in the world and their capacity to 'infect' human beings. The term *väki*[29] in Finnish folk belief was used specifically to refer to a system of belief in which impersonal forces of a supernatural nature were seen to inhabit a wide range of objects and spaces in the natural and cultural environment: forest, water, animals, fire, iron tools, etc.[30] According to this belief, many beings and categories of beings carried within themselves power charges, and since this dynamistic force could be dangerous, using it or being in contact with it required the taking of precautionary measures. Some of these beings and categories were more dynamistically powerful than others, or their väki forces were incompatible (Apo 1998). The notion of *väki* was the basis for other dynamistic categories in folk thought, such as *nenä*, *vihat*, and *luonto* (see Stark-Arola, 2002).

The concept of *väki* was first documented by that name in the late 18th century,[31] but was a fundamental part of the Finnish-Karelian mythico-magical world view already long before this (see Vilkuna 1956). At the same time, *väki* could refer to a 'group' or 'mass' of supernatural beings, and in many folk beliefs these two *väki* concepts are blurred. However, in this book I am primarily concerned with the first definition of *väki* as a theoretical underpinning of the concept *nenä* (see pp. 77–110).

Väki has been compared to the Melanesian concept of *mana*, the Iroquois concept of *orenda* (Haavio 1942:51; Hautala 1960:13; Honko 1960:88), and its closer Old Scandinavian counterpart *meginn* (Siikala 1992:173, 220). It should be made clear, however, that the term *väki* as used in Finnish-

Karelian rural communities never denoted an 'all-pervading' ,'immanent' or 'universal' force, but rather an impersonal 'power charge' of more limited scope ascribed to a tangible object or entity in the physical world. The folk or emic concept of *väki* in Finnish magic is therefore much more restricted and 'concrete' than either *mana* or *orenda*: in order for *väki* to have had an effect on its target, it had to be in close proximity and there had to be a clear, unobstructed path, if not actual physical contact, between the two. *Väki* was therefore not the supernatural principle operating in long-distance sorcery, for example, nor did the *väki* of the hunter defeat the *väki* of its prey, as with *orenda* (see Mauss 1974/1904:113). Unlike the case with *mana*, there were no specialized *väkis* to make people wealthy and to kill people (see ibid:109). *Väki* was the essence of an object or animate being, but not the power evoked by a magic ritual or incantation. Thus unlike *mana* in classic dynamistic theory, *väki* cannot be seen as the logical or historical underpinning for all religious or magical beliefs and practices (Mauss 1974/1904; Alles 1987). In other words, *väki* was not the same as magical or mystical force *in general,* as Mauss argued for *mana* and *orenda* (ibid:108–121). *Väki* and *mana* do share one aspect in common, however, and that is that they were forces that could be described in terms usually reserved for substances, indeed they were in some sense conceived of as substances: while *mana* could be described as 'heavy' or 'hot' (ibid:109), *väki* and other dynamistic forces in Finnish-Karelian folk thought could be described as 'hard' (see Stark-Arola, 2002).

When humans were in some way 'open', vulnerable or unguarded vis-à-vis certain *väki*-forces, it was thought that contact with *väki* could 'infect' humans, resulting in an illness which could take any number of forms in different parts of the body. Such illnesses were known by the emic terms *nenä, viha, hinku, vigahine, hinkautuminen, heittäyttyminen, nakkautuminen, and tartunta,* among others.[32] Holy icons and the wind were other sources of dynamistic infection, but were usually referred to only after infection had occurred, as *obrazanenä* and *tuulennenä* respectively. Kaarina Åstedt (1960:320–321) has suggested that the term *nenä*, 'a mysterious illness which results from infection by the forest, water, cemetery, etc.,' is linked etymologically to a wider field of meanings associated with 'taking offence, becoming angered, being indignant, etc.' (compare Finnish *nenäkäs*) and thus refers to the concrete result of the nature spirit's or dead person's *hostile nature* or *angered state*.

There were a number of different types of *väki* in Orthodox Karelian folk belief. These included, but were certainly not limited to *kallionväki* (*väki* located in rocky outcroppings, cliffs), *kalmanväki* (the dynamistic force associated with death and believed to reside in corpses, cemeteries and other things associated with gravesites and burials), *löylynväki* (*väki* contained in sauna steam), *maanväki* (*väki* located in the earth), *metsänväki* (*väki* located in the forest wilderness, trees, bears, game animals), *tulenväki* (*väki* located in fire, ash or a blacksmith's forge), and *vedenväki* (*väki* located in natural bodies of water, as well as wells and patches of wet, swampy ground). I discuss each of these briefly below:

kallion väki: cliffs and rocky outcroppings had their own *väki*, which was used among other things to help defendants achieve a favorable ruling in court proceedings. According to one informant, *kallionväki* was more difficult to control than other types of *väki*, and only elderly men handled it in former times. Another informant from Archangel Karelia[33] described how *kallionväki* was obtained and handled so as not to 'infect' the user: the *kallionväki* was to be obtained from a rock which was perpetually wet (known as a 'crying rock' (*itkevä kallio*), and which never saw the sun. From this rock one had to find a place where the rock had broken crosswise, and drop 3 silver coins into the cracks formed from this break. After this, one recited an incantation asking the rock for its *väki*, and took small pieces of rock from the crack using an old knife. These pieces were then wrapped in a bundle so that the sun never shone on them, and the bundle was kept in the user's pocket. According to the informant, all other *väkis*, with the exception of water's *väki*, were believed to fear this *väki*. The bundle containing *kallionväki* could be kept forever as long as the pieces of rock were never exposed to the sun, because if they were then their owner would fall ill from infection by this powerful *väki*.

kalman väki: the dynamistic force of *death* believed to reside in corpses, cemeteries, and other things associated with gravesites and burials. Infection by this *väki* could occur through consumption of things containing it (for instance, when soil from a grave was added secretly to the victim's food or drink), by being startled near a corpse in the laying-out room, or by offending the dead in some way, by thinking bad thoughts while walking past the cemetery, or not behaving properly at a funeral. Objects containing *kalman väki* were believed to be powerful aids in many types of magic.

löylyn väki: the dynamistic force located in sauna steam. This steam was not only seen as infectious in its own right, it was considered to be capable of transmitting illness and disease between two bathers who had both visited the sauna but had not necessarily been in contact. Certain magical precautions had to be taken in order that the *löylyn väki* would not infect or transmit disease to persons bathing in the sauna.

maan väki: the dynamistic force located in the *earth* or *ground*. This force was seen to be different on different farms, or in different types of ground used for different purposes. The illness resulting from an 'attack' of this *väki* could be precipitated, for example, when a bride did not greet the earth spirit when she first arrived on her husband's farm.

metsän väki: the dynamistic force located in the *forest* or its representatives (trees, bears, game animals). Infection by this *väki* could be precipitated by being startled by something in the forest or by not observing certain norms when hunting or trapping.

tulen väki: the dynamistic force located in fire, whether an open fire, or fire in a baking oven, sauna stove or blacksmith's forge. Although this *väki* had the potential to 'infect' if the fire was offended or treated badly by humans, it was in many cases considered to also be a 'healing' *väki*. Fire-*väki* was sometimes described as the most powerful *väki*, as well as being the youngest of 'siblings' (water was seen to be the 'eldest' sibling).

veden väki: the dynamistic force located in natural bodies of *water*, especially lakes and ponds, but also springs, wells and patches of wet, swampy ground. Infection by this *väki* could be precipitated by being startled when falling into the water, for example, or by accidentally splashing when drawing water from a well.

According to Satu Apo (1998:22), included in the Finnish-Karelian idea of *väki* was the notion that compatible *väki* forces could be combined, and that antagonistic *väki* forces could collide and wage battles in which the stronger defeated the weaker. Evidence of the incompatibility of various *väki* forces can be seen most clearly in the case of fire-*väki*, which was both extremely powerful and incompatible with numerous other *väkis*, and thus used by human magic-users to control and defeat the *väkis* in their environment (see Stark-Arola, 2002).[34] Fire-*väki* was seen, for instance, to be incompatible with cemetery-*väki*, and it was believed that the two types of *väki* (stored in the pockets of two different magic-users, for example) could not remain in same room together, otherwise they would begin to "clatter and roar". [35] Fire-*väki* was also used to drive out forest-*väki* and particularly water-*väki*. For example, if one wanted to make the water spirit angry, an oven-broom containing fire-*väki* was submerged in the lake where the water spirit resided.[36] It was also believed that persons who were infected with water-*väki* could be cured with fire-*väki* ("*Veden väki karkoitettiin tulen väellä*").[37]

Sacred agents

The present study deals with several different types of sacred agents. The **Christian saints and holy personages** who appear most often in Orthodox Karelian folk religious ritual were Jesus (*Spoassu*), the Virgin Mary (*Maaria, Bohoroditša*), St. Nicholas (*Mikkula*), the apostle Peter (*Pietari, Petri*), St. Blaise (*Valassi, Ulassie*, or *Olassii*), St. Elijah (*Ilja*), Ss. Florus and Laurus (*Frola* and *Laura* or *Bourei* and *Laurej*), St. Anastasia (*Nastassie*), and St. George (*Jyrki* or *Jyri*). In official church tradition there were actually two different saints named George, but in the folk tradition these two were melded into a single figure.[38] The sacred **dead** were those deceased relatives who could still be personally remembered by the living, and who were considered to 'reside' in the village cemetery. Sacred **monastery figures** (*pyhittäjät*) in belief legends, folk beliefs and ritual descriptions included: Ss. Sergius and Herman, the founders of Valamo monastery;[39] SS. Zosimus and Sabbatius (*Savatij* and *Sosima* or *Isossim*), founders of Solovki (*Solovetski*) monastery;[40] St. Aleksander of Svir, (1449–1533; also known as *Oleksi Svirskoi*), founder of the Monastery of the Holy Trinity (*Stroitsa* or *Troitsa*);[41] St. Arsenius of Konevits (1360–1447), founder of the Konevits (*Konevitsa*) monastery; [42] St. Nicholas (*Mikkula*), who was connected to Valamo monastery because of a monastery church dedicated to him;[43] and St. Adrian of Andrusov (also known variously as *Ondrei Ondrayski* or *Antrei*

Antonski, for example), founder of a small monastery in Olonets on the eastern shore of Lake Ladoga.[44] Sacred monastery agents tended to be depicted as 'holy' not because of their saintly qualities of character such as kindness, mercy, patience and charity, but because of their supernatural control over the natural environment: they cured diseases, fed multitudes single-handedly, defied the laws of gravity by sailing on flat rocks across the water, or their buildings built themselves overnight. In some stories they also are said to have driven out demons, for example.

Nature spirits included spirits of the forest (*metsänhaltia*), water (*vedenhaltia*), and earth (*maanhaltia*), among others. In referring to the forest spirit in their narratives, informants used a number of different terms, including *piru*, *karu*, *piessa* and *metšiine*. When ritually addressing the forest spirit, on the other hand, different names and titles of respect were used, for example "forest master (*metsän isäntä*)" and "forest mistress (*metsän emäntä*)", as well as "forest's golden king (*metsän kultainen kuningas*)", "forest groom, silken-beard (*Metsän sulho, sulkuparta*)" "Mielikki daughter of the forest (*Mielikki Metosen tytti*)", and "Tapio's precise wife (*Tarkka Tapion vaimo*)". The epithets used for the forest spirit most commonly referred to its gender and sometimes its age or social status as well, and for female spirits, whether they were wife or daughter of the patriarch-like male forest spirit. The main categories of nature spirits could also be further subdivided into highly specific types of say, earth spirits or wind spirits. For instance, one supplicatory ritual incantation recited by a female informant from Olonets Karelia addressed four different kinds of wind spirits: *pohjazen tuuli* ("northerly wind"), *koillizen tuuli* ("easterly wind"), *merituuli* ("the sea wind"),[45] and *suvizen tuuli* ("the southerly wind").[46] A male informant from Ladoga Karelia addressed nine different wind spirits in his incantation: *koilline tuuli* ("easterly wind"), *ahava tuuli* ("March wind"), *ranta-tuuli* ("southeasterly wind"), *suvi-tuuli* ("southerly wind"), *töine tuuli* or *šoloiniekku*, ("southwesterly wind"), *luuveh tuuli* ("northwesterly wind"), *kaltaine tuuli* ("westerly wind"), *pohjaine tuuli* ("northerly wind"), and *maalline tuuli* ("northeasterly wind").[47]

In another example, a woman from Olonets Karelia named five different kinds of earth spirits (*moahizel*): *tulimoahizel* ("the earth spirit occupying land cleared by burn-beating"), *kylymoahizel* ("the earth spirit of the sauna"), *ligamoahizel* ("the earth spirit of waste land"), *vezimoahizel* ("the earth spirit of swampy land"), and *pihamoahizel* ("the earth spirit of the barnyard"). A female informant from a different village in the same district classified the earth spirits in her verbal greeting differently. According to her, there existed earth spirits occupying "reddish land (*ruskei moa*), white land (*valgei moa*), black land (*muštu moa*), grey land (*harmoi moa*), multicolored land (*kirjavu moa*), land for growing grain (*eloi moa*), land on which humans live (*kanzoi moa*), land on which the sauna is built (*kylymoa*), and burn-beat land (*tulimoa*)". The classification of nature spirits thus appears to have been closely associated with the cultural classification of one's natural surroundings in terms of different points of the compass and different areas of land-use. On the other hand, the different colored 'earths' mentioned above may not necessarily have referred to actual land, but may be a reference to various categories in the "other world". The mythical or 'otherworldly' nature of animals, topographic features, spirits, etc. was often signalled by describing them using epithets referring to colors such as red, black, and "multicolored" (see Siikala 1992), or the 'golden' appearing in numerous incantations in this volume.

Nature spirits lived unseen in their surroundings, but could reveal themselves to humans in various forms, usually human or animal. Finnish and Karelian nature spirits were often single beings, the lone occupant of a particular locality (Vilkuna 1963:354), but in some contexts, ritual formulas address an entire kin community of nature spirits, complete with fathers, mothers, grandparents, children, etc., as well as representatives of a class society: judges, priests, kings, servants, slaves. In these incantations it is clear that the place spirits were thought to inhabit another world which was the approximate mirror-image of the human world, at least in terms of social organization (see Köngäs-Maranda 1967).

Sacred agents in Karelian folk religion were seen to be empirical beings, that is, rituals were an *encounter* with the supernatural, but memorates describing actual sensory experiences (the agent appeared in some visible form, spoke, made noise, etc.) are few. Generally the assumption appears to have been that the sacred agent was present in some invisible form, nearby or omnipresent, and was able to 'see' and 'hear' what the human participant said or did, but did not reveal itself, at least not directly.

All of the sacred agents discussed in this study were supernatural agents in a reciprocal exchange relationship with humans, in which the exchange was guided by moral codes and obligations seen to be shared by both parties. The present study does not, therefore, deal with entities or objects which were not explicitly *sentient* (i.e. sacred groves, trees, rocks, etc.), or with whom there was no *two-way ritual communication* (i.e. numen-type hauntings, sightings of water nymphs, beliefs concerning the Devil, appeals for aid made to the Virgin Mary, Ukko, or Väinämöinen). An important criteria for sacred agency in this study is *anthropopathy*, the attribution of human-like emotions and desires to the supernatural being, as well as its ability to act in a morally prescribed manner.

The most common emotion attributed to sacred agents was *anger*. This anger was expressed when human beings offended, violated or trespassed the sacred agent's area of concern, as in the following description: "In former times, several places were considered to become angry and offended if they were approached at an improper time or manner. They sent diseases into people, they 'became angry (*snieppaantuivat*)' and many eye and skin diseases were caused by this…"[48]

The water-spirit or simply 'water' in a personified sense was the most commonly mentioned 'angry' agent in these narratives. For example, as was explained by informants from Ladoga and Olonets Karelia, "the well in Radila village in Kolatselkä is a very angry well. One can easily be infected with illness (*maahinen*) from it";[49] "it was also the custom to give offerings of pieces of bread to the river running through the village of Palomylly in

Suistamo when it 'became angry'";[50] or "when water is not angry, then it does not want any gift. When it is angry, then one gives the gift".[51]

Although sacred agents were seen to dwell in the other world, they were also *proprietary* beings in this world, occupying and reserving privileges either in a particular physical *space* which bordered that of the human community, or requiring particular respect and caution from humans at certain *times* in the annual or diurnal cycle. These times could include, for example, certain days of the year when foods were to be brought to the cemetery and rituals performed for the dead, or times when one was supposed to avoid the 'territory' of a sacred agent believed to be easily aroused or angered. The water-spirits residing in wells were reported to be particularly quick to anger when disturbed at improper times. According to one informant from Olonets Karelia, "after the sun goes down one must no longer chip ice from a well. If one must do so, then the well must first be given, for example, coffee as payment."[52] A folklore collector in Ladoga Karelia explained, "…in Äimäjärvi village in Suitsamo parish there was a deep well owned by my informant's father, and it was not good to go past it at night or in the evening. When somebody showed symptoms of a strange skin disease, it was soon said: 'You have walked past that well in the evening, that is the cause of this disease.'"[53]

Ritual incantations addressed to nature spirits also referred to their anger: "Forest masters, forest mistresses / forest's mighty elders… / since you have become angry / we must ask forgiveness!"[54] One informant from Archangel Karelia, in describing a ritual of appeasement made to the forest spirit following infection from the forest, reported that the patient was brought to the site of infection, bowed facing the northeast, and spoke the following words of greeting: "Forgive me Mielikki, forest mistress / My golden king of the wilds," etc., after which "the patient had only to remember not to look back when returning home, because if the place spirit happened to be in a bad mood, then despite those eloquent words, it might make a horrible racket, and if one looked back at that moment, one was in danger of becoming the target of its anger."[55]

The notion of a sacred agent having certain territorial rights runs through nearly all folk beliefs and ritual descriptions concerning them. Any person or animal, for instance, arriving on an unfamiliar farm for an extended stay had to receive permission from the farm's own earth spirit, or even had to "buy" a piece of earth from the earth spirit, in order to avoid angering or offending it. Those at risk from the earth spirit included brides moving into the household of their husband's kin,[56] new servants,[57] newly-bought cows[58] and even newborn babies[59] and calves.[60] Ritual greetings and sometimes concrete gifts such as food and silver coins were given to the earth spirit in order to placate it and ensure its acceptance of the newcomer: "then the earth spirit knows that the person is part of the household",[61] and during a funeral, money was thrown into the grave in order to "buy" the plot of earth from the earth spirit for the dead person (examples 4a and 4b below):

4a)

[At the funeral] one throws a copper coin into the grave and while throwing, says three times: "this earth is purchased". This is said so that the dead person (*pokoiniekku*) will become the *moal izändy* [=earth spirit, lit. 'master of the earth'] there.

(Säämäjärvi. 1936–38. Jefim Popoff E 141).

4b)

A copper coin was thrown on the grave and it was said to the dead person: "buy this earth" (with the money) .

(Tulemajärvi. 1932–38. Maija Juvas 75. –Katri Markström. Parentheses in the original).

Pilgrimage and monasteries

As a universal human phenomenon rich in history, symbols, ideas and behaviors, pilgrimage has become an increasingly popular object of study in several humanistic fields. Pilgrimages are journeys undertaken as acts of devotion to places considered by a community of believers to be holy. In various religions these places can be mountains, shrines or caves to name but a few, and many cities such as Jerusalem, Rome and Mecca have historically been, and continue to be, pilgrimage goals. The renewed scholarly interest in pilgrimage within Europe and the Holy Land has given rise to numerous scholarly studies appearing in the late 1980s and early 1990s.[62] Along with these have been a number of studies devoted to *popular* or *folk* dimensions of pilgrimage, for when anthropologists began to study pilgrimage in the field as it was actually practiced by devotees, they began to appreciate that popular pilgrimage, as a cultural form of its own, could differ markedly in its aims from those of the official Church regarding devotional journeys.

In cultural anthropology, much of the new interest in pilgrimage has been in response to Victor and Edith Turner's formulation of pilgrimage as a liminal phenomenon which tends towards anti-structure and *communitas*, a paradigm which they put forward in their influential study *Image and Pilgrimage in Christian Culture* (1978). Subsequent scholars in the fields of anthropology and cultural geography who have tested the Turners' theories in the field across a variety of cultures have generally found them inadequate; the current consensus among anthropologists of a slightly more postmodern bent is that pilgrimage is an arena of competing discourses, pilgrims are motivated by mixed agendas, they bring with them their own beliefs and attitudes, and that pilgrimage often reinforces rather than dissolves social boundaries – *communitas* is clearly neither the outcome nor even the goal of all pilgrimage journeys.[63]

In Greek and Russian Orthodoxy, *monasteries* have historically been among the most popular sites of pilgrimage, and this is also true for the region of Orthodox Karelia. Pilgrimages were made primarily to four monasteries in Orthodox Karelia: **Valamo** and **Konevits** on Lake Ladoga,

Solovki on the White Sea, and the **Monastery of the Holy Trinity** in Olonets Karelia along the Syväri river.[64] Smaller chapels, for example the chapel at Orusjärvi in Salmi which was built on the site of a destroyed monastery, were also popular sites of pilgrimage. Each year, tens of thousands of pilgrims visited these monasteries, chiefly Valamo and Solovki. Pilgrimage was usually a collective experience rather than an individual one, since persons travelled together with fellow villagers and those from neighboring villages to the monasteries and their festivals.[65]

Over the past decade there has been heightened interest among Finnish scholars in re-examining and mapping out the various social, cultural and historical features of Orthodox monasteries in Karelia prior to World War II.[66] A major focus of this research has been Valamo monastery on Lake Ladoga and its history during this century, including the composition and dynamics of the monastery community in the 1930s,[67] the cultural geography of Valamo before World War II,[68] and pilgrimage to Valamo in the 1930s.[69] This interest in monasteries and pilgrimage in Finland can be traced to the works of historian Heikki Kirkinen, which first appeared in the 1960s to challenge the prevailing view of Orthodox Karelia as a cultural backwater and to highlight the important role of monasteries in bringing Byzantine culture to Northwest Russia as early as the 11th century.

While recent scholarship has tended to focus on the *institutional* and *official* aspects of pilgrimage in Karelia from the viewpoint of the monastery inhabitants and intellectual and cultural leaders,[70] the view of monasteries and pilgrimage held by the semi-literate rural population has received little attention in historical or religious studies scholarship. In earlier articles (Stark 1995, 1997, Stark-Arola 1999), I have compared and contrasted 'folk' views of pilgrimage with 'official' and 'intellectual' perspectives on pilgrimage in the 1930s. In the present study, I again raise the issue of folk pilgrimage, but this time I place it *alongside other forms of Orthodox Karelian folk religion* and analyze them together as elements of a single folk religious system. I explore how pilgrimage and monasteries were viewed by the same segment of the rural population which participated in religious festivals (*praas-niekkas*), sacrificial festivals of pre-Christian origin, memorial rituals for the dead, and ritual communication with nature spirits. My assumption that the same rural segment of the population was involved in both local folk religious rituals and pilgrimage to monasteries is supported by the fact that in my material at least eleven folk informants gave descriptions of both forms of devotion. From Ladoga Karelia, these are: Martta Kuha, Maria Kuosmanen, Martta Kähmi, Paraskeeva Makkonen, Nastja (Natalia) Rantsi, and Outti Feudorantytär Torgouttšu; from Olonets Karelia: Anni Agafonov, J. Avoketo, Maksima Jevlona, and Solomanida Petrov, and from Archangel Karelia: Marina Takalo.

My point of departure in analyzing the folk experience of pilgrimage is that sacred messages and meanings are never contained in fixed form within the pilgrimage site itself but are constructed and transmitted both by pilgrims and by the institutions controlling the site. Such image-making takes place through the stories, legends and anecdotes which make up what Morinis

Festival of Apostles Peter and Paul (*Pedrunpäivä*) at Valamo monastery, 1909.
Photo: T.H. Järvi. National Board of Antiquities.

(1992:18) calls the 'informational field' of the sacred center. Because the pilgrims' knowledge of this informational field affects their perception and experience of the pilgrimage site once they reach it (e.g. Bowman 1991), in my view it is not possible to speak of the pilgrimage experience without taking the informational field into consideration. Rather than a monolithic institution, pilgrimage should be viewed as "a realm of competing discourses" (Eade and Sallnow 1991:5). This can be clearly seen in Orthodox Karelia, where the stories told by the 'folk' represent, on the whole, a different tradition than the one transmitted by monastery and church officials (Stark 1995, 1999). A contributing factor in the divide between popular and official tradition surrounding the monastery was the fact that the monastery monks were almost exclusively Russian-speaking, while most pilgrims from surrounding areas spoke Karelian as their mother tongue.

A dichotomy between 'official' and 'popular' perspectives on pilgrimage is nonetheless too simplistic to describe the complexity of the social interaction which took place at the sacred center. At Valamo monastery in the late 19th and early 20th centuries, for instance, there were at least six categories of persons involved in pilgrimage: (1) monastery monks, mostly Russian-speaking, who dwelled at the monastery; (2) Finnish-speaking Orthodox church officials, priests, seminary teachers and students, and like-minded intellectuals who undertook pilgrimages (see Stark 1995); (3) Lutheran tourists from among the political and intellectual elite of Finland (especially after 1918, see ibid.); (4) Russian-speaking pilgrims from St. Petersburg and other parts of Russia; (5) the literate, Karelian-speaking members of the rural population who maintained written correspondence and personal contact with monastery monks and who mentioned personal visits with them as part of the pilgrimage sojourn (see Kilpeläinen 2000); and (6) those Karelian-speaking persons from the lowest socio-economic levels of the rural community, who, in their accounts of pilgrimage or narratives concerning the monastery, never mentioned living monks by name or gave any indication that they had any personal contact with monastery residents. I have argued elsewhere (Stark 1995) that the goals and motivations of this last category of pilgrims were not strictly spiritual in the sense of an intimate, personal relationship with the divine, but were also supernaturally-oriented, that is, part of a broader view of the 'other world' which was not derived solely from Christian teachings. It is this last group of pilgrims which is the focus of the present study.

What was the function of pilgrimage in the lives of these rural peasants? Historians have noted that at various times and places Christian pilgrimage has been conceived of as a spiritual exercise, an imitation of Christ and his Saints (Davies 1988: 184–202), and some scholars have likewise tended to emphasize pilgrimage as a form of communication with the divine which allows the pilgrim to deepen his/her relation with the Supreme Being (Preston 1992: 45), or experience a spiritual transformation, (Gothóni 1993: 108). Here I understand 'spiritual' to refer to an inner process of self-examination in a personal, intimate relationship with God. Karelian folk narratives, however, do not address these motives. There is no mention of a longing for a closer union with God or individual spiritual growth, no emphasis on sin and repentance, no evident self-reflection or even mention of the afterlife. Spiritual exercises such as prayer are only mentioned in the narratives in an active, communal and immediate goal-oriented form, usually with direct effects on the weather, as in one story where prayer resulted in a sudden storm which saved the monastery from a pirate attack, and another in which prayer brought badly needed rain for monastery crops.[71]

We do not know whether folklore collectors ever asked folk informants about their intimate religious experiences, but it is clear that informants viewed the collectors' questions and conversations as open-ended, given the great diversity of the information they provided. People did not only tell collectors their folklore repertoires but also recounted their personal and idiosyncratic experiences of pilgrimage. Insofar as language is the only key to the experiences and perceptions of other persons and we are unable to speculate on what may or may not have been left unsaid by informants, Karelian folk narratives concerning monasteries and pilgrimage suggest informants' interest in a *tangible* sacredness rather than a *mystical* one.

According to the informants themselves, a primary motivation for pilgrimage was the receipt of some concrete benefit bestowed by God, the Virgin Mary or legendary holy hermits in return for having made the pilgrimage journey. Pilgrimage in the folk narrative tradition comes across not so much as a spiritual transformation but as a type of *exchange* or *transaction* with a specific aim or reward in mind. Persons made holy vows in which they promised to undertake a pilgrimage journey in order to receive something in return. This seems to have been viewed by informants as a straightforward exchange: children were pledged to monasteries in return for a cure, or a 'substitute' pilgrim could make the pilgrimage journey in order to seek a cure for another person too ill to travel (Kilpeläinen 2000). The role of pilgrimage and sacred centers in exchange transactions between humans and divinities appears to be a nearly universal phenomenon, as John Eade and Michael Sallnow (1991:24) point out:

> In most cases, the dominant motive for going on a pilgrimage is to request some favor of God or the shrine divinity in return for simply having made the journey or for engaging in ancillary devotional exercises. As transformation stations between the earthly and heavenly realms, pilgrimage shrines are the pre-eminent centres for dealings between human beings and the divine. In many ways, they represent the stock exchanges of the religious economy. Using the shrine divinity as a mediator, physical suffering and penance are exchanged for material and spiritual favors, contracts are forged with the saints, sin is amortized by means of a tariff of devotional or ascetic practices, and in many instances indulgences may be earned merely by dint of having attended the shrine festival and having expended earthly time in doing so.

A second reason for popular interest in monasteries was linked to the folk belief system of traditional Karelian culture. For ordinary pilgrims, the monasteries were *not* places to experience the divine in terms dictated by the official church (see Stark 1995), instead they offered glimpses of the *supernatural* as seen through a different set of cultural models and images. Supernatural motifs familiar from Finnish and Karelian belief legends abound in narratives told by pilgrims and others. Informants told how monastery founder St. Arsenius of Konevits drove a dragon-like demon from Konevits island, [72] how the body of St. Adrian of Andrusov refused to remain buried after death,[73] and how monastery buildings under construction raised themselves overnight. [74] The monasteries were places where monks and priests had used 'magic' to conceal their treasure,[75] and had the power to foresee the future.[76] The monastery was also, for example, seen to contain magical coffins which 'spoke' and were possessed by place spirits (*haltias*), which could be seen and heard by the pilgrims themselves:

5a)
At Valamo, in the church of Nikolai, there was a chapel which contained a place spirit (*haldiekas*). There in the chapel was an ancient coffin which was able to speak. When you hit the coffin with a birch branch, it said: 'Nikolai, Nikolai, Nikolai'. A lot of people have heard that coffin speak. (Suistamo. Siiri Oulasmaa a) 6211. 1961. –Ivan Ladovaara (Plattonen), 78 years).

5b)
At Valamo there is the grave of Ss. Sergei and Herman. 'It is a *haldiekas* chapel'. They have the best guardian spirit (*haltija*) because they are real holy hermits. They can be compared to Christ. People's sicknesses are cured in the chapel when they pray there in true faith.
(Suistamo. Siiri Oulasmaa a) 6214. 1961. – Mihaila Shinda, 64 years).

A motif of floating rocks commonly found in Finnish-Karelian legends of witches and giants (Haavio 1936) was also used to describe how monastery founders sailed long ago to the monastery islands. This theme of holy hermits sailing on floating stones or stone rafts, even mill stones, was particularly widespread, with over twenty variants recorded from Archangel, Ladoga and Olonets Karelia, as well as districts in northern and eastern Finland: [77]

6a)
The monastery island of Konevitsa was formerly "Horse Island" (*Hevossaari*), where the people of Sortta Bay let their horses out to pasture. There came two Russian pilgrims looking for a site for a monastery. Having arrived at Sortta Bay, they began to want to go to Horse Island. But there were no boats. They hardly let this worry them, but rather went down on their knees on some stones and prayed to God for help and for a way to reach the island. After they prayed for a time, the stones became so light that the praying men could sail on those stones just like a boat over the sound, 5 kilometres from Sortta Bay to Horse Island. Who knows how long they might have prayed, but one can still see those two stones in front of the guesthouse of Konevitsa monastery...
(Pyhäjärvi V.l. 1935–36. Yrjö Kinnari KRK 126:256. –Heikki Kuranen, 51 years).

6b)
Sergei and Hermann (...) were Russian by birth and left a certain island by sailing, each standing upon a separate stone, and they sailed the seas and rivers and then the stones came to rest on the shore of Valamo monastery and they came to land and praised God...
(Suojärvi. 1936. Juho Koivunen KT 128:8.)

6c)
When Konevitsa monastery was founded, and its founder went to view the site, he travelled the seas and rivers on a stone. The stone is still on Ukonsaari Island, with a cross on top of it.
(Impilahti. 1939. J. Hautala 1243. –Paavo Jaatinen, 53 years).

6d)
In former times the old people said that Sroizza, Valmoija and Solohkoi were brothers. They rowed to *Solovetski* on a stone raft...
(Suistamo. 1936. M. Kähmi 16).

6e)
There were once three brothers, three holy men, who lived at Valamo. One of them remained at Valamo, but two of them sailed away on stone rafts and each founded a monastery, one at *Troitsa* [=Monastery of the Holy Trinity] and the other at *Orosova* [=Orusjärvi]....
(Salmi>Impilahti. 1936. Eino Toiviainen 17. –Jaakko Kämäläinen, 52 years).

6f)
Oleksei Svirskii was a holy man…He sailed on a stone over the lake and didn't drown. In his memory the monastery of Oleksei Svirskii on the eastern shore of Lake Ladoga was founded.
(Salmi. 1946. O. Harju 3868).

6g)
An old story tells how the brothers Sergei and Herman, who founded Valamo monastery, had rowed to Valamo on a millstone.
(Harlu. 1936. Siiri Vaarna KT 141:14. – J. Sokkanen, former police constable, b. 1861 in Ruskeala).

A focus on the popular aspect of pilgrimage and its informational field allows us to grasp the complexity of the dialectic between official and folk perspectives on pilgrimage. This was not merely a 'top-down' process in which the teachings from the monastery institution were transmitted to the rural laity, but also a 'bottom-up' one, in which pilgrims brought to the monastery their own unique syncretic world view and experienced the monastery through their own frame of reference. The way in which pilgrims responded to the monasteries was a continuation of their daily attitude toward the sacred in which they fulfilled their obligations and asked for aid in return. I argue, therefore, that journeys to the sacred center represented for rural pilgrims an extension of the same strategies that were utilized in everyday village life to alleviate ordinary crises.

Types of ritual examined in this study

On the basis of both formal and functional criteria, including the purpose of the ritual as reported by informants, the ritual sequence of events, and the use or non-use of Kalevala meter incantations, the source materials used in this study can be divided into seven different ritual types. When we consider where these rites took place, we can group these seven ritual types into two main classes: (A) those performed on the smaller scale of farm, village, and home district, and (B) those directed at pilgrimage goals located at greater distances from the pilgrims' home districts, as can be seen below:

A. 'Folk religious rituals performed in and oriented toward local surroundings'

1) *proškenja* rituals to cure *nenä*-type illnesses deriving from the forest spirit, water spirit, dead and cemeteries, earth spirit, wind, and holy icons.

2) rituals for letting the cows out to pasture in the spring (addressed to forest spirit, bear, Christian saints).

3) rituals to release lost cows or children from the forest cover (aimed at forest spirit).

4) rituals to maintain contact with the dead (memorial rituals, ritual 'feeding' of the dead, dreams).

5) sacrificial festivals (oriented toward Christian saints/to provide protection against forest predators).

6) offerings made to Christian saints at local village chapels in return for healing and protection (*jeäksintä*).[78]

B. 'Supralocal folk religious rituals'

7) pilgrimage to monasteries and sacred vows (*jeäksintä*).

I wish to make clear at the outset that I locate *both* of these ritual classes at the level of folk religion (as opposed to official religion). The pilgrimage journeys carried out by the semi-literate laity were *not* necessarily more closely connected to official Orthodox teachings than was exchange with nature spirits and the dead, since all of these were manifestations of *popular* belief and practice.

All seven types of ritual listed above share in common the fact that they favored the tendency toward social and economic equilibrium achieved through exchange and reciprocity, both within the peasant community and between humans and sacred agents. The seventh type of ritual analyzed here, *pilgrimage to monasteries*, differs from the preceding ritual types in that it did not take place within the local community of the performer (farm or village milieu). Nevertheless, pilgrimage shares a number of features in common with ritual types 1–6 above. For instance, all of the seven ritual types possessed the *formality* and *distinctiveness* mentioned earlier as the key criteria of ritual. Local folk religious rites were formalized sets of behaviors following a certain pattern and utilizing specific distinctive elements such as symbolic gestures and the use of traditional Kalevala meter incantation formulas. Similarly, although different meanings may be attributed to pilgrimage cross-culturally, it is never an ordinary journey but a formalized one, with certain rules and expectations which make it distinctive (the trip must be arduous, made on foot, certain places along the way are set apart by the practice of special customs, the journey is made to fulfill a holy vow, and so forth). Second, pilgrimage, like the other rituals discussed in this book, involves social knowledge acted out through the body.

Finally, and most importantly for this study, both popular pilgrimage and local folk religious rites represented a form of communication and exchange with sacred monastery agents. In both types of folk religious ritual, this communication and exchange could take the form of fulfilling a holy vow. A thematic bridge is thus formed between the two main classes of rituals A and B by the common features found in ritual types 6 and 7, namely that both offerings to local chapels and pilgrimage involved holy vows or promises that the supplicant would visit the sacred site (village chapel or monastery). In both cases, such vows were referred to using the term *jiäksie, jeäksintä* or *jiäksinta*. The fact that rural peasants conceived of these two types of ritual activity as related can be seen in the following description of *jeäksintä* which mentions both as elements of the same idea:

7)
In order to remove or prevent illness, misfortune or injury, people made a holy vow (*jiäksittih*) to take for example a candle to the village chapel (*tsasounah*) or church; often an candle was promised to a particular holy icon. One could promise to give a horse, cow or heifer to a monastery or chapel. It was told that in Kontu village, on the other side of the border, the informant's mother had promised a heifer to St. George when the cattle were let out to pasture in spring so that St. George would protect the cattle. The heifer was sold and the money was given to benefit the chapel, in that chapel there was a holy icon of St. George, among others. The informant's grandmother, on the other hand, had "jiäksinnyh", that is, made a holy vow to visit the Orusjärvi chapel from Miinala village either by foot or with bare feet, she did not remember exactly. It was recalled that the reason for the vow was some illness, most likely an ailment in the legs. (Salmi. 1932. Martta Pelkonen. KKTK-KKA, entry: *jiäksie*)

Even if not specifically referred to as *jeäksintä*, all seven ritual types listed above involved a pledge or oath of some sort to sacred agents. It is this formal promise or contract found in all of these ritual types which makes it relevant to compare them within the same analytic framework.

The classification of folk religious behavior into the foregoing seven ritual types provide one means of showing the reader, at a glance, the scope of ritual activity dealt with in this study. However, such categories in and of themselves reveal little about the meaning and function of folk religious rituals for the people who practiced them. This is particularly due to the highly syncretic nature of the rituals, and the fact that in actual accounts by folk informants, the distinctions between these divisions are often blurred. Ritual typologies such as the one presented above tell us more about categories in the researcher's mind than they do about the way in which Orthodox Karelian ritual participants saw the world. In order to approach the emic or folk models of thought reflected in folk religious ritual, we must first take a closer look at its fuzzy categories and ask ourselves whether this 'fuzziness' might operate according to an identifiable pattern. This is the topic of the next section.

The problem of folk religion's fuzzy taxonomies

Earlier in this century, Karelian folk religion was examined by Finnish folklorists from a diachronic, comparative, and historical-geographic perspective (e.g. Waronen 1898; Krohn 1915; Holmberg (later Harva) 1916, 1948; Mansikka 1941, 1943). These older studies aimed at uncovering the most ancient layers of religious practices and beliefs of the Finno-Ugric or Finnic peoples, and revealed formal similarities among rituals across a broad geographic region and a large number of cultures. The present study, by contrast, is an attempt at a systematic mapping of folk religious cultural models and their function *within a single cultural area*, as well as the interrelationship between these models in the late 19th and early 20th centuries.

One reason for the researcher to adopt a synchronic perspective and seek functional rather than formal similarities among agents and events in Orthodox Karelian folk religion is that the rituals examined here, oriented as they were toward everyday goals and specific *communicative* objectives with supernatural agents, generally strove for clarity in expression and therefore eschewed the archaisms and mythological images which would lend themselves to a diachronic or comparative study (cf. Siikala 1992). A second, more important reason, is that within Orthodox Karelian folk religion, categories of divine figures and key ritual concepts were often hazy (Järvinen 1993). Ritual concepts and designations could have multiple meanings, and the sacred agents described in the texts were often only vaguely identified, or appear to have been 'fusions' of two different categories of sacred agents. This was not due to ignorance or confusion among uneducated Karelians so much as the fact that among the ordinary people, the sacred was kept relevant and practical for everyday needs in 'this world' (making a living, preserving one's health, keeping out of harm's way), and was also important for communal identity.

The folklore materials used in this study provide numerous cases in point. Strict identification of a particular saint, for instance, was often not important: an informant might not necessarily know a saint by name, but rather by his or her appearance in holy icons or function in healing for example toothache, as was the case with the Ladoga Karelian women who reported the following:

> 8a)
> ...and then they put a *jumala* [=god, saint, holy icon] in the monastery, I don't know the *jumala's* name. He wore birchbark shoes, they were not tied with laces...
> (Salmi. 1934. Martti Haavio 1694. – Nastja Rantsi, 49 years).

> 8b)
> ...There are also other icons there too. One is St. Nicholas, then there is St. Elijah, and then the Virgin Mary, then there is the "tooth-saint" (*hammazjumal*), I don't recall his name, he is in the entryway, above the *tsasouna* door, on top of the lintel...
> (Salmi. 1935. Martta Pelkonen 362. – Outti or Oudottu Feudorantytär Torgouttšu, nee Lammas).

A holy icon depicting a Biblical event or legendary event in the history of the Church could be interpreted as a sentient agent able to provide help and prosperity. This is evidence that the folk tended to 'read' the images or visual 'texts' of the holy icons in a manner different than what the Church intended. In one case, the icon known in the vernacular as *voznesennal*, depicting the event of Christ's Ascension and replete with numerous human figures, was treated as a sacred *agent* to whom one could turn in time of crisis, for example when boating on Lake Ladoga. Help would arrive if one promised to buy and light a taper in front of the icon.[79] Another such agent was *sviizoi*, the folk name for the icon and Orthodox holy day which commemorated *The*

Exaltation of the Cross (September 14). Yet another was "Uspenja Bohorooditsa", to whom one prayed in order that the flax would grow. According to one collector's notes, Uspenja Bohorooditsa was really "a festival commemorating *The Dormition of the Mother of God*, actually the icon depicting this event, which the informant has understood to mean a saint by this name."[80] The icon for *The Presentation of Christ in the Temple* was similarly seen as a supernatural agent known as "St. Sreitenny the provider",[81] who cured people of toothache in the chapel of Palojärvi village (see Part III, example 4a), and in Suojärvi parish, persons venerated "St. Kasan", the personification of an icon painted in the style of the Kazan icon of the Mother of God. St. Kasan was seen to be able to infect with supernatural *nenä* illness if angered or offended (see Part III, example 5a).[82]

Another curious religious figure was 'Saint' Pokrova, the name deriving from the holy day commemorating the *Intercession of the Virgin* (October 1).[83] In one account, Pokrova was believed to be a supernatural protector of cattle, but also the cause of headaches in women, associated with a holy tree in Suistamo.[84] Women who wished to cure their headaches left their hair ribbons at the tree and said: "Release me, holy Pokrova, if this is your fault, from this ailment!" In another text, "Pokrovu" was described as an angel who watched over a person and his/her possessions if that person honored the day of *Pokrova* by refraining from work:[85]

> 9)
> On Pokrova one should not cut down any tree. She loves trees, the old people said. Then she looks after one's prosperity the entire year, she takes care of the cattle and the people herself. Pokrova is an angel. She says: "Whoever honors me, does not work on Pokrova, then I spread my wings over his livelihood, so that God does not touch it."
> (Salmi. 1935. Martta Pelkonen 391).

According to recent cognitivist theories in the study of religion, humans show a tendency to construe religious concepts as agents with something counter-intuitive about them.[86] In high or official religious concepts, agents like God do not necessarily possess the characteristics we normally attribute to agents. God is invisible, has no physical body nor indeed any physical properties at all, he can never die, and possesses limitless powers. Folk religion, too, is rife with counter-intuitive agents, one example being icons depicting events rather than persons which are nonetheless construed as sacred agents.

Yet the agents construed in high religion and those of popular religion are generally different *sorts* of agents. The fact that counter-intuitive agents in high or official religions, especially monotheistic world religions, must be universally relevant and theologically correct means that while they may possess those attributes cognitively most important to human interaction with them – intention, motivation, moral consciousness, and access to strategic information (Boyer, forthcoming) – they may lack most other features which would make them more human-like and individual in character. Sacred agents in folk or popular religion may be counter-intuitive in certain respects, but when compared to their counterparts in high or official religion, they often appear more human in terms of physical form, needs or desires: there seems to be a continual tendency for them to be rendered more concretely anthropomorphic. In many cultures, for example, sacred agents at the popular level are offered food because they are thought, like humans, to require or at least desire nourishment.

In high religion, the function of counter-intuitivity is to transmit or convey abstract, perceptually difficult and even contradictory philosophical statements which would be difficult to spell out verbally but are somewhat more easily encompassed in the form of an invisible, omniscient and omnipresent sentient agent; this is true at least of Christianity. In folk religion, the aim is not the embodiment (or disembodiment) of philosophical or abstract concepts, so the sentient agents involved are conceived of differently: in general, they are seen to be closer at hand, linked more closely to local concerns. In folk religion, non-agents such as objects may be recruited for transformation into agents, or disembodied divinities become reinterpreted in more physical, human-like terms, in order to facilitate inference-making in real-time problem solving (Barrett 1999). This may mean that abstract concepts become simplified, but it also means that seemingly simple concepts (such as the idea of one, universal Virgin Mary) are made more complex (splintering into dozens of 'different' Marys), depending on the cognitive, cultural and ideological needs of the culture in question. In Orthodox Karelian folk religion, as I strive to show in this study, what people needed were agents with whom they could negotiate the boundaries of 'this world' versus the 'other world', 'this world' being the sphere of an ordered cultural universe, while the other world was the sphere to which ritual specialists relegated any 'dirt' which did not fit into the symbolic Order.

There is a certain irony to Orthodox Karelian icons being transformed into sentient agents in the context of folk religious ritual. Sentient agents such as Pokrova and "Uspenja Bohorooditsa" represent basic-level concepts which helped ordinary people in everyday problem-solving. Yet such icons were originally intended by the Church as institutionalized visual memory aids to bolster *abstract, complicated* and *theologically-correct* religious ideas (such as ideals of saintliness) in the minds of the uneducated and non-literate faithful and to prevent these ideas from being whittled down to basic-level notions (cf. Barrett 1999:337). Ultimately, even these pictorial memory aids were so much grist to the mill of agent-production in folk religious thinking.

In an early account of folk religious beliefs, linguist Arvid Genetz (1870:103) describes a conversation with an elderly woman living in a remote area of Ladoga Karelia. The conversation as reported by him highlights the conflict between theological religious concepts and basic religious concepts used in everyday problem solving:

> **Genetz:** "How many *jumalas* [=gods, saints] might there be?"
> **Woman:** "I don't know how many *jumalas* there are: *Mikkula miilostivoi* [St. Nicholas], *Jyrgi* [St. George], *Sviizu*,[87] *pyhä Nastassu* [St. Anastasia], and *valgeivalassi syöttäi* [lit. 'White (St.) Blaise the provider'].
> **Genetz:** Isn't there a God in heaven?

65

Woman: There is one, or two, or nine.
Genetz: Doesn't God have a son Jesus Christ?
Woman: How should we know, us ignorant people! He is likely on God's side.
Genetz: When you have some pain, doesn't God in heaven help you?
Woman: They don't know anything in heaven; this here icon helps [taking from the corner a small picture of St. Nicholas in bronze].

Genetz' informant here indicates that abstract, theologically correct religious concepts are of little use to her in solving the problems of daily life, what is relevant to her instead is a *concrete* representation of the sacred, here the icon of St. Nicholas, the most popular saint in Orthodox Karelia.

Overlap and ambiguity in the identification of sacred agents suggests that formal taxonomies based on the identification of the sacred agent may not be the most useful way of organizing the Orthodox Karelian folk religion material. For instance, the nominal distinction between *saints* and *nature spirits* was often blurred. As Mansikka (1943:197) has pointed out, the figure of St. George in particular was linked to the role of the forest spirit. In numerous texts, St. George was called upon to prevent *his* forest predators from harming cattle in the summer pastures, likewise holy hermit St. Adrian of Andrusov was depicted as the *water spirit* responsible for supernatural *nenä*-illness in five examples of 'healing' incantations,[88] and as the *forest spirit* responsible for livestock trapped in the 'forest cover' in one known example (see pp. 128–133).[89] The purpose behind this may have been so that both types of sacred agent could be recruited to the same end: to serve as agents on the 'other side' of the human/wilderness boundary, agents with whom, moreover, humans could negotiate.

Because the ritual roles of sacred entities appear to have overlapped to a large extent, I suggest that they can be seen more fruitfully as part of a larger system in which their *function*, rather than their formal identification, was of primary importance to ritual performers. Moral obligations and ritual expectations, rather than the precise identity of the sacred agent, are where we should be looking for meaning in folk descriptions of exchange with sacred agents. As Archangel Karelian informant Marina Takalo (b. 1890) remarked to researcher Juha Pentikäinen (1971:257) concerning an incantation prayer spoken to increase fishing luck:[90] "The *jumala*[91] or the water's king or water spirit, how should I say it, drove the fish into the net". For Takalo, the significant aspect of the sacred agent was not its name nor even the class of beings to which it belonged, but *what it did*, the concrete role it played in human livelihood.

Not only sacred agents but also actual rituals defy strict classification in Orthodox Karelian folk religion. *Pominominen*, for instance, referred to rituals in which food was brought to the cemetery and placed on the grave for a dead relative or friend to 'eat' on various anniversaries of the person's death, or on certain ritual holidays (Kemppinen 1967:48). But it also described a ritual by which drink or bread was left for *living cows* and *children* trapped by the 'forest cover'.[92] The term 'forest cover' (*metsänpeitto*) referred to the belief that the forest was capable of hiding or imprisoning cows, horses and even children in a magical or supernatural domain from which they could not escape, and in which they were invisible to persons searching for them. In this latter type of *pominominen* rite, a ritual prayer was also read to invite the lost member of the household to return to eat and drink. According to three informants, *pominominen* was performed for the lost animal "just as if for a dead person":[93]

10a)
One released farm animals, cows and calves from the forest cover in the following manner: "one put a small piece of bread which had remained unnoticed in the oven while the other breads were taken out, into a drinking pail. On top of that one prepared the cow's drink. After sunset one went to a plowed field and there one invites [the cow] to the pail to drink just as one does for a dead person. One performs *pominominen* and invites it to eat and drink its supper. Then the forest can no longer keep the animal in its cover. One continues to invite it until the cow comes to drink." Once, Marfa's calf remained in the forest. It came home when it was summoned in this manner, but it was thin and its eyes had come out of its sockets.
(Tulomajärvi. 1943. Helmi Helminen 2358. – Marfa Jogorov, 70 years).

10b)
…"Both were elderly people", they *pominoi-ed* with the drinking container of the cow trapped in the forest cover. *Pominominen* for a cow is done with a drinking pail, for a horse with a bridle and for a Christian [i.e. human] with food. One went into the yard in the evening and there invited [the lost creature] to eat and drink, as if for a dead person. One made the sign of the cross and asked that the forest would release it.
(Tulomajärvi. 1943. Helmi Helminen 2357. – Okulina Kondradjev, 70 years. Parentheses in original).

10c)
A cow in the forest cover is *pominoi-ed* using bread that has been found somewhere.
When a cow is in the forest cover, then one performs *pominominen* with 'found' bread: "Lord have mercy on Brownie [=cow's name] (*pomeni hospodi ruskoidu*). Come to this bread. Come and eat this bread."
(Once there was a cow in the forest cover). People went to perform *pominominen* on top of Kuurannenä hill, then the cow was released.
(Salmi. 1936. Martta Pelkonen 210. – Irinny Juudin, 77 years. Parentheses in original).

10d)
…The drink or bridle is left on the threshold. During the next 24 hours, some stranger or the ritual performer him/herself will see the animal which has been covered by the forest. Usually the *tietäjä* to whom one has turned for help announces that this or that person is coming to tell where the lost animal is. Without *pominominen* (*pomenintaa*) the animal cannot be seen, no matter how many times someone walks past it…
(Tulomajärvi. 1944. Helmi Helminen 2360. – Solomanida Petrov, b. 1862).

Another ritual term, *jeäksintä* (and associated verb forms *jeäksie/jeäksitteä*), most commonly referred either to 1) a ritual vow to undertake a pilgrimage to a monastery, or 2) the dedication of children to a monastery where they would later serve for a period of weeks or even years, in return for protection from illness or a miracle cure (see Tilvis 1989; Kilpeläinen 2000). But *jeäksintä* also referred to vows and promises not necessarily associated with monasteries or pilgrimage, whose roots lie in practices which may go back to indigenous pre-Christian tradition.[94] These included: (3) the act of bringing to a local or more distant village chapel gifts promised to a saint in return for the alleviation of sudden pain (toothache, headache, leg pain), or in return for a good catch of fish or protection from storms when on the open water. Such gifts included livestock, butter, cabbages, flax, wool, tapers and money.[95] Examples of this type of *jeäksintä* can be seen in the descriptions below (11a and 11b), in which the promise was made to give a ram or cow in sacrifice to St. George so that the entire herd would be protected, and flax and cabbages were given to the chapel of St. Kosman. (4) Offerings were also given to nature spirits either to increase the giver's prosperity or to be healed from illness, as in the examples below (11c and 11d) in which a sheep was promised in sacrifice to the water spirit in order to improve success in fishing, and a supernatural *nenä*-type illness was cured through offerings to the water spirit. As explained by one informant, *jeäksitetäh* means "to make the illness go back whence it infected. If for example the 'earth spirit has infected (*moahini on hinkautun*)' it is 'sent back to the earth (*jeäkšitetäh moaha*)' by, among other things, making an offering of silver coins to that place".[96] A related term was *jeäksintähine*,[97] the name for the illness itself. *Jeäksintä* is thus associated not only with pilgrimage to monasteries, but also with exchange relations with nature spirits and saints, and is linked to the same semantic field as concepts of *nenä* and *proškenja* (see pages 77–110).

11a)
On Lunkilansaari Island in Salmi it was the custom to donate a ram, a "woolly hide (*villavuona*)", to the village chapel on St. George's Day. Somebody made a vow (*jääksiytyy*) to do it in order to prevent future misfortune or to ensure success with the cattle. The promise is made already when the sheep is born. In former times the ram was eaten at the chapel, nowadays it is the custom to sell it, and the money goes to the chapel. (Salmi. 1909. U. Holmberg 545).

11b)
In Suona village is Kuzmoi's [St. Kosman's] chapel. As a donation to the chapel, flax was taken to Kuzmoi. And three cabbage heads. The best cabbages were given to the chapel and sold to benefit the chapel. "It was *jeäksitty*".
(Tulomajärvi. 1944. Helmi Helminen 3421. –Houri Gregoljanov, 71 years).

11c)
We had, you see, the sort of belief in Olonets that in spring if few fish were caught, then the farm master might *tjääksiä* (promise) a sheep or some

such to the water master; and then when he began to net more fish, then the sheep was to be killed and the meat tossed into the river or lake from which the fish were netted; if he did not do so, then the water master might become angry and take the farm's sheep, or drown people. The promise had to be kept.
(Salmi. 1939. Ulla Mannonen 11024. –Martta Kuha, 54 years. Parentheses in original).

11d)
Something was wrong with my daughter's eyes, and I healed (*jeäkšitim_mie*) my daughter's eyes (…) For example if the eyes became ill from the water, then one had to go at midnight to the water's shore, and the healer (*jeäkšittäjä*) took a cupful of water which was then given to the ailing person to drink, one gave a silver coin as an offering to "water, the provider (*vesikormenitšalla*)" and prayed for a cure.
(Petsamo-Kiestinki-Sohjanansuu. 1932. Hannes Pukki. KKTK-KKA, entry: *jeäkšittöä*).

The broad semantic fields glossed by *jeäksintä* and *pominominen* suggest that these terms index deeper patterns of logic, patterns which provide important insights into Orthodox Karelian folk religious worldview. The extension of a term from one ritual field to another requires that there be some cognitive association shared by the two fields. In the case of *jeäksintä*, it is possible to see a connecting thread running through all of its meanings, which could be summed up as: "some promise or obligation to a sacred agent which results in a reciprocal benefit from that sacred agent". In the case of *pominominen* as well, the homology is not difficult to locate: in both types of *pominominen* ritual, human performers offered sustenance to beings of 'this world' which had crossed over to the 'other side', in the hope that those on the other side would return to partake of the food. Both types of *pominominen* thus show a desire on the behalf of the ritual performers to maintain ties with the boundary-crosser and to continue to view the deceased person, lost person or lost animal as part of the 'inner sphere' of the community of the living. It also suggests that food and drink created bridges between this world and 'other worlds', between the living and the dead, and between humans and the forest.[98]

In Orthodox Karelian folk religion, rites in which humans communicated or interacted with supernatural agents ultimately dealt with the question of *disorder*, in other words, they mediated between 'pure' or 'impure' categories of phenomena. In some cases these rituals could be classified as *crisis rituals* because they were carried out in response to some unforeseen event requiring immediate remedy, such as illness or the disappearance of a child or farm animal in the forest. Other such rituals could be designated *calendrical rituals* because they were carried out on a particular day or at a particular point in the annual agrarian cycle.[99] This separate classification, however, tends to mask the fact that from the emic or folk point of view, calendrical rites were in many cases carried out not simply in order to follow a time-honored tradition or celebrate a good harvest, mark the passage of time in the annual cycle, etc., but in order to stave off some possible, or even likely, misfortune.

69

An example of this includes the rites performed when cows were let out for the first time in spring on St. George's Day (*Jyrki*), so that the cattle would thrive and be protected from attacks by bears and wolves (see pages 111–113, 121–124, 128–131). Other examples include sacrificing a ram or bull to the village patron saint once a year in order that forest predators would not attack the villagers' livestock in the ensuing year; or the honoring of the dead on certain holidays so that the dead would not be angered and infect the living with a supranormal illness (see pages 79–80, 117–119). Like crisis rituals, these calendrical rituals were concerned with misfortune, disaster, and social breakdown: in short, systemic disorder. The underlying concerns of calendrical and crisis rites were therefore the same: calendrical rites differed from crisis rituals only in that *the crisis in question had not yet occurred*, the forest predators had not yet attacked, the dead had not yet become angered. Yet these crises were both anticipated and recurrent, woven into the structure of peasants' and pastoralists' everyday lives.

Thus while descriptions of Orthodox folk religion appear fuzzy from the perspective of our formal categories based on the identification of the sacred agent or ritual typology, they make good sense from the standpoint of their functional distinctions. Classifications which distinguish between ritual 'types' such as village festivals and sacrificial feasts, rituals associated with the dead, and offerings to nature spirits have little relevance from the emic perspective of their function, which was to minimize disorder in everyday life, either before or after it struck. In a similar vein, we can better understand the fact that sacred agents (nature spirits, the dead, and Christian saints) were often only vaguely or ambiguously defined if we consider that their most important characteristic was their role in (1) the signalling of a possible threat or impending danger which set ritual practice in motion and (2) negotiating boundaries between purity and impurity. A focus on a nominal taxonomy, therefore, may only obscure the broader meanings which can be traced out for Orthodox Karelian folk religious ritual activity as a whole. These patterns emerge when the focus is on functional rather than formal similarities, and when a large amount of intertextual material is synthesized with particular attention paid to the moral operating principles which underlay the rituals.

Two ritual complexes: sacred boundaries and sacred centers

Let us now return to the two categories of folk religious ritual given in the previous section: category (A), "Folk religious rituals performed in and oriented toward local surroudings"; and category (B), "Supralocal folk religious ritual". Based on my analysis of their function, I hypothesize that these local and supralocal rituals formed two ritual 'sets' or complexes which were responses to 'disorder' in everyday life. In both of these complexes, the concept of the sacred was used to promote a sense of social continuity and coherence. These two ritual complexes fostered social continuity and coherence by separating things which were pure from things impure, but they did this in two different ways, according to two *different* models. In ritual complex A, the model was one in which the ordinary peasant's farm/ community was separated from the 'Other': the deceased members of the community and the forest environment. Here the self, farm and community were aligned with purity while impurity was ascribed to the 'other world' (forest, cemetery). In other words, *a conceptual boundary line was drawn between the farm and forest*, so that the farm (and local community) were situated on the 'inside' of the boundary line, with the forest on the 'outside' (and as we shall see later on, the cemetery was also seen to be part of the forest in folk religious ritual and belief). In complex B, however, the model was that of *center versus periphery*, where farm and community were now located at the periphery, along with impurity, while purity was seen to be located at the sacred center, which was the distant monastery or pilgrimage goal. In moving from periphery to center through pilgrimage, the individual pilgrim journeyed from impurity to purity.

In these hypothetical models, ritual complex A is composed of reciprocal rituals and communication carried out between peasants/pastoralists on the one hand and nature spirits, saints and the dead on the other. This interaction took the form of ritual offerings, prayers, confessions of wrongdoing, requests for forgiveness, ritual coersion and negotiation, ritual feeding, dream interpretation and divination. I argue throughout this study that the purpose of these ritual activities was always *either* to reinforce boundaries in order to control the relations between the community and the 'other world' of the forest wilderness, *or* to mediate the boundary between the living and the dead in order to reincorporate the dead into the community of the living in a ritually-controlled manner. In both cases these local rituals were primarily concerned with the maintenance and negotiation of *boundaries* between the inner sphere of the human community and 'other worlds'. I therefore refer to this entire folk religious complex as the *sacred boundaries* complex.[100]

The second folk religious complex in Orthodox Karelia involved interaction between rural Karelians on the one hand and the sentient supernatural agents associated with monasteries (God, Jesus, monastery founders, holy hermits) on the other. This interaction took the form of pilgrimages and holy vows to undertake such pilgrimages, or the pledging of oneself or one's child to perform labour or service in a monastery for a period of time. Since the purpose of these ritual activities was to solicit aid from a reservoir of powerful symbols within the culture itself, to seek order from a closer identification with the highest and most-difficult-to-attain ideals of Karelian peasant culture, I refer to this folk religious complex as the *sacred centres* complex. [101]

My model of the monastery as a *sacred center* in Orthodox Karelian folk religion derives at least in part from the emic or folk recognition of the religious and secular authority of the monastery, as well as its political and economic influence over surrounding areas (see Kilpeläinen 2000). Yet, despite the fact that the monastery represented an 'official', institutional sacred center, the picture of it revealed through 'folk' descriptions differs in key aspects from descriptions authored by church officials and intellectuals

(Stark 1995, 1999). The two sacred complexes outlined in this study, the (A) *sacred boundaries* and (B) *sacred centres* complexes, did not therefore represent 'low' and 'high', or 'unofficial' and 'official' and orientations toward the sacred. Both can be characterized as 'unofficial' perspectives, because even the peasants' relationship to the monastery was uniquely their own, in every sense as much an expression of folk or popular religion as the cults surrounding nature spirits, saints and the dead.

Sacred boundaries –
Nature spirits, saints and the dead in the
maintenance of cultural Order

Boundaries against disorder

An implicit assumption which underlies much of scholarly writing on the subject of Orthodox Karelian traditional rites and cults is that peasants and pastoralists engaged in rites directed at saints, nature spirits and other sacred agents in order *to ensure material prosperity* in hunting, fishing, and agriculture. In fact, a closer examination of informants' descriptions reveals these rituals to have been most often *a direct response to disorder or the threat of disorder* in individual and communal life. The aim of the rituals was a return to equilibrium. By this I do not mean to imply the actual existence of stasis or permanency in either real life or the cultural Order, only that ideals of equilibrium and order were expressed through ritual, and can be said to have existed *in the temporary cognitive universe which the rituals evoked.*

An emphasis on equilibrium was a key part of the model of 'limited good' in peasant life. Because those persons and households intent on 'getting ahead' materially were seen as a communal threat and could be the target of aggression, most members of the community wanted to simply 'keep up' and avoid any misfortune which would deny them their rightful place in the social and economic order (cf. Foster 1965:302–303). Events which motivated most folk religious rituals were those which *diminished a sense of order and equilibrium* (illness, attacks on cattle by forest predators, cattle lost in the forest, deaths in the community). The desired outcome of ritual responses to disorder was thus *the restoration of health, the return of lost cattle, and the maintenance of relations with the dead* (which preserved their membership in the community).

As stated in the previous section, within the wider system of reciprocity and exchange I distinguish *two* folk religious complexes: (A) local rituals taking place within the community (sacred boundaries complex), and (B) supralocal pilgrimages to distant monasteries (sacred centers complex). Both of these ritual complexes addressed the problem of disorder in individual and communal life, but they operationalized the *sacred* in different ways. By this I mean that first of all they *sought to isolate purity from impurity in different ways*, and secondly, they *extended moral expectations to different supernatural agents using different means.*

The sacred centers complex in Orthodox Karelia involved interaction between ordinary pilgrims and the sentient supernatural agents associated with monasteries and famous chapels. This interaction was motivated by disorder (illness, wrongful acts perpetrated against the community) in the same sense as were the reciprocal rituals in the sacred boundaries complex. However, this disorder was not seen to come from *outside the community* but from *inside* its own moral universe: from the actions of God or community members. The response to this disorder was to seek aid from a more distant cultural *center*, to pursue a closer identification with the highest, purest ideals of Karelian peasant culture. This ritual complex will be dealt with in Part II of this book.

The focus of Part I is the *sacred boundaries* complex of communicative rituals carried out with nature spirits, saints and the dead. These rituals were performed as a response to **three types of disorder** in individual and social life:

a)   Disorder in the human body (=unexplained illness).

b)   Disorder in the resource spaces shared by humans and the wilderness (=attacks on cattle by bears and wolves and the entrapment of cattle, horses and children by the 'forest cover'). Disorder types a) and b) were analogous: mysterious illness was seen as a transgression by the sacred agent across the boundaries of the human body, just as attacks by bears and wolves on cattle represented violation of the boundaries which separated the farm from the forest wilderness.

c)   The third type of disorder dealt with in local folk religious rituals, **disorder threatening internal communal cohesion**, was seen to derive both from the death of community members and from socio-economic inequality. One communal response to this disorder was the drawing of ritual boundaries in order to renegotiate and control the relations between the community and the dead. Another response was rituals which mediated the boundary between the living and the dead and which served to reincorporate *both the dead and the poor* into the community of the living in a ritually-controlled manner. This ritual reincorporation of the dead and the poor dealt with these two marginal, potentially disruptive elements of the community by setting up restricted 'zones' of time and place in which this reincorporation could take place, while at the same time reifying the boundaries between them and the rest of the community.

Illness: disorder in the human body

Nenä illness and proškenja rites

Physical illness, particularly unexplained illness, disrupts the coherence of meaning in everyday life because it poses a problem for cultural categories of experience, representing disorder not only for the individual but also for the community. An essential part of the 'cure' in many cultures is the restoration of this coherence of meaning through the initial step of diagnosis as well as the organizing symbols, images and categories produced in the healing ritual through the guidance of the ritual specialist (see Lock 1993:137). According to Clifford Geertz (1973: 105), healing rituals focus on the problem of suffering, and attempt to deal with suffering by placing it within a context of meaning and providing a "mode of action" through which it can be expressed, understood and thus endured. Healing rituals thus "give the stricken person a vocabulary in terms of which to grasp the nature of his distress and relate it to the wider world" (ibid).

This sort of healing process can be seen in Orthodox Karelian ritual cures for sudden, inexplicable pain or illness which were diagnosed, through divination, to be the result of bodily penetration by various powerful elements or agents: the forest, water, wind, dead persons, and even holy icons. In the procedure to cure these so-called *nenä* illnesses (also known as *vigahine* and *heittäytyminen*, among others), the afflicted person usually visited a ritual specialist who first 'divined' the cause of the illness through various means before leading the patient *to* and *through* a ritual of exchange and appeasement known as *proškenja* or *prostitus*.

The sequence of events leading up to the ritual began when a person began to experience various physical symptoms such as pain, discomfort, or dizziness which did not lend themselves to immediate classification. The afflicted person sometimes guessed the cause of the discomfort to be 'infection' from the forest, a body of water, the cemetery, wind, etc., but in most cases the final cause was determined by a ritual specialist. The ritual specialist then either accompanied the sick person or went alone to represent the patient and perform the *proškenja* ritual on his/her behalf. This ritual was carried out, where possible, at the site of 'infection', for example in the forest, by a lake shore, or in the cemetery. Gifts or offerings were brought to appease the place spirit or dead person, and the actual request for forgiveness was usually accompanied by the gesture of bowing low to the ground. The appeal for forgiveness and health was made through verbal formulas in a kind of loose Kalevala meter modified to fit the needs of a straightforward request expressed in the vernacular. Ritual formulas often addressed an entire kin community of nature spirits, complete with fathers, mothers, grandparents, children, etc., as well as representatives of a class-based society: judges, priests, kings, servants, slaves. In these incantations it is clear that the place spirits were seen to inhabit another 'world' or sphere which was an approximate mirror-image of the human world, at least in terms of social organization (see Köngäs-Maranda 1967). A typical description of a *proškenja* rite can be seen below:

1)
When forest-*nenä* infects, one is supposed to go with the sick person (the infected person) to the forest to bow down. Then a *tietäjä* (*tietoniekka*) is supposed to go with the sick person. Then you should bow [and say]:

Terveh, metsän isäntä,	Greetings, forest master,
(Terveh, metsän) emäntä,	Greetings, forest mistress,
Terveh, ostetut orjat,	Greetings, purchased slaves,
(Terveh), palkatut piiat,	Greetings, salaried serving-maids,
Päästäkää minuo ta pellastakaa,	Release me and save me,
Kui lienen minä kun laatinut vääryttä,	Since I have committed a wrong,
Ku olloo minun väärys,	Since it is my wrong,
teidän syy,	and your doing
Minä tuon tuohukset,	I bring tapers,
Laitan lahjukset.	Set down gifts.

Then one takes linen clothing or reddish string and draws these in a circle about oneself and places them at the foot of a spruce tree. These are given as gifts. One should go at nighttime when nobody can see you or hear you. (Suistamo. 1884. Kaarle Krohn 5533. –Irini Paramoona, 70 years).

The formulas used in the *proškenja* ritual expressed, in first-person voice, the blame or fault of the ailing person who had offended the sacred agent. They also sought forgiveness from the sacred agent through negotiation, appeasement and offering. The incantation formulas usually followed the pattern of the examples presented below:

2a)
Metshän ishännät	Forest masters,
Metshän emännät	Forest mistresses,
Metshän kuldaset kuningahat	Forest golden kings,
Minuo brostikkua!	Forgive me!
Midä lienen pahua ruadannuh,	Whatever evil I may have done,
Duuminuh, ajatelluh!	Pondered, thought!
Metshän sarounat,	Forest conjurers,

Metshän papit,	Forest priests,
Metshän pabatjat,	Forest priests' wives
Brostikkua!	Forgive me!

(SKVR VII$_4$:2495. Suojärvi. 1900. – Outotja Petrouna Kuutti, 80 years).

2b)

Prosti, joki joukkoneš,	Forgive me, lake, with your kin,
Umpilampi lapšineš,	Pond, with your children,
Vejen tuatot, vejen muamot,	Water grandfathers,
	water grandmothers,
Vejen vellet, vejen sisäret,	Water brothers, water sisters,
Vejen suuri sukukunta,	The kin of the water's father,
Vejen helie heimokunta...	The kin of the water's mother...

(SKVR I$_4$:1033b. Kivijärvi. 1911. – wife of Sisso).

It was generally considered that if a person was infected by *nenä* illness, this was because he or she had committed some transgression against the infecting agent, as can be seen from the following description:

3)
Metsätalo farm is about 7 kilometres from here. There the people were in the meadow cutting hay. In the meadow is a artesian well. A man took a pole and started to measure the depth of the well. The man's "hands and feet became swollen". "The man himself saw in a dream", how the water spirit came and said: "we were drinking tea, when you smashed our tables". The man had to visit the well on a *proškenja* visit, to ask forgiveness. In the evening he went to the well, did not make the sign of the cross, and said:

Vein izändy, vein emändy,	Water's master, water's mistress
vein valgied vanhembat,	water's white elders,
vein kuldazet kuningahat,	water's golden kings
kai minulla prostikkaa."	Forgive me."

(Tulomajärvi. 1944. Helmi Helminen 2320. – Nikolai Sykköjev, b. 1873).

After the incantation was recited, the ritual specialist and/or client departed the scene of infection and the client awaited recovery.

Disorder in the human body also motivated the continuation of interpersonal relations even beyond the grave. In a ritual form of devotion known as *pominominen*, food was brought to the cemetery and placed on graves for the dead to 'eat' on various anniversaries of a relative's or loved-one's death, or on certain ritual holidays. The most common ritual holidays for honoring the dead were *ruadintšat* (Russ. *radunitsa*), occurring on the second Tuesday after Easter, *muistinsuovatta* occurring on the second to last Saturday in October (Harva 1948:507), and the Saturdays preceding Shrovetide and Whitsuntide (*Stroitsa*).[102] All of these days for honoring the dead were also recognized by the local clergy, and priests held services in local churches and chapels on these days. *Pominominen* did not merely represent the 'honoring' of the dead: there are a number of examples which demonstrate that *pominominen* was part of an ongoing system of exchange in which the living hoped to persuade the dead to assist them in various crises or difficulties. Failure to keep up the exchange could result in a penalty which was usually *nenä*-illness. If an ailing person was diagnosed with *nenä* illness which had infected from a dead person, *pominominen* was also used to appease this sacred agent, thereby persuading him or her to remove the illness.[103]

4a)
When a dead person infects, then any kind of illness can come of it: one can become dizzy, one's leg or hand can ache, or something else. It starts to show itself in dreams, it is a nuisance when one is sleeping, and during the day it makes one afraid and weighs upon one's mind. The dead person disturbs in this way so that it can demand that one visit the cemetery and give memorial gifts. One should take *tuulipaikkas* [=long white strips of cloth which were tied to the grave crosses]. Only *tuulipaikkas* are taken to the grave, in memory, food is given to relatives, some of every kind one has on hand.
When putting the *tuulipaikkas* in place one asks forgiveness, says the dead person's name and says: "Whatever ill I may have caused, wrong I may have thought, forgive me, when you seem to have demanded that I come and visit."
(Archangel Karelia. 1932. Samuli Paulaharju 18193. –Anni Lehtonen).

4b)
Hilippä was buried, and then he became angry at me. When I went to the graves, I said: "I'm going to my own son's grave first". That made him angry. My leg began to hurt terribly, and for that reason I did not visit his grave. I tossed the baked turnip on the floor of the icon corner, and made the sign of the cross in the direction of the cemetery. Then I *pominoi*-ed: "Lord, provider, remember Hilippä, come and eat this baked turnip! If I have done something wrong, forgive me this once! Take your own away! Forgive me, a great sinner!
One should not perform *pominoimen* in the evening, for in the evening he is moving about, one should do the remembering in the early morning and ask forgiveness.
(Salmi. 1934–36. Martta Pelkonen 665. –Fodossu Stopanovna Homa).

4c)
Collector: Where does *cemetery-nenä* (*kalmannenä*) come from?
Informant: [...] if you go to the cemetery and think 'I should go and visit the graves' but you don't go.
Once there were a husband and wife who were at church. The wife says: "Let's go and visit the graves!" The husband says: "We'll go on the next holy day". Then his legs gave out. He came to me that same week. His [dead] father had been angered. We visited [the father's] grave, and [the afflicted man] was released.
(Salmi. 1936. Martta Pelkonen 195. –Natalju Timofjouna Mironov, healer and diviner).

Proškenja and *pominominen* rituals, which were both performed in order to remove *nenä* illness, were predicated on a series of assumptions concerning the rights and responsibilities of both humans and sacred agents: humans were obligated not to offend the nature spirit or the dead person, and although the offence which led to infection was often unintentional, the nature spirit or dead person was still seen to have the right to infect with *nenä* illness. Humans were motivated by the illness to perform the *proškenja* ritual and give offerings, and the nature spirit was in turn obligated to remove the illness after being appealed to in this way.

Moral orientations and the tietäjä's *authority: aggressive versus conciliatory healing rites*

Rituals represent particular ideologies and involve particular moral orientations toward a given issue, and in some situations ritual participants have the freedom to choose which ritual to perform based on the stance they wish to take. In Orthodox Karelia, the attitude adopted towards illness-agents could differ widely, and the different types of rituals used in curing *nenä*-type illnesses indicate a range of moral orientations or responses to the 'Other'.

In Orthodox Karelia, the most common ritual mode for the curing of *nenä* illness was the aforementioned *proškenja* ritual, which can be characterized as a type of 'prayer' incantation rite (see Hautala 1960:22–25; Siikala 1980: 78–79) including apologies, a sense of personal responsibility for transgressions committed against the illness-agent, an acknowledgement of the illness-agent's rights and territories, offerings for the illness-agent, and a sense that there existed a justifiable explanation for the illness. Alternative, and more aggressive ritual methods for dealing with illness-agents were known in the 19th and early 20th centuries in both Orthodox Karelia and across the border in Lutheran Finland, particularly in its eastern and northern parts. [104] These aggressive ritual modes included: 1) rituals in which the healer utilized knowledge of the illness-agent's origins (*synty*) to force it to remove the illness; 2) and rituals in which the healer invoked his or her own power and the aid of supreme beings (esp. *Ukko*) in order to expel or banish the supernatural illness agent (*manaus*, see Hautala 1960:27–36; Siikala 1980:73–79; 1994:76–83). These last two ritual modes were often combined within a single incantation rite.

In the *synty* and *manaus* modes of ritual healing, there was no sense of obligation toward the agent of illness, nor did the rituals express any respect for the illness-agent's right to a particular territory. In addition, neither the *synty-manaus* incantation formulas, nor the descriptions surrounding them, gave any explanation as to *why* the supernatural agent had infected its victim, other than its fundamentally dangerous nature. These aggressive modes of healing were usually performed by a *tietäjä*, the highest level of ritual specialist, who drew upon his knowledge of the other world, knowledge which reflected a highly archaic and multilayered world view (see Siikala 1992).

Proškenja rites appear to have been used in the same areas as aggressive *synty*- and *manaus*-type rites in Orthodox Karelia, and during the same period. What were the criteria for selecting one ritual mode over another in

Bowing or prostitus *was performed not only to sacred agents, but to other persons in many everyday life situations. Here a bride performs* prostitus *to her family and childhood home as a sign of respect and expression of farewell when departing for her husband's home. Jyvöälahti. 1894. Photo: I.K. Inha. Finnish Literature Society.*

dealing with supernatural illness-agents? Although it is difficult to answer this question based on the scarcity of available information regarding healers' and *tietäjäs'* motives and decision-making processes, one thing is clear: a fundamental difference between these incantation modes concerns the type of *authority* invoked when interacting with supernatural agents.

Ultimately, the efficacy of any healing rite which addressed supernatural agents rested on the notion of authority: the only way for the patient to be healed was if the illness agent obeyed or submitted willingly to the authority vested in the healer. But this authority could be of more than one type: in the case of *proškenja* rituals, the authority in question was a *moral* authority born of a collective agreement on the 'rules of the game', on what was right, fair, and permissible in relations between humans and illness agents. In *synty* and *manaus* incantation rituals, on the other hand, the authority in question derived from the performer's, that is the *tietäjä's*, own knowledge, competence and power (*luonto*-force) which enabled him or her to manipulate illness-agents and thus 'force' rather than persuade them. This manipulation included, for instance, knowledge of which supranormal beings and forces to call upon for assistance, knowledge of the illness-agent's true origin and essence, and knowledge of how to use *väki* forces for maximum effect in a sort of dynamistic alchemy. The *tietäjä's* authority was seen to be extended simultaneously over the participants and audience who deferred to him, over the supranormal agents of harm or illness addressed in the incantation ritual, and over other competing ritual specialists (who were not present but were known to all or some of the participants).

The *tietäjä's* authority over his audience and clientele derived from his knowledge and ability to convince others of his knowledge through feats of memory, verbal expression of supernatural relationships, use of secrecy and poetic and ritual performance technique. The authority of the *tietäjä* in aggressive healing rituals was based in part on a sense of mystery: he or she used actions and objects which were often baffling and opaque to the participants, and emphasized his/her possession of a secret knowledge, a form of cultural capital (see Lyotard 1984:20; Luhrmann 1989, Stark-Arola 1998:39–43). This possession of secret, exclusive knowledge enhanced the individual authority of the *tietäjä* and may explain in part why the *tietäjä* selected and preserved in this repertoire archaic poetic forms for his or her performance. The more obscure and archaic the formulas sounded to the audience, the more exclusive they were perceived to be. It should be stressed, however, that while the incantation imagery associated with older models of thought and expressed in archaic language may have been at times incomprehensible to the audience, for the *tietäjä* initiated into the incantation tradition it reflected systematic knowledge of the supernatural world (see Siikala 1992).

The language of *proškenja* rituals, on the other hand, was closer to the spoken vernacular than the language of aggressive incantations. This is obvious not only from a comparison of the incantation texts, but also from the fact that *proškenja* formulas contain numerous Russian loan words, while the language of the aggressive *synty* and *manaus* incantations preserved its original Finnic form to a greater extent and was thus more "western", that is, more archaic (see Siikala 1992:289).

A repeated emphasis on the *tietäjä's* authority and the illness-agent's submission to that authority can be found in incantation formulas, for example in the use of the verb *totella* (to 'obey') in the commonly encountered threat addressed to the illness-agent: "If you do not obey this...(*Jos et sitä totte-le...*)". Informants also brought up the issue of obedience in their descriptions of rites performed by *tietäjäs*. Even divination devices, used in diagnosing the source of *nenä* illness, were supposed to 'obey' those who used them. In a North Karelian text explaining healing rites to alleviate toothache (*hammas-tauti*) caused by a supranormal illness-agent known as a *hittara*, a male informant born in the latter half of the 19th century explains the necessity of forcing *obedience* from the illness-agent before healing can take place. The magic-workers referred to in the text were famous *tietäjäs*, while the ineffective 'magic tricks' were the rites used by minor household healers:

5)
When such magic tricks were usually of no avail, then people complained, moaned and marveled over the fact that what sort of strange toothache is this, when it does not obey anyone or anything. Such an illness could no longer be something ordinary, in other words caused by a small *hittara*, it

had to be an attack by the powerful *kalama* [=*kalma*]. That blackguard was not about to obey anything. There had to be an especially renowned and skilful magic-worker (*velho*) in order to make it obey, and those sorts of magic-workers were few and far between. But Uncle Pekka and a certain woman named Margetta as well as Hason Eerikäinen, they were the sort from which the *kalama*, even the Devil himself fled.

(Kitee. 1921. Pekka Vauhkonen VK 107:1)).

In describing the divination rites performed by *tietäjäs* in order to determine the origin of *nenä* illnesses, one informant from Archangel Karelia pointed out that "not everyone was able to carry out divination, naturally, but whoever was privy to its secrets and was able to make the divining device obey them, then to that person it never lied."[105]

In *proškenja* rituals, on the other hand, the authority invoked was the authority of society, of collective norms and expectations which were now extended to include supernatural agents. The purpose of *proškenja* rituals was not to overpower or threaten supernatural agents with secret knowledge but rather to appeal in simple, easily understood terms, to the supernatural agent's moral sensibilities and to request that both parties submit to a prior agreement.[106] For this reason, *proškenja* rituals used collectively-understood symbols rather than secret formulas or enigmatic rites to underscore their claims concerning moral authority. One of these collective symbols was the act of bowing carried out in order to ask forgiveness from the sacred agent. The meaning of this act was assumed to be immediately clear, since it was also performed by human community members to each other in order to show respect and subordination. So-called *proškenja* or *prostitus* bowings were carried out, for example, by a bride when leaving her natal home and again to those who had given wedding gifts, by the new wife to her parents-in-law when entering her husband's home, when saying the final farewell to the dying, when kissing the icon placed on the dead person's chest during a funeral, or when asking forgiveness for a wrong committed against another person.[107]

Different orientations to the illness-agent were thus expressed through different types of incantation rites. Below, I illustrate this with incantations spoken to remove infection by water-*nenä*. In the first three incantations, *proškenja* formulas derived their authority from a shared code of ethics between humans and illness-agents which specified that when forgiveness is asked, it must be given:

Proškenja formulas:

6a)

Veen isäntä, kultahattu,	Water's master, golden hat,
veen emäntä, kultarinta,	water's mistress, golden breast,
tule suostumaan, sopimaan,	come accept this agreement,
(Mari) lahjoi hyvät lahjat,	(Mari) has offered good presents,
(Mari) kenkkii hyvät kenkit,	(Mari) has donated good gifts,
sulkkuset sukan sitehet,	stocking bands of silk,
hopiaiset housun nauhat,	silver trouser-strings,
itselläs, akallas, lapsellas,	for yourself, for your wife,

	for your children,
perehellä kaikell,	for your entire family,
piijoilla, kasakoilla…	for your serving maids and
	farmhands…

(SKVR VII₄:3114. Korpiselkä. 1908).

6b)

Vesi kultanen kuningas,	Water, golden king,
Vein isännät, vein emännät,	Waters' masters, waters' mistresses,
Kulta kassat, kulta kulmat,	Golden tresses, golden brows,
Annakkoa tämä kerta andeiksi	Forgive me this once
Jos että anna anteiksi, siitä tuloo	If you forgive, then between us
suuret sovat meille.	there will be great harmony.
Jos että uskone,	So that you believe,
niin tuoss' on vierasmies.	there stands my witness.

(Porajärvi. 1884. Kaarle Krohn 6696. –Luka Ondrianen, 39 years).

6c)

…Vein isännät,	Waters' masters,
vein emännät,	waters' mistresses,
lapset suuret, pienet,	children big, small,
keskkertaset,	and middle-sized,
piiat, kasakat,	serving-maids, farmhands,
papit, d'iekat.	priests, sextons,
niekkunat, ponommarit,	servants of the church, vergers,
vein kuningahat.	waters' kings.
Vein keisarit,	Waters' emperors,
keisarin keisarit	emperors' emperors,
ja vein valdakunda kaikki,	and the whole of waters' empire,
proštikkua, antakkua anteeks…	forgive me…
…siks ilmoist igiä,	…for eternity,
rauhoa ja tervehyttä.	peace and health.
Ei ole puuta	There is no tree
linnun istumatointa,	in which a bird has not perched,
eikä ihmistä	There is no person
hairahtumatointa.	who has not strayed.
Omassein tuhmuuves tullu,	I have come in my own wrongdoing,
riähäkkäisen ristkansal,	to a sinful Christian
andakkua nyt andeeks,	now grant forgiveness,
siks ilmoist igiä,	for eternity,
kuun valgeuks,	as long as the moon is white
päivän selgeyks.	and the sun is bright.
Jos lienen mitä pahoin ajatellut,	If I have thought wrongly,
pahoin duumainnut,	evilly pondered,
proštikkua.	Forgive me.

(Suojärvi. 1966. Senni Timonen KT 374:602. –Aleksi Rakki, farmer, born 1896).

By contrast, in more aggressive incantations based on the ritual performer's personal authority, the *tietäjä* calls attention to the fact that the patient is a blameless victim and that the illness-agent had no right to infect. In the incantation below, the *tietäjä* announces that the illness-agent must obey or be banished by means of the *tietäjä's* own knowledge and competence ("If

85

this you do not obey / I will surely give you passage…"). In it, the *tietäjä* also appeals to the power of divine helpers such as *Ukko*, the supreme deity. Note also the use of references to archaic, mythical imagery in this incantation: *Ukko's* fire, the *tietäjä's* helper-animals (a mythological rooster and colt), and the place of the banishment in the other world, a frothing body of water.[108]

Aggressive *manaus* formula:

7)

Veen isäntä, veen emäntä,	Water's master, water's mistress,
Vein kultanen kuningas,	Water's golden king,
Vetten herra voimallinen,	Mighty Lord of the waters,
Miksi syyttä suuttununa,	For what reason are you angered,
Vinnistä vihastununna,	By what wrongdoing made hostile,
Miksi laitoit lapsia,	Why did you send your children
Panit palkalaisiasi,	Dispatch your servants,
Sata miestä miekka vyöllä,	A hundred men with belted swords,
Tuhat piipelo pivossa	A thousand holding sabres
Puremahan, nielemähän,	To bite, to swallow,
Syömähän, kalvamahan,	To eat, to gnaw,
Siäri luita särkemähän,	To shatter shinbones,
Polvi luita polkemahan,	To trample kneebones,
Syäntä sykertämähän,	To knot up the heart,
Maksoja maistamahan,	To taste the liver,
Keuhkoja kietämähän,	To bind the lungs,
Silmiä sinoamahan,	To shoot the eyes,
Kulmia kolottamahan,	To pain the eyebrows,
Leuka luita luistamahan?…	To dislocate the jawbones?
…Pui, Ukko, tulinen riihi,	Thresh, Ukko, a fiery threshing-barn
Säkähinein säiskähytä,	flash like a spark,
Tuli tuikki ikkunoista,	Fire glimmered from the window,
Säkeheti ovesta läksi.	A spark flew out the door.
Nouse, kukko rauta harja,	Arise, iron-crested rooster,
Kavaha, kannus jalka,	work magic, spur-foot,
Tätä konnoa koprimahan…	To grab this villain…
	[to prevent him]
…Puremasta, nielemästä	…From biting, from swallowing,
Syömästä, kalvamasta,	From eating, from gnawing,
Ristittyjä rikkomasta,	From breaking the baptized,
Kastettuja kaatamasta!	From killing the christened!
Jos ei sie sitä totelle,	If this you do not obey,
Saan mie muitaki sanoja…	I can procure other words…
…Jos sie ett sitä totelle,	…If this you do not obey,
Kyllä mie sinulle kyyin annan,	I will surely give you passage,
Annan ajoheposen,	I will give you a horse to ride,
Soimelta valitun varsan,	A colt chosen from the forest,
Joll' ois lampi lautasella,	With a small lake on its hindquarters,
Lähe länkihin välissä,	A font between its shoulder-blades,
Synnyn suitset päässä olis,	born with a bridle on its head
Joka ei kilpisty kivehen,	whose hooves do not founder,
Eikä kaavu kalliosen	nor slip on the rocks

Kotisehen mennessänsä.	As it takes you home.
Tuonne ma sinut manoan:	To this place I banish you,
Kosken kuohuvan kitahan,	Into the jaws of frothy rapids,
Hettehesen heiluvahan,	Into a sloshing spring,
Lättehesen läikkyvähän,	Into a bubbling font,
Siell' on hyvä ollaksesi...	There it is good for you to be...
...Siell' on luutonta lihoa,	...There is meat without bones,
Sekä päätöntä kaloa	And fish without heads,
Syöä miehen nälkähisen,	for the hungry man to eat,
Haukata halun alasen.	A bite for the one in want.

(SKVR VII₄:3097. Suistamo? 1847)

The *synty* and *manaus* incantation modes offered the ritual specialist a means of banishing, removing, or counteracting the threat of an illness agent. For this reason, I suggest that persons in Orthodox Karelian communities did not perform *proškenja* rituals because they felt they *had to*, or because they saw themselves as powerless to do other than placate the illness agent. Participants in the *proškenja* rituals *chose* to place themselves in a reciprocal, obligating relationship with the sacred agent.

This possibility for choice between the two different ritual modes was expressed in a description of a procedure to cure infection by water-*väki* recorded from Ladoga Karelia. Live coals containing fire-*väki*, a force believed to be incompatible with water-*väki*, were dropped into the well thought to be the source of *nenä* illness, thus demonstrating the performer's knowledge of how to play different *väki* forces against each other. This act of aggression against the water-spirit was accompanied by a verbal formula which parodied the apologetic *proškenja* ritual, a formula said to have been used when "headstrong" ritual performers who were "furious" at the supernatural agent did not wish to "subordinate themselves by asking forgiveness":

8)
If a child has been startled by the water so much that it starts to cry during the night, one determined the location of the harm, whether a well or spring. If the harm was found, one was supposed to ask forgiveness and persuade the well or spring. One was supposed to recite to them a good incantation. And one was supposed to bow. But not everyone subordinated themselves by asking forgiveness, rather the more headstrong were furious at that sort of evil-doing. "Three live coals were taken from the sauna stove and one took them to the well and dropped the live coals through the child's clothing into the well and said:

Täs siulles gostšintšat	Here are gifts for you
Dai muud kumarrukset.	And other bowings,
Elägä tämän paremboa vuaji!	Don't ask for better!

I remember when grandmother performed this cure on behalf of our crying daughter. Red-hot coals were dropped hissing into the water of the well. Grandmother went into the farmhouse without looking back. The magic-doer was not allowed to look back before he/she had entered the house. (Suistamo. 1959. Siiri Oulasmaa b)4265. –Paraskeeva Makkonen (Makko)).

The *synty* and *manaus* ritual modes treated pain or disorder as an inexplicable attack by an impersonal illness agent which carried no moral significance for human relationships with the 'other world'. For if an illness agent is not recognized to have a legitimate territory, or legitimate motives for infection, if it does not have a reciprocal relationship with humans, then its infection is a random event, unpredictable and without overt importance for the signification, categorization and evaluation of the *social* world. The same illness-agent, on the other hand, could be treated instead as a sacred agent by bowing down to it, apologizing to it, giving it gifts, in other words incorporating it into a relationship of moral obligation and exchange. *Proškenja* rituals, therefore, were a way of treating the physical complaint as a manifestation of the sacred. In the context of *proškenja* rituals, illness became a departure point for a dialogue with a 'sacralized' agent, a dialogue which in turn had implications for the human participant's moral self-awareness and self-image.

Divination: the role of the ritual specialist in the production of knowledge

The archival descriptions analyzed in this study suggest that the client who came to the healer seeking help was often unsure about whether or not a sacred agent was responsible for the onset of his/her illness. The sensation of disorder in the self was the signal or catalyst which encouraged the afflicted person to seek an explanation, but such explanations were not necessarily obvious or ready at hand. Sometimes clients guessed that contagion from the outside environment was responsible for their ailment,[109] yet it was the *ritual specialist* who nearly always gave the final, authoritative interpretation of the illness, narrowing and clarifying exactly what type of *nenä* illness the victim suffered from, and whence it had infected. The 'gaps' in the ailing person's knowledge concerning the meaning of the illness lead us to enquire how the illness received a culturally-agreed upon meaning, and if that meaning was a manifestation of the sacred, then how the patient became consciously aware of it. The first step in explaining the illness, that is, fitting the patient's sensation of bodily disorder into a system of cultural meaning, was *divination*. In Orthodox Karelia, the ailing person was diagnosed by ritual specialists who used various traditional means to determine the source of the illness. In divination, the participants had not yet entered into a relationship with an illness-agent governed by a specific type of authority: they were first led through the divination, and only afterward told the meaning of the relevant 'signs' by the diviner him/herself. Divination could then be followed by either mode of ritual healing: the *proškenja* ritual based on moral authority, or the more aggressive *synty-manaus* banishment ritual relying on the *tietäjä's* individual authority.

The various symptoms complained of by *nenä* victims were toothache, aching pain in leg, hand, joints, back, eyes, ears, etc., stomach ache, vomiting, swollen tongue, bluish lips, eczema or rash, feeling light-headed or dizzy, and general weakness and poor health. *Nenä* illnesses did not display any coherent class of symptoms and there is no evidence from the available information that a diagnosis of *nenä* was ever made on the basis of *the symptoms alone,*[110] rather, it was arrived at through the interpretive efforts of diviners who used their own modifications of the divination tradition.

The cure was not only the 'removal' of the symptoms but also the 'naming' of the illness, the identification of its source and explanation of the contagion which restored the coherence of meaning. Divination was therefore much more than the ritual posing of a question and the receipt of an answer from an oracle-like device. The divination rituals performed in Orthodox Karelian culture in order to determine the cause of suspected *nenä* illness simultaneously evoked a new universe of categories and values. These new categories and values, as is typical of those elicited through ritual, were seen to come from a higher, more authoritative source than the ritual specialist him/herself, or than, indeed from the society or community (cf. Bell 1992:110).

Divination of *nenä* illness was usually carried out by arranging a series of objects on a flat-bottomed sieve which had been overturned, and dangling a 'pointer' of some sort (needle, cross pendant, etc.) over the arranged objects. The diviner asked a number of questions, in a certain order, and according to the movement of the 'pointer' either between or towards the objects on the sieve, he or she divined the answers.[111] The most common divination arrangement made use of small chunks of bread and charcoal from charred wood. Additional items such as a cross pendant, money, knife, salt, water, clay, or a kindling splint might also be used, but bread and charcoal were generally always 'opposed' to each other as categories or meanings. Bread usually indicated a positive response from the divination device, while charcoal indicated a negative response. One possible explanation for this symbolism may be that bread, which was food and was treated as sacred object in itself, represented positive growth values and thus the right-hand aspect of the sacred, while charcoal, a substance depleted of its energy, represented by contrast an absence of growth values and thus the left-hand aspect of the sacred (cf. Anttonen 1996:77–78, 95).

This collection of objects used in divination was then asked to give an answer, not one based on human knowledge and desires, but one based on 'objective' truth, using the following formula:

Sano arbu, arboa myöte,	Say, oracle, according to your divinations
Elä miehen mieldy myöte!	Not according to the wishes of man!
Sanonet miehen mieldy myöte,	If you say according to human wishes,
Sinuo tungietah tuleh,	You will be pushed into the fire...
(Genetz 1870:95).	

The Folklore Archives contain several detailed descriptions of this sort of divination ritual, [112] two of them recorded by educated collectors, Arvid Genetz and K. Karjalainen, who in the latter half of the 19th century recorded folk customs from Ladoga and Archangel Karelia respectively:

9a)

Generally, when one wants a particular piece of information which cannot be obtained through natural means, for example if an animal or child is lost and it has been sought for a long time with no result, or if one cannot guess the source of a physical discomfort and how it is to be removed, or if a young man would like to know in advance in which village his courting efforts might succeed, then one goes to the *tietäjä,* who sets up the divination device (*arpa*) in the following way. A sieve is placed on the table and on top is placed the cross worn around the neck of the person asking the question, along with its string, so that the string lies along the edge of the sieve. Opposite to the cross, also on the edge, one places a piece of charcoal and obliquely from the charcoal, two pieces of bread; then the *tietäjä* puts a third piece of bread on the end of a needle hanging from a thread and recites, while holding the other end of the thread:

Sano arbu, arboa myöte,	Say, oracle, according to your divinations
Elä miehen mieldy myöte!	Not according to the wishes of man!
Sanonet miehen mieldy myöte,	If you say according to human wishes,
Sinuo tungietah tuleh,	You will be pushed into fire,
Kivet kuvotah,	The rocks will fuse together,
Lagih manatah,	The law will be invoked,
Vedeh vellotah.	The waters made to churn.

After which the piece of bread dangling from the needle is commanded to move from the cross to the charcoal if, for example, the lost [animal or child] should be sought from the north: if this happens, then the bread is commanded to move from bread to bread, and if it does this as well, then to "stand like a wall". If the oracle now shows for the third time that the [animal or child] must be sought from the north, then there can no longer be any doubt about it. But naturally this occurs only rarely, and the *tietäjä* often gets to enquire long and repeatedly from the oracle, before he can give his final statement.
(Genetz 1870:95).

9b)

This same Poahkomie offered to see through divination whether one of my wishes would come true. With pleasure I agreed to his suggestion and asked him to set up his device. He went to fetch a sieve, a thick loaf of bread and three pieces of charcoal about as large as the end of a person's thumb. From the bread he cut a piece of crust and divided this piece into four parts, each as large as the pieces of charcoal. The bread was put on the table, on top of this the charcoal into the configuration of a triangle, and a piece of bread and my ring, and on top of this arrangement the sieve was placed upside-down. At the bottom of the sieve Poahkomie made a square by placing the charcoal opposite charcoal and bread opposite bread, the fourth piece of bread he stuck on the end of a large needle at the end of a braided string. Winding the braided string a bit around the first finger of his right hand, he stabilized this pendulum in the middle of the square formed by the bread and the charcoal and lifted it from the bottom of the sieve.

"Još ajatukšeš käy toteh,	If the wish will come true,
kulkekoh leivästä leipäh,	travel from bread to bread,
još ei, hiileštä hiileh,"	If not, from charcoal to charcoal,

said the old man, and after a few moment the pendulum, visibly under the influence of the old man's finger, began to move from bread to bread; my wish would thus come true. It was still necessary to test whether there were any enemies, opponents, and now the piece of bread travelled from charcoal to charcoal, there were no obstacles, no one would put their hooks in my path. It would have been nice to now know the future, but unfortunately I had been so engrossed in watching what was happening that I had not remembered to wish for anything. This divination device always spoke the truth, according to the old man...
(SKVR I$_4$:2025. Akonlahti. 1894. Karjalainen p.59)

Although a number of interesting features of this divination rite call for further analysis, I would like here to focus on one in particular. From the standpoint of evoking a new universe of categories and values, the *questions asked of the divination device* by the diviner may have been more important than the answers received from it. As is suggested in the following example, the divination device always worked with a limited range of possible answers. This is because the ritual specialist set the parameters of the questioning in advance, by naming only a few possible sources of *nenä* infection:

10)
How to find out from which water the illness has infected
One cuts four crusts from bread, and gives two of them the names of local bodies of water, and the third is called wind-*nenä*. The fourth is placed on the end of a needle with thread, one lifts it from the bread loaf and watches towards which piece of bread crust the sharp side of the hanging piece of crust turns, and one finds out from which body of water the illness has infected or whether it comes from the wind. One must first remember the names one has given to the bread crusts.
(Salmi. 1938. Vilho Vinui 143. –Ivan Rajakka, b. 1897).

The divination process specified which among several possible 'sources' (water, wind, forest, cemetery, etc.) was the cause of the illness in each case, but it was *the ritual specialist, rather than tradition*, which specified the alternative sources *in the first place*. The diviner limited the field of possibilities already at the outset of the divination ritual when he/she asked whether the *nenä* illness had come from the water or the cemetery, for example, but did not mention the forest. Some diviners favored water and wind as the culprits responsible for *nenä* illness (example 10),[113] others the forest, cemetery and earth (example 11b), and some even included 'gods' (=holy icons,[114] see example 11c). The seemingly supernatural source of the divined information mystified the actual processes taking place in the production of knowledge, in which the healer designated in advance the relevant cultural categories for sources of illness. In this way, the diviner guided the patient towards a new understanding of the boundaries between self and environment, since only particular aspects of the patient's surroundings were presented as dangerous, potential sources of body pollution:

11a)

By divining with a sieve and bread and charcoal, one can discover whence earth-*nenä* (*maahinen*) has infected. It's better in the morning on an empty stomach. But one can also divine in the evening. Underneath the sieve was placed the patient's clothing, preferably some unwashed garment which had been worn next to the skin. A scarf or cap is best. The sieve is put on the table. On each side of the sieve, across from each other, are placed pieces of bread, and perpendicular to them, pieces of charcoal. "Then a needle", and a piece of bread is put on the end of the needle. The diviner blows on the piece of bread and says:

"Sano pyhä illu syöttäi,	Speak, St. Elijah, provider,
sano praudu.	speak the truth.
Ku ollou Niinan ristkanzan	If something from the earth
moas rodinnu	has infected Niina, a Christian,
käy leivän leibäh,	go from bread to bread,
Kei olle, sid hiiles hiileh."	If not, then from charcoal to charcoal.

(Tulomajärvi. 1944. Helmi Helminen 2530. –Anni Jogorov, b. 1894).

11b)

Divining *nenä* illnesses
A sieve is turned over and on top of it is placed three forked alder branches and next to them, first a piece of bread, second a piece of burnt clay and third a piece of charcoal; a needle is placed in the bristles of a brush, and at the other end of it, an unwashed filament of flax or hemp, and the brush is dangled from the filament over the sieve and one asks:

"does my pain come from the forest, the earth or *kalma*?"

And at whichever word the brush swings, from there has [the illness] come. (SKVR VII$_4$:1599. Korpiselkä. 1908. Ida Mikkonen 267).

11c)

The words of the divination device
When it was not known which illness plagued the sick person, the divination device was asked. The magic-worker took matches, put them in a star formation on the table and in the middle of them put something representing the sick person, for example a hair, a button, etc. To each match he/she gave the name of an illness, for example illness from a well, from the river, from the lake, forest-*nenä*, curses, illness from icons (*jumaloista tullut tauti*), etc. After this he/she took a flax brush, put two matches crossways between the brush hairs and recited:

Sano arva asioita,	Say, oracle, things as they are
älä miehen mieltä myöten	Not according to the mind of man
arvalle da Jumalalle.	but to that of the oracle and of God.
Jos ei arva totta sano	If the oracle does not tell the truth
arva pätsiin viskataan,	the oracle will be tossed into the oven
mies mereen paiskataan.	the man hurled into the sea.

The magic-doer then took hold of the string attached to the other end of the brush, dangled the brush over the matches and let it spin until it stopped by itself. Then the match attached to the brush pointed to the illness which plagued the sick person.
(Impilahti. 1933. Rauni Rantasalo VK 79:8. –mistress of Jyrkinen farm, approx. 50 years)

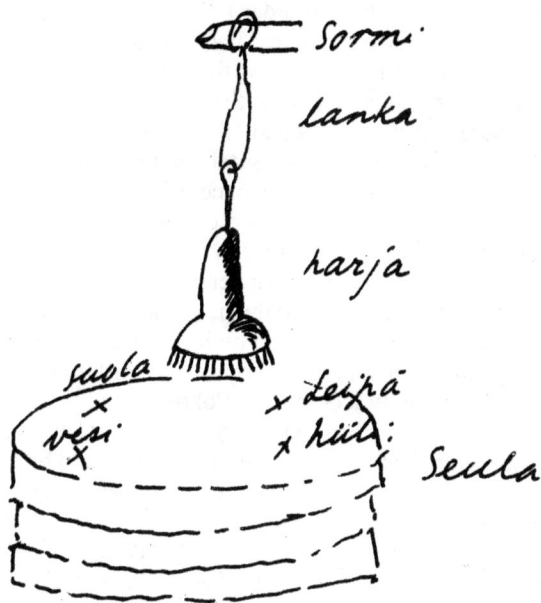

Sketch of divination device by Martti Haavio showing overturned sieve (seula)
with objects placed upon it: salt (suola), *water* (vesi), *bread* (leipä), *and charcoal*
(hiili). *According to the 90-year-old informant Marppa Solehmainen, "one put a*
needle in the brush (harja), *and hung it from a thread* (lanka). *In one section of the*
sieve one placed bread, in another salt, in the third water, and in the fourth
charcoal. One then attached the [thread] at the end of the needle to one's finger
(sormi). *If [the brush] goes to the bread or salt, this indicates "true". If to the*
water or charcoal, the answer is "false"...
(Korpiselkä. 1933. Martti Haavio 895)

These descriptions of the divination process suggest that different ritual
specialists set up the divination process so as to reflect different cognitive
categories of the dangerous 'Other'. These categories were also spatial
categories, since the different sources of illness usually corresponded to
concrete places. Thus the ailing person's mental landscape was influenced
by the diviner in the context of each divination ritual.

It is worth noting that in most cases the client's own guesswork concerning
the site of infection does not seem to have played a significant role in
divination. After the healer had arrived at an answer, then the client was
expected to recall an event leading to infection which was compatible with
the healer's conclusion:[115]

12)
...But sometimes there occurred more complicated illnesses than those
whose source was known for certain. And it often happened that there was
not the faintest clue concerning the cause of the illness, and then a skillful
tietäjä was needed. When this sort of illness was at issue, then the *tietäjä*

turned first to divination in order to discover the origin of the illness, in other words, "whence the illness had infected". For infected it must have done, since illness is not a good thing and therefore it is not a natural phenomenon in human life. Thus the folk believed and for this reason they were so sure that the illness had "thrown itself" from somewhere or had possibly come through another's deliberate sorcery (*rikkomalla*). And for this reason one had to divine whence it had come: from the water, or the earth, or was it sorcery? Not everyone was able to carry out divination, naturally, but whoever was privy to its secrets and was able to make the divining device obey, then to that person it never lied. The *tietäjä* who told me about divination explained that it happened in the following manner: a sieve is turned upside down and on it is placed three pieces of bread and three pieces of charcoal, each representing different cardinal points. One ties a string to a holy icon of "St. Pokrova" and holds the string over the sieve, and if the illness has come from the place he/she inquires, for example from the water, then the icon swings from bread to bread, but if it is from somewhere else, then it swings from charcoal to charcoal, and then one must inquire a new possibility of whence the illness might have "thrown itself". On the basis of the divined result, healing can be carried out. If the illness was from the water, one had to "ask the waters' mistress for forgiveness". But the patient had to remember – if he or she were an adult – in what situation the illness had infected. Had the net, for example while seine fishing, snagged on the bottom of the lake and in dislodging it the patient accidentally let out a curse? ...And there are countless other possibilities for infection. But a knowledgeable *tietäjä* will be certain to discover the real one.
(Kontokki. 1936. Vasili Jyrinoja E 132, p. 8–10).

In this process, naming the possible sources of illness turned the undifferentiated space of the patient's natural surroundings into meaningful 'places' which could be negotiated with and therefore controlled. In the case of *nenä* illnesses, the divination process situated the original source of the physical disorder away from the body itself to the 'outside' realm. It then organized reality by mapping unexplained physical suffering onto the natural surroundings outside the body, and by dividing the amorphous, threatening environment into two or more categories of "Other". Divination turned an ambiguous experience of bodily disorder into a controlled relationship with a specified, identifiable illness agent, thus yielding a measure of order and comprehensibility where previously there had been only unexplained suffering. In doing so, divination simultaneously privileged the difference between *the human domain* and the *wilderness*, as we shall see later on.

Dreams were an alternative source of knowledge (Siikala 1980:65–66; 1994:220–223), and often a last resort if divination failed to indicate the source of a supernatural illness.[116] In dreams, the sacred agent itself might indicate the transgression which had led to the infection, as well as what sort of compensation it demanded. According to one informant from Olonets, "the water himself shows in a dream what he might need: tea, bread or alcohol."[117] In an account of his travels through Archangel Karelia, Juho Lukkarinen (1918:74) gives an example of divination through dreams that he heard on his travels:

13)
A certain person broke branches from a tree growing near a spring in order to make a sauna-whisk. He became immediately ill and lay bedridden for 28 weeks. Finally one evening as he prepared for sleep he implored that he would receive in a dream an explanation of where he must go to find the cure. And the explanation came. In his dream he saw how a naked female figure rose from the spring and advised him to bring some sort of offering to the spring, for example shards of glass, and to take water from the spring for bathing. When morning came, the offerings were taken and the ointment water was brought according to instructions. And soon the ailing person recovered.

It was also common practice for ailing persons to give articles of their clothing to ritual specialists who were known for their ability as seers (referred to as *tietäjä* or *noita* in the examples below). The seer would place the clothing under his or her pillow at night in order to see a dream that might reveal the origin of the illness and how it could be cured:

14a)
When someone became ill, it was necessary to go to a *noita*. The *noita* was supposed to be given the sick person's cross or some article of clothing to put under his head during the night so that he/she could know where the illness had come from: from the earth, the water, or from holy icons (*jumali*). If it came from a holy icon, one had to go on the third night with the *noita* to "bow", without anyone knowing. One had to then make a promise to go to the village chapel of the *jumala* who is said to have caused the illness and take some kind of gift, a cow or something else.
(Jyskyjärvi. 1936. Osmo Niemi 518. –Joosef Ragneff, 40 years).

14b)
One diagnosed an illness by taking the sick person's cross to a *tietäjä* so he could have it under his head overnight. The *tietäjä* saw in a dream whence the illness had come.
(Sarviniemi. 1932. H. Hilippälä 153. –V. Koski, 50 years).

14c)
In December of 1912, the son of Huoti Puavilainen from Kivijärvi had fallen ill with some sort of illness in which his bones ached. The boy's grandmother had, in addition to other cures, used the following method: she had sent the sick boy's shirt to some acquaintances of hers in Porklahti village so that they would put it under their heads when sleeping and see dreams of whence the boy's illness had infected. The dream was seen and the grandmother was told that the infection had come from the water.
(Kivijärvi. 1913. Iivana Marttini 1403).

14d)
Whoever can divine according to dreams can also find out whence the illness has infected. One should put the person's clothing, about whom the information is desired, under the head of the person who wants to know, without the former's knowledge, [and ask:] Did you see anything in your dreams? When there is a diviner of dreams, then that person can know. My daughter-in-law had a toothache. When you dream that horses are coming

towards you, then the fault lies with the holy icons in the village chapels (*tsasounas*). My daughter-in-law said: I was travelling from Koito village and the horses came towards me. [I said:] Your teeth will ache until you take a taper to the chapel at Koito. She remembered that she had been at the Koito cemetery once with her boyfriend – so she took her aunt with her, and donated a taper. Immediately it took the toothache away. From whichever direction the injury comes, the horses race to that place. (Suistamo. 1935. Martti Haavio 1997).

The role of the ritual specialist did not end with the *diagnosis* of the *nenä* illness through divination and dreams, however. There is ample information in the ritual descriptions to indicate that the ritual specialist played an active and key role in directing the patient both *to* and *through* the appropriate healing ritual:

15a)
When I young, I was weak and sickly until my fifteenth year. My mother tried to do her best for me so that I would grow up to be healthy. She took me to the *tietäjäs* to have me treated. When I was a girl, there were many times when I had to carry out the *proškenja* visit with a *tietäjä*. Arhippa's widow, a *tietäjä*, came many times to our home to take me on a *proškenja* visit. When she was unable to help me, my mother invited "grandmother Fedota"[118] to cure me. Grandmother was a superior *tietäjä*, she cured me. – The divination showed my ailment to be from the forest. Ahead was therefore a *proškenja* visit in the forest. Grandmother took hold of my hand and led me to the forest. When we were at a sufficient distance and grandmother was sure that there was no one to see us, the bowing started...
(Suistamo. 1958. Siiri Oulasmaa 3981. –Paraskeeva Makkonen, 72 years).

15b)
When a person has become ill, the diviner may say that the sick person has water-*nenä* (*vedenvigahine*). Then the diviner decrees that the *proškenja* visit must be made. He/she also stipulates whether the person making the visit must be light- or dark-blooded, a man or a woman. The sick person is either present or is represented by a walking stick.
(Impilahti. 1936. Niina Saarela KRK 153:37. –Marfa Kirjavainen, 51 years).

15c)
One spoke incantations to and asked forgiveness (*prossitettih*) from the water, whatever incantations may have been said—it was the *tietäjäs*, naturally, who were supposed to be the ones who knew.
There were diviners who divined from whence the *nenä* (*heittäytyn*) came. If it was from the water, then one went to the shore and asked for forgiveness, asked for "proskenjoa" from the water. Ontippa showed me how to ask forgiveness...
(Virtaranta 1958:126. –Mari Kyyrönen)

Ritual specialists who functioned as both seers and healers thus occupied a key role in giving meaning to the physical complaint. This meaning was nothing less than an entire universe of causality evoked by the divination rite, as well as a new moral orientation expressed through the bodily movements, spoken formulas and offered gifts of the *proškenja* rituals. In

Poahkomie Omenaini demonstrates the divination ritual for collector K.F.
Karjalainen and photographer I.K. Inha. Akonlahti, 1894. Photo: I.K. Inha.
Finnish Literature Society (see no. 9b, pp. 90–91).

this cognitive universe, the illness-agent was expected to respond with healing and thus maintain the reciprocal dialogue because the moral force of the gift required it (cf. Mauss 1967). Maurice Godelier (1999:11) sums up Mauss' idea of the gift's moral force thus: "what creates the obligation to give is that giving creates obligations [between actors]." By receiving a gift and accepting it the sacred agent became indebted to the giver (in this case the patient): equilibrium in the form of equality between the two actors could only be restored by a return gift (in this case health). This awareness of reciprocal obligation, however, was actualized *only when the ritual specialist chose to use the 'proškenja' ritual*, since as we have seen earlier, alternative moral universes, in which an entirely different attitude was taken toward the illness-agent, were also possible. The 'patient', as a witness to the ritual specialist's supplication on his or her behalf, was invested with this moral universe simply by participating. Even when the patient was too ill to accompany the ritual specialist to the site of infection in order to witness and participate in the specialist's performance, the crucial ritual evocation was still communicated to the patient during a prior bathing rite. As one ritual specialist describes:

97

16)
...During the bathing, I read the same formula [as I do in asking forgiveness from the forest, water, wind and cemetery]. The bathing occurs beforehand. Then I go to ask of the wind, forest, and cemetery "are you wrong or right", and only then do I ask for forgiveness (*proškennua*).
(Salmi. 1936. Martta Pelkonen 194. – Natalju Timofjouna Mironov, female professional healer, aged 90 in 1935).

This suggests that the most critical aspect of the *proškenja* ritual was seen to be its effect on the patient's way of perceiving the world, rather than mere communication with sacred agents, which could have been carried out by the healer without the patient ever having had to know the details of this communication.

The reciprocal relationship between humans and supernatural agents did not only take place through ritual: dreams also played an important role, as has been suggested earlier. *Communication between humans and sacred agents was a two-way street*: while humans communicated with nature spirits through ritual gestures, verbal formulas and offerings in the context of *proškenja* rituals, nature spirits communicated with humans through dreams, as in the following examples:

17a)
In Keikkula village lived a sorcerer (*tiedoiniekka*), Gauroi. He had an adopted son, whose tongue was swollen by the water spirit. Since the old man was a *tietäjä*, he soon discovered what had made the water spirit angry. The boy had, cursing, thrown a plow into the lake. In a dream, the "water master" whose dwelling place is right underneath Keikkula village, said to Gauroi: "You did wrongly, when you put the plow on my back. And with a curse."
(Tulemajärvi. 1943. Helmi Helminen 2318. –Olga Fomin, b. 1905).

17b)
A woman was washing potato skins near a well, and some of them dropped into the well. "*Nenä* (*vigahine*) infected, my teeth began to ache." It occurred on a Saturday evening. If that happened, one was supposed to go alone at midday or late in the evening to the well and fill a bottle with water. And then put the bottle on the top of the roof. This the woman did. At night while sleeping she sees: "He opens the door and comes in." His hair is long, an old person he is. "Why did you have to bring me here?" he says. "I would have forgiven you in any case."
(Tulemajärvi. 1943. Helmi Helminen 2327. –Nikolai Sykköjev, b. 1873).

17c)
The informant himself had, as a small boy, filled up an old well together with another boy. After that he felt pain in his leg and it began to atrophy without any outwardly visible symptoms. The doctors ordered that the leg undergo surgery. But one night the boy had a dream in which a man came to him and said, "little boy, why did you fill the well with stones and other rubbish, was the well in your path?" and having said this the man departed. The boy awoke just then and in the morning told the dream to his older brother. The brother wondered whether the illness in the boy's leg had come from the well. And that same morning the brother took the boy with

him to the well. He emptied it and cleaned it out thoroughly, and the boy, too, threw several stones out of the well. The next day the leg was already improved and finally it returned to normal all by itself.
(Salmi. 1935. Pekka Pohjanvalo KRK 151:249. –Miko Hattara, 32 years, laborer).

By construing illness and health as the result of conscious acts perpetrated by supernatural beings, and by entering into a dialogue with them, ritual participants were able to reorder a cognitive world made chaotic by the intrusion of bodily disorder and ailment. The psychological and mental aspects of the ritual are therefore important here. We cannot, however, understand the full meaning of the *proškenja* ritual without attention to bodily experience. The body was the site of both transgression and reconciliation between the two parties: the beginning and endpoint of the sequence of events were played out in the body, which functioned as a *field of meaning*. Physical disorder was a sign of discord between the human and the sacred agent, and the return to health signified the return to normal, harmonious relations on both sides.

Proškenja rituals and the 'open' body

Recently, anthropologists, folklorists, sociologists and historians interested in the function and meaning of ritual have begun to grant the body a primary role in the social construction of reality (Grimes 1985:18, Bell 1992:95). The human body is the ultimate mediator of our experiences with the outside world, as well as our social experiences with other human beings, and is "foremost of all metaphors" for how society perceives and organizes itself (Benthall and Polhemus 1975:10, 59–73). According to George Lakoff and Mark Johnson (1980), bodily experience is the ultimate source for structures of human understanding and spatial orientation, including those of 'up', 'down', 'inside' and 'outside', etc.

For the present discussion there are actually three relevant 'bodies': first, the phenomenological body/self, which is also the locus of consciousness, the source of the way we see the world. Second, the human body is a potential map for cognitive representations of other relationships, whether natural, supernatural, social or even spatial (see Lock and Scheper-Hughes 1987). This is Douglas' notion of the body as a *natural symbol* (1966, 1975), in which bodily boundaries are seen to correspond to social boundaries and bodily pollutions are symbolic expressions of undesirable contacts threatening the social order. Finally, there is the ritualized 'social body' (Bell 1990, 1992), referring to the body's social presence, its awareness of its place in a universe of sentient agents and the relations among them, the body situated and contextualized in social practice and discourse. In a worldview which sees the supernatural 'Other' as a sentient being capable of intention and conscience, the human body also becomes the instrument which shapes and is shaped by dialectic relations with the supranormal.

How are social bodies constructed? Here the notion of ritual discussed earlier is crucial. Scholars of ritual see the movement and self-positioning acted out by the body as somatic or corporeal "ways of knowing", and bodily experience is closely involved in the production of knowledge (Sklar 1994:9–12; Utriainen 1998b). Put another way, the spare, simple movements and postures which are the "elementary" repertoires enacted through the body in ritual can be seen as mnemonic schemes inscribed in physical form (Connerton 1989:57). Rituals thus work to impress cultural and ideological systems on the body and to alter individuals' perceptions of identity and social reality (Bell 1990:299).

If we view ritual *as a way of socializing the body*, as a primary way in which the body comes to internalize an understanding of its own place in a network of social relationships and discourses, then we must ask what sort of schemes were being impressed upon the body through the *proškenja* rituals, what sort of embodied knowledge these rituals represented. We must also ask, conversely, what sorts of cultural categories and divisions the body in turn imposed upon the cultural landscape through its enactment of the ritual.

Let us first consider the diagnosis of *nenä*-illness through divination. Here we see that the body/self was not construed as bounded, discrete and separate from its environment, but was treated as highly vulnerable, permeable. The perimeter of the self was seen to be easily infiltrated, and bodily boundaries were experienced as vulnerable to forces from an animated, threatening environment.

This view of the body is not surprising, given the fact that cultural body concepts reflect broader schemas regarding the structure and nature of society and the cosmos. There is ample evidence pointing to the fact that the body was perceived and experienced in distinct ways within traditional cultures in which persons were under threat of supernatural and magical harm. In the older magical worldview which prevailed in premodern and early modern European popular thought, the boundaries between oneself and the natural world were thought to be more permeable. This older magical world view entailed nothing less than the alternate construal of the self, as scholars like Charles Taylor (1989) and Lyndal Roper (1994) have pointed out. Bodies in these cultures have been described as conceptually 'open' (Falk 1994), their body images 'fluid' (Sault 1994). Basically, a culture in which the body is conceived of as open or fluid sees these bodies as having weaker, fuzzier boundaries between themselves and the outside world (including other bodies and the natural environment), and therefore as more vulnerable to intrusion from the outside, than is the case in what are considered the more 'closed' bodies of modern societies. At the same time, however, the open or fluid body can also be a 'projecting' body, whose image, energies and sensory information can spread far beyond its own boundaries and have a concrete effect on its surroundings.

Pasi Falk (1994) posits the schema of an 'open' body as a feature of traditional, face-to-face societies in which a collective sense of community is strong. The boundaries between 'open' bodies and the outside world are experienced as more hazy or blurred, making the self more vulnerable both to others and to forces in their surroundings. In an 'open body' culture, symbolic representations depict bodily boundaries as weaker, and the flow of meanings and effects across them stronger, than is generally the case in the modern West. Falk compares the 'open body' in traditional societies with the 'closed' body of modern societies as follows:

> (…) the stronger the cultural Order and the community bonds in which the subject is constituted, the more 'open' is the body both to outside intervention and to a reciprocal relationship with its cultural/social context. In general terms, this is the situation in a primitive society in which the constitution of the subject acquires the form of a 'group-ego' or 'group-self' defining the boundaries between inside and outside primarily in collective terms. And second, the less rigid the cultural order and the weaker the community bonds, the more intertwined are the boundaries of the self with those of the individual body. In other words, the constitution of the subject takes the form of an individual self – especially characteristic of modern society – articulating the inside/outside distinction primarily at the boundaries of the individual self, and thus the body surface (Falk 1994:12).

The existence of 'open' versus 'closed' body images and the importance of body image for the social behavior of individuals have long been recognized by psychologists and psychoanalysts in studies of "high barrier" versus "low barrier" body boundaries (Tiemersma 1989:60). While the 'open' or 'fluid' body remains a somewhat vague concept which must be explicated for each culturally-specific case, it also offers a valuable theoretical framework for perceiving the important ways in which magic interfaced with social life in 19th-century agrarian Finland and Karelia. Without it, much of the significance of magic beliefs and practices for actual, embodied persons is lost.

The most prototypical example of the open, fluid or projecting body in rural-traditional Finland and Karelia is the case of dynamistic *väki* forces. The human body had its own dynamistic force, *luonto*, which could infect other persons or could be used to resist intrusion from outside forces (see Stark-Arola, 2002). A closer look at ritual tradition in Finland and Karelia reveals that it is not simply dynamistic beliefs which are based on an 'open' body or projected body image schema, but practically all magical beliefs related to the body, especially those linked to the body's orifices: mouth, eyes and vagina. These included the 'evil eye' (*silmäykset*); 'mouthings' (*suutelus*, in other words magical harm in the form of spoken praise); 'love magic' in which a woman's menstrual blood was secretly placed in alcohol or coffee to be ingested orally by men; the idea that menstruation could be transferred to men; and symbolic pollution emanating from the vagina (see the 'wrath of the vagina' and negative *harakointi* in Stark-Arola 1998). The notion of an 'open body' is thus an important starting point for understanding the social construction of human experience in a supernaturally-permeated universe. In the next sections, I consider the implications of *nenä* illness and *proškenja* rituals for concepts of social structure.

101

Falling down and "standing up straight"

In *proškenja* rituals, the ultimate responsibility for infection by sacred beings was seen to lie with the human patient, who usually admitted or implied his/her culpability during the course of the ritual. Many ritual descriptions also include mention of the act which was assumed to have provoked the sacred agent in the first place. Such offensive acts include: not making the sign of the cross when passing a grave in the forest, disturbing anthills or forest animals, disturbing the peace in the forest by whistling, talking loudly, etc., offending a dead person by not attending the funeral procession, not kissing the corpse at the funeral, going to the cemetery when not wearing a hat, disturbing the water in a well or pond, quarrelling, cursing or uttering profanity while near a body of water, in the forest, in the cemetery, in the fields, etc., or going swimming without saying a prayer beforehand.

While some folk informants thus explained *nenä* illness as arising from human wrongdoing or oversight, in actuality many events thought to lead to *nenä* illness do not fit this description. Three instances in particular which gave rise to *nenä* illness were (1) being startled or taking fright, (2) 'thinking' about infection, and (3) 'falling down'. These causes of *nenä* infection were part of the folk model of illness not only in Orthodox Karelia proper, but in neighboring parts of Eastern and Northern Finland as well. They are interesting in that they were viewed in informants' descriptions of illness as deliberate acts. I will discuss the last of these, "falling down", first.

Falling, collapsing, tripping, etc., as a cause of *väki* infection (*nenä* illness) was mentioned for example, by Archangel Karelian informant Marina Takalo (Pentikäinen 1971:237). As another informant from Ladoga Karelia explains,

> 18)
> the earth spirit and the farmyard spirit are one and the same. If you fall hard, it infects, the earth spirit does. Then it brings pain. Then one must go to the shore to ask forgiveness.
> (Salmi. 1934. Martti Haavio 937. –Oksenja Petrovna Karhu, 81 years).

In another example from Ladoga Karelia, an informant describes how "a certain boy happened to fall while moving about on the rocks along the bank. At the same moment, the boy heard a loud bang from the mill, although there was nobody there at the time. In falling the boy was not badly hurt, receiving only a small scratch on his chin..."[119] The boy, however, immediately became ill and was diagnosed as having been infected by water-*väki*.

Being in contact with the ground in a horizontal position may have been seen as a dangerous state:[120] since humans normally stood vertically to the horizontal plane of the ground, to do otherwise, and without permission, may have represented unauthorized contact with the 'Other'. Moreover, it may have signified a *lack of agency*: when humans are lying down, they are most often sleeping, sick, injured or dead, all cases characterized by a non-capacity to act or exert one's conscious will over one's surroundings. The danger of such a state may explain why persons asked permission from the ground before lying down to sleep on the floor even in their own homes,[121] and why travellers in the forest had to ask permission from the ground and surrounding nature when wanting to sleep in the open:

19a)
When you go to lie down you greet the earth:

Maan isändät,	Earth's masters,
maan emändät,	earth mistresses,
Maan kultanen kuningas,	Earth's golden king,
(Repeat)	
Maan kaiken papit, papadjat,	All the earth's priests and priests' wives
Maan kasakat, piiat,	Earth's farmhands, serving maids,
Maan vernoit sluugat,	Earth's faithful servants,
Maan suuret, pienet,	Earth's great ones, small ones,
Maan keskikertahiset,	Earth's middling ones,
Maan nuoret, vanhat, jne.	Earth's young, old, etc.
Suuri teiän sukukunta,	Your father's kin is great,
Helei teiän heimokunta,	Your mother's kin is bright
Pitkät peräntiet;	With long roads behind you;
Prosti luupostis,	Forgive my stupidity,
Prosti gnievostis	Forgive my rashness
Prosti vinnostis!	Forgive my guilty deeds!
Rakenda rauhutta, tervehyttä!	Build peace and health!

(SKVR VII$_5$:5066. Suistamo. 1884–5).

19b)
Permission to spend the night in the forest
When in the forest one might sometimes stay overnight in the open but then, however, one had to ask permission to spend the night in the following way:

Panen maata maan luvalla,	I lie down with the earth's permission,
puun luvalla,	with the tree's permission,
kaiken kartanon luvalla.	with the permission of the entire manor.
Spuassan miekka pieluksiin,	Christ's sword as my pillow,
Muariin kivi katteeksi,	Mary's stone as my roof,
Rauhaks' terveydeksi.	for peace, for health.

(Salmi. 1936. Eino Toiviainen 30. –Jaakko Kämäläinen, 62 years).

'Standing up straight', on the other hand, seems to have been the proper posture for both humans and nature spirits when interacting with each other, and this is most clearly expressed in *proškenja* rituals. In a standard phrase used in ritual greetings to nature spirits or the dead in Orthodox Karelia, the otherworldly agent was asked to 'stand straight' at the same time that it was asked to forgive the supplicant or fulfill the reciprocal obligation of 'fairness', and in some incantation-prayers, humans stressed that they, too, would continue to 'stand straight' in their relations with sacred agents:[122]

20a)

Vesi kultane kuningas,	Water, golden king,
Ole oigein seiso selgein,	Be right, stand straight,
Ja anna entinen rauhus,	And give to this Christian
tervehys ristikansalle...	his former peace, health...
...Ristikansa on oigei	...This Christian is right
ja syytöin ja viatoin.	and innocent and blameless.
Jos työ etto ole oigein,	If you are not right,
seiso selgein,	do not stand straight,
Antakkoa sanani anteiksi,	do not forgive my words,
Mie teiät manuutan	I will banish you
Laatuskoih järveh,	to Lake Ladoga,
Vesi kultasel kuninkaal.	To the water, the golden king.

(SKVR VII$_4$:3095. 1884. Salmi. –Stopa Jakoljov, over 60 years).

20b)

...When you first go in front of the cemetery gate, you should take off your hat and compose a greeting to them:

Terve puhtahil kalmalaisil,	Greetings, pure cemetery-dwellers,
Terve kaunehil kalmalaisil!	Greetings, beautiful cemetery dwellers!
Olkoa oikein,	Be right,
seisokkoa selkein,	stand straight,
Antakkoa rauhus, tervehys,	Give peace, health,
Minä tulen azetta	I (name) come to
sellittämäh (nimi).	explain matters.
...Antakaa tämä	Forgive this
ristikansan syy anteiksi,	Christian's fault,
Olkoa oikein,	Be right,
seisokkaa selkein,	stand straight
Yhdeksän polveh sai,	Nine generations back,
Kaksitoistakymmeneh kantah sai,	To the twelfth ancestor,
Kaikki prostikkoa!	Everyone forgive!

(SKVR VII$_4$:1984. Salmi. 1884. –Stepana Jaakonpoika, over 60 years).

20c)

...täz on mettšy potarkat	Here forest, are your gifts,
kun annat omat itšel eäreh	Since you gave my own back to me
älä sinä koske	do not touch
meiiän omi enämbi,	ours again
emme myö sinun koske.	and we will not touch yours.
olemme oigei	We will be right
seisomme selgei	stand straight
täs päiväs edehpäi.	from this day forward.

(Tulemajärvi. 1929. Iina Seppänen. KKTK-KKA).

20d)

St. Blaise looks after the cattle.[123] People pray to him as follows:

Spoassu da pyhä Olassii,	Jesus and St. Blaise,
kormelitsa,	provider,
Kaitse miun lehmäin	Guard my cows
da kasvata.	and help them grow.

Olla oikein, seisuo selvin,	Be right, stand straight,
Lypsättäkkää...	Milk them...

(SKVR I$_4$:1449. Vuonninen. 1915. –Anni Lehtoni).

In his book *How Societies Remember*, Paul Connerton (1989) suggests that the equation between standing up straight and being upstanding, honest, and fair on the one hand, and the association between falling and a negative lack of social or bodily control on the other, is nearly universal, based on the vertical orientation of the body that humans share in common (see also Bourdieu 1977:94; Lakoff and Johnson 1980). As Connerton explains,

> ...in all cultures, much of the choreography of authority is expressed through the body. Within this choreography, there is an identifiable range of repertoires through which many postural performances become meaningful by registering meaningful inflections of the upright posture...when we speak of someone as being 'upright' we may use the expression descriptively and literally to mean that they are standing on their own feet, or we may use it evaluatively and metaphorically to express admiration and praise of someone whom we judge to be honest and just, to be loyal friends in difficulties, to stand by their own convictions, and in general not to stoop to low or unworthy actions...when we speak of misfortunes of all kinds we express the change of circumstances as a fall; we fall into the enemy's hands, we fall upon hard times, we fall from favour. Nor are such metaphoric turns of phrase ad hoc; they remind us of patterns of authority because they form not simply individual metaphoric turns of phrase but whole systems of metaphoric expression. Our oppositional concepts 'up' and 'down' arise out of our bodily experience of verticality...It is through the essentially embodied nature of our social existence, and through the incorporated practices based upon these embodyings, that these oppositional terms provide us with metaphors by which we think and live. Culturally specific postural performances provide us with a mnemonics of the body (p. 74).

If 'standing straight' represented the embodiment of proper social behavior, 'falling down', therefore, may have represented a blurring of boundaries between self and the natural environment, a negative loss of bodily control and thus a case of a person not being fully 'human', that is, not having full agency or volition.

The role of 'thinking' in nenä infection

'Falling down' was not the only act seen to blur the boundary between the two spheres of human and 'Other': the most commonly mentioned causes of *nenä* were associated with the ailing person's inner cognition and affective responses: these included taking fright when walking through the cemetery or a dark forest, or when recalling that a certain shore was the site of a former drowning (see Lintinen 1959; Utriainen 1992:171–172). As informants from neighboring North Karelia pointed out: "Forest-*nenä* infects, when one happens to take fright in the forest";[124] "when you are startled in

105

the forest, the forest-*nenä* intrudes, in other words, *'mehäh hiimosti'*, the forest realm begins to make you ill, you see."[125]

One could also be infected simply by 'thinking' of the possibility of infection: as one informant explained concerning wells, "…if one spits into them or otherwise disturbs their water, they infect. Especially if one 'thinks about it'".[126] The role of 'thinking' in *nenä* infection was already pointed out by Ilmari Manninen (1922) in his study *Die Dämonistichen Krankheiten in Finnischen Volksaberglauben* when he noted: "Übrigens spielen die gedanken eine grosse rolle bei der ansteckung" (p.15); "Eine ansteckung vom wasser (*hingaundahine*) kann man auch durch den blossen gedanken an diese möglichkeit bekommen…" (ibid:88).

The examples below from Archangel and Olonets Karelia suggest that bodily infection deriving from the 'other world' could result entirely from internal cognitive processes:[127]

21a)
Water infects, when one takes fright anywhere on the water, it infects. When one wonders whether something will infect, then it infects and begins to afflict that person.
(Archangel Karelia. 1932. Samuli Paulaharju 18566. –Anni Lehtonen, b. 1868).

21b)
Holy icons infect when you walk past them and don't make the sign of the cross and think: maybe it will infect?
(Archangel Karelia. 1930. Samuli Paulaharju. 13732. –Anni Lehtonen, b. 1868).

21c)
If, for example, you happen to tread on *kalma*[128] and there you think and regret it, "then it forces its way inside." One should cough, make oneself inwardly stronger. One has to audibly clear one's throat, one must not take fright…
(Tulomajärvi. 1944. H. Helminen 2380. –Olga Tomin, b. 1905).

21d)
Forest-*nenä* comes for example if the wind whistles in the forest and frightens you and you think: "dear me, I caused something bad." One's own thinking brings it.
(Tulomajärvi. 1943. Helmi Helminen 2349. –Solomanida Petrov, b. 1862).[129]

21e)
For this reason, no one broke off branches in the spruce copse, for one will receive cemetery-*nenä* if one "thinks, what will come of it."
(Tulomajärvi. 1944. Helmi Helminen 3864. –Jevdokia Kohlojev, b. 1874).

Incantations from Ladoga Karelia spoken during the *proškenja* ritual also refer to the notion that the cause of the infection was the victim's own 'thinking' of the possibility of such infection:

22a)

Hyvä ilta metsän isännät,	Good evening, forest masters,
hyvä ilta metsän emännät...	good evening forest mistresses
...anna rauha, terveys,	...give peace, health
anna rauha, anna rauha,	give peace, give peace
anna anteeksi,	forgive me
jos on tuhmin tuuminut,	if I have badly pondered
viärin ajatellut...	wrongly thought...

(Impilahti. 1933. A.V. Rantasalo 160. –master of Jyrkinen farm, n. 60 years).

22b)

...vezi kuldane kuningas	...water, golden king
prosti minuu riähkahisty	absolve me of my sins
midä minä olen duumainnuh	of what I have pondered,
ajatelluheze,	thought,
prosti minuu riähkähisty.	absolve me of my sins.

(Salmi. 1936. Martta Pelkonen 152. –"Irinny" Juudin, 77 years).

Furthermore, we find from several descriptions recorded in Olonets and Ladoga Karelia the idea that if one did *not* 'think', that is, did *not* allow any suspicions of *nenä* infection to form in one's mind, then one could not be infected:

23a)

Nothing more is needed than that you spit in the yard and at the same time think: "hopefully it doesn't infect me", then wind-*nenä* has already intruded. There are some people into whom no sort of wind-*nenä* nor water-*nenä* nor forest-*nenä* ever intrudes, since they don't think about it.
(Porajarvi. 1943. Helmi Helminen 1485. –Ivan Hermonen, 75 years).

23b)

If while walking past the church or chapel one thinks of the cemetery residents (*kalmanväki*)[130] without sufficient reverence, the church or cemetery spirit (*snievaija*) may infect and produce some illness, and one is not released from it until one visits the church or cemetery and bows to its residents, until one pays a *proškenja* visit, asks for forgiveness. For this reason one *should not be thinking of anything* when at the church or cemetery, just make the sign of the cross and go past.
(Suistamo. 1900. Iivo Härkönen 416. Emphasis mine, parentheses in original).

How can we understand the idea of humans being infected because they "thought" wrongly, were startled or fell down? This question leads us back to the issue of body image and the 'open body' or fluid body boundaries discussed earlier. In a culture where people may have been socialized to view the boundary between self and other as relatively weak and vulnerable, I suggest that 'thinking' of the possibility of infection or being startled led to a perceived *breach in the boundaries of the patient's own body-image*. The boundary between 'this side' and the 'other side' was marked not only by the body's physical boundary (skin) but also by the person's awareness of the outer limits of their body image. This is why boundaries violated in 'thought' were violated in the embodied experience of self, and why 'falling down', that is, loss of bodily control which brought one closer to the 'ground', may have been seen as a dangerous loss of the distinction between self and the natural environment.

The emic view that 'inner' thought processes led directly to *nenä* infection and thus boundary transgression has important implications for understanding the purpose of the *proškenja* ritual. The ritual, I suggest, was not merely intended to heal the body nor even to reinforce the image of the forest, water, cemetery, etc. as the 'Other', but to repair *a perceived breach in the patient's body image*, to restore the boundary separating self from 'Other' in the patient's own perception. The boundary between 'this side' and the 'other side' was marked first and foremost on a person's *awareness* of his/her bodily boundaries. The most common causes of *nenä* – falling down, taking fright, inadvertently thinking a thought – were all *involuntary* acts. Was the very fact that a person had momentarily lost his volition seen to open the door for the 'Other', the forest environment, to exert its agency over the now defenceless person?

The interlinked concepts of fright, *nenä* infection, body image and agency were also bound up with the Eastern Finnish and Karelian notion of *luonto*, a term used in ritual descriptions to refer to a dynamistic force present in humans which derived from the self and acted upon the outside environment. *Luonto* is etymologically related to idea of agency (> *luoda* 'to create, make' (SKES:108)). According to information from folk belief sources, all persons were thought to have some kind of *luonto*, which in its *non-raised* state was thought to be either hard/strong or soft/weak. A person with a soft or weak *luonto* could be easily frightened and infected by outside *väki* forces in the form of *nenä* illness (see below). Ordinary persons could make their *luonto* harder or stronger through contact with more powerful, *väki*-filled (*väekäs*) sources (Stark-Arola, 2002). Raised *luonto*, sometimes referred to as a *haltia*,[131] on the other hand, represented a different state, one usually only achieved by *tietäjäs*, who were normally supposed to have hard *luonto* in any case, as long as they still had their teeth. In order to perform magic, a *tietäjä's luonto* needed to be rugged (*karkea*), brisk, crisp (*raikas*), strong, solid (*luja*) or 'of stone' (*kivikäs*).

Luonto could be raised deliberately or in some cases unintentionally, as when a *tietäjä* saw a bad dream,[132] or began to brag and boast.[133] *Luonto* was raised by physically grinding one's teeth and jumping up and down, clapping one's hands, spitting, coughing, and being 'angry'.[134] Physical manifestations of successfully raised *luonto* were most commonly the *tietäjä's* hair standing on end: "when he grinds his teeth, then his *luonto* rises and his hair stands on end"[135] (see also Siikala 1992:207–208).

As can be seen from such incantation verses as "Rise my *luonto* from the *lovi*, from the undergrowth, my *haltija*…",[136] the word *haltia* or *haltija* was often a parallel term for *luonto* (Siikala 1992:213–214). As one informant from Uusimaa in Finland pointed out, "if there was a person with such a hard *luonto* (*kovaluontoin*), then it was said that that person has a hard *haltia*".[137]

A person's *haltia* could warn of dynamistic danger: in one text recorded by Samuli Paulaharju in 1916, a female informant 'mumbles' something about how her 'haltia' began to move inside her when she was in danger of infection from the forest-*väki* (forest-*nenä*):

24)
Forest-*nenä*
I came across three squirrels, first a rabbit, then three squirrels then after that a reindeer – the forest-*nenä* is on the move (I thought), but it didn't infect me. My *haltia* began to stir inside me. The wife of Miina Kliimo had performed sorcery – the squirrels screeched and screeched. The forest was set in motion, that is certain…The old woman had visited our place and performed sorcery so that… (1916. Latvajärvi. Paulaharju 7807. – "Mumblings of a woman from Latvajärvi").

Descriptions from informants from Orthodox Karelia and neighboring northern and eastern Finland tell how persons with 'soft' or 'weak' *luonto* were infected by the wilderness environment, while those with 'hard' *luonto* were not:

25)
Bears contain forest-*nenä*. When a person with a slack *luonto* (*löyhäluontoinen*) startles a bear, then forest-*nenä* infects, begins to torment that person. One must call for a *tietäjä*, who knows how to release the victim.
(Kuhmo. 1916–1917. Samuli Paulaharju 7622. –Old Man Lehmivaara).

One informant from Olonets Karelia, when speaking of *nenä* illness, mentioned that "I was infected many times". According to the collector Helmi Helminen, the informant explained this susceptibility by saying that he had a "soft *luonto*".[138] In a description from Ladoga Karelia of a rite to cure infection from water-*väki*, the patient was supposed to hold a stone in his hand and say:

26)
May my *haltia* be as hard as stone,
May no more *nenä* infect me ever again.
(SKVR VII$_4$:3105. Suistamo. 1884. –Irina Paramoona, 70 years).

Not only were sudden fright and falling down the most commonly-mentioned causes of *nenä* infection, they were also connected to the 'loss' of *luonto* or personal *haltia* (Harva 1948:255–256; Siikala 1992:214–215; Stark-Arola 2002). By taking fright when in proximity to the forest or a body of water, persons were seen to allow the boundaries of the self to be momentarily 'opened' or 'blurred'. For example, an informant from South Karelia stated that "when a person takes fright, his/her haltia departs and the person falls down…"[139]

Possessing a hard *luonto* or *haltia* was also linked to the *tietäjä's* agency and authority – that is, the ability to make others obey (see pp. 81–88 for a discussion of the role of authority and obedience in the healing of supernatural illness). For example, it could be said of a *tietäjä* in Finland that "he has such a hard *haltia*, that he must be obeyed."[140] It was said of one woman in South Savo who possessed a hard *luonto* that "what she wills, it happens".[141]

We can extrapolate from informants' descriptions that *nenä* infection was perceived as the *väki* of the attacking agent which had penetrated the victim's bodily boundaries (see also Stark-Arola 2002). Those boundaries did not correspond to the physical (skin) boundary, but instead to the patient's body-image boundary defined in terms of the extremities of his/her *luonto*-force. According to the models of thought surrounding Finnish-Karelian belief in dynamistic *väki*-forces, the *väki* of agents and substances (forest, water, fire, cemetery, etc.) and the corresponding *luonto*-force in humans could be either 'hard' or 'soft'. Furthermore, anger was seen to make this *väki*- or *luonto*-force 'harder' and 'sharper', and fear was seen to make it soften and weaker (ibid.). We have seen earlier how sacred boundary agents capable of infecting with *nenä* illness were usually also those that could be easily angered, and in fact *nenä* infection was often explained in terms of the sacred agent having become angry. Conversely, *nenä* infection could be caused by the victim's own fear or fright. I suggest that *nenä* infection, or violation of this '*luonto*-boundary', operated according to two mechanisms: (1) the sacred agent's *väki* was able to penetrate the victim's *luonto*-boundary because anger had made it 'hard' or 'sharp' enough to penetrate; or (2) the victim's *luonto*-boundary was inadvertently 'opened' or weakened through fright, 'thinking' of infection, or 'falling down' so that the *väki* was able to penetrate and cause *nenä* illness.

If we look at belief in *nenä* illness from the perspective of the cultural Order, it would appear that disorder, manifested as illness in the human body, may have been the signal that the boundary between self and other in the patient's body image had been blurred and needed to be redrawn through ritual. Patients' own perceptions of themselves as bounded, inviolate and distinct from their natural environment had momentarily vacillated, and it was *this* vacillation which was seen to be the true danger. The persons who were primarily responsible for identifying this danger, the ritual specialists, were also those who re-erected the mental barrier between the two worlds in the patient's consciousness.[142] If *nenä* illness represented contamination by *väki*-forces inherent in certain (but not all) entities existing in the outside environment, then perhaps these entities were seen to contain *väki* for the same reason that many religions contain a distinction between the sacred and the profane: because contact or even contiguity between these things and the body "would contradict too violently the dissociation of these ideas in the mind" (Durkheim 1965/1912: 55). Precisely which associations were viewed as threatening can be seen from which entities were believed to infect with their *väki*-force. Clearly, the main categories of dangerous, *väki*-filled agents were (1) things connected to the forest nature or wilderness, and (2) things connected to the dead. It was these categories which were seen to stand in opposition to the human body and the man-made cultural universe in which humans lived and worked. In the summary to Part I, I delve deeper into a discussion of symbolic pollution and the fundamental divide between culture and nature.

Farm versus forest: disorder in the resource zone shared by humans and the forest

Cattle and the forest spirit

In the foregoing, I discuss the first boundary between 'self' and 'Other': the *luonto* boundaries of the body, which corresponded to the outer limits of a person's body image. As such, violations of this boundary manifested as a supranormal illness were at the same time the first and most intimate context for human exchange relations with sacred agents. The second context, explored in the sections which follow, concerns the resource spaces shared by humans and the forest. These resource spaces represented a boundary zone encompassing the outer edges of fields wrested from the forest through burn-beating, the zone of new regrowth just beyond the fields in which the cattle grazed, and the beginning of the old growth forests. The boundary between the 'inner sphere' of the farm or human community and the 'outer' wilderness was thus **not** a clearly delineated 'line' between the two, especially because farmers might also cultivate distant fields on the other side of forested land. Negotiations with the wilderness over the use of these resource-rich areas usually took place *when the cattle were let out to the forest pasture for the first time in spring*. The entire community let their cows out to graze on the same day, which was usually St. George's Day (*Jyrki*). After this day, the cows grazed during the day in the grassy glades located between the fields and the coniferous forest, and as evening fell they returned home to be milked. Various dangers faced the cattle in the forest, including attacks from bears and wolves, becoming lost, drowning in the swamps, or being trapped in the 'forest cover' (*metsänpeitto*).

In this section I discuss the rituals which created the spatial and temporal arrangements by which forest resources were shared by the human community and the wilderness, and the boundaries between them negotiated. Ritual appeals to the forest spirit made when letting the cows out for the first time in spring were intended to protect the cattle grazing in the forest, and were often expressed in the form of an exchange agreement. Bread, an egg, or money was given by humans to the forest spirit, and the forest spirit (or its representatives) was asked to guard the cows in the forest pastures or to simply refrain from doing them harm:[143]

27a)
On St. George's Day, before the cattle were let out to pasture, the mistress took a loaf of bread or some pasties to the forest spirit in order to placate it, so that the forest spirit would grant good cattle-luck during the summertime and protect the cattle from forest predators.
(Sortavala. 1937. J. Hyvärinen 1247. –Maria Pärnänen, b. 1880).

27b)
When letting animals out to the forest

Metän sulho, sulkuparta,	Forest groom, silken-beard
Minä jos lasken lehmiäni,	If I let out my cows,
Sinä kytke koirijaisi,	You tie up your dogs,
Karhut rautakahlehisin,	Put the bears in iron chains,
Suvet rautasuitsiloihin!	iron bridles on the wolves!

(SKVR I$_4$:1366. Akonlahti. 1877. –Iivanaini Prokko).[144]

In some cases, the forest spirit or spirits (sometimes referred to in this context as *piru* (devil) or *karu*, see Järvinen 1996), were actually asked to take over the cowherd's job and keep the cattle together while grazing in the forest. In this case, 'payment' for this service was usually one or three eggs, or a cow from the herd itself.[145] According to informants from Ladoga and Archangel Karelia,

28a)
Bears attack the cattle three times each summer, but when the forest spirit is the cowherd, the bears don't touch them – the bear is the forest spirit's cow…the forest spirit (*piru*) was paid to be the cowherd. If one of the cows disappeared, the forest spirit came to talk – he had to give the animal back.
(Salmi. 1934. M. Haavio 1656–1657. –Natalia Rantsi, 49 years)

28b)
Cowherds herded with the aid of the forest spirit (*piru*). In our village there was a cowherd who had never even gone into the forest. For a chicken's egg the forest spirit (*karu*) herded for the summer, that's not a large payment. The cowherds addressed the forest spirit and gave him the egg, whoever knew how to say the right spell, knew how to make him come and talk. Or it was promised that some cow would be lost, each person promised something. The color of the cow was also mentioned: black, white, or whatever color. Even the farm mistress [=the cows' owner] does not know of it.
(Salmi. 1934–36. Martta Pelkonen 656. –Ina Plaketti).

28c)
When one forbids the forest to eat the cattle, so that one does not need a cowherd, then the cows have drivers to drive them home, so there is no need to herd them. But the cowherd demands his payment, each year he takes one cow. There were three hundred cows that the old man herded, he herded them for 45 years without ever having to be in the forest. One had only to go to the end of the lane and throw the herding equipment, to go in the morning with the cattle and in the evening to go again, to blow the horn three times to the forest and go home without looking back.

The forest's men then drive the cattle home. The old man had three cattle drivers: one behind the cattle and one on each side. The last evening that the cattle were in the forest, one was supposed to go oneself to the forest and bring out the cattle and remove the herding equipment.

But every year one lost a cow or calf or some other animal...

The old man's son, during the last week when the herding was almost finished, was waiting at the end of the lane to receive the cattle, and looked at the cattle when they came and saw the drivers. Then the drivers said: "but here there are cowherds, we are not needed", and disappeared. The next evening when the boy went again and blew three times on his horn, the cattle did not come. The boy went into the forest, but the cattle fled like wild elk when they saw the boy, nor did the boy get them home, instead the old man had to go look for them. The old man said: "Why did you look?"

(Venehjärvi. 1917. Paulaharju 7400. –Ontippa Suolanen)

While the bears and wolves belonging to the forest spirit posed the greatest natural threat to the cattle grazing in the forest glades, the greatest *supernatural* danger encountered by livestock in the forest was the 'forest cover' (*metsänpeitto*), a term which refers to the belief that the forest or forest-spirit had the ability to trap cows, horses and children so that they could not find their way out of the forest and others could not see them (see Holmberg (later Harva) 1923). Ritual specialists or *tietäjäs*, who were usually male in this case, employed various methods to force the forest spirit to release the animal from the 'forest cover'. The most popular methods were (1) 'binding' the forest (tying the tops of two or more saplings together over a path (*sitominen*, see example 30a below)), (2) 'trussing up' the forest, (tying a stone so that it hung down from the bound tops of the aforementioned saplings, weighing them down (*tyrä tekeminen*, see ibid:30–44, examples 29b and 30d below)), and (3) 'mixing' or 'closing' the forest spirit's paths and roads (i.e. forest trails used by the forest spirit) by placing crosses on such paths (see 29a, 42 below).[146] According to collector K. Karjalainen, it was believed that as a result of these measures "the *piessa* [=forest spirit] is now under duress and will release the animal from its clutches."[147] Likewise an informant from Archangel Karelia asserted that the forest would surely release the trapped animal because "it's difficult for the forest spirit, too, to be a prisoner".[148]

29a)
When the forest spirit (*metšiine*) takes a cow, one must go to the far end of a field, stand on the fence and shout: "Hey, release my cow or I will tie up your roads and paths so that you no longer have any paths".
(Soutjärvi. 1943. Sylvi Sääski 3256. –Maria Karkkine, b. 1878).

29b)
Releasing a cow from the 'forest cover'
One takes the collar of the lost cow and goes into the forest, and, using three easily-seen lengths of string, binds the tops of three spruce saplings and hangs the [lost cow's] collar from them. During the binding, one person asks the other:

'What are you doing?'
The second one says:
'I am trussing up the forest spirit's son.'
The first person walks a short distance, comes back and asks again:
'What are you doing?'
The one doing the binding says:
'I am trussing up the forest spirit's son, since he won't return my cow.'
The same is done a third time and then the saplings are left tied together. If the cow is not found on the first day, then one goes to tighten the arch. On the second day it is tightened in the same way. But if it has not been found on the third day, then the saplings must be released. Then it is not the forest spirit's fault.
(SKVR I$_4$:1474. Kiisjoki. 1888. –Mikittä Kontulaine, heard in Finland, on the Kuusamo side).

As can be seen from the above example, the forest was not 'bound' indefinitely. Numerous informants alluded to an unspoken 'agreement' between humans and the forest when they warned that the forest spirit should be bound for only three days and nights, after which time the 'binding' or 'lynching' apparatus was to be dismantled even if the cow or horse had not been found, since if the forest did not respond within three days, then it was not responsible for the animal's disappearance. [149] Informants claimed that if bound for longer than three days, "the place spirit would become angry", [150] "the forest would begin to disturb the one who bound it", [151] or that the forest would "deal with the binder", in other words he or she would go insane: [152]

30a)
When a cow or some other living thing is 'covered' by the forest, then one must rope two trees together with a red string over a cattle track and say three times:

Jos et sie miun ommoin piästä,   If you do not release my own,
niin en mie siun ommoin piästä.   Then I will not release your own.

When one does this, then the cow will surely come home soon or be found. One must not keep the forest in its bonds for longer than three days, otherwise the place spirit becomes angry.
(SKVR VII$_5$:3966. Ruskeala. 1894).

30b)
...And when the cow is found, one must immediately dismantle the truss and pour silver into an anthill and read the words of offering. And if it is not found within three days, then it is not the fault of the forest's folk. Then one must release the apparatus, otherwise the forest begins to disturb the 'binder'.
(SKVR I$_4$:1473. Uhut. 1889. Mihhei Niikkaanoff; heard on his travels).

30c)
If one keeps the forest bound for longer than one should, or if the animal is not, after all, in the 'forest cover', then the "forest will deal with the binder": he or she goes insane. Nobody has ever kept [the forest] bound for more than three days, in order that there would be no consequences. It is the forest spirit who keeps things 'covered': nobody else there.
(Salmi. 1934. Martti Haavio 1070. – the elderly wife of Jehor Lammas).

*Livestock were released from the forest-cover (*metsänpeitto*) by holding the forest "prisoner". Taivalkoski, northern Finland, 1917. Photo: Samuli Paulaharju 1917. National Board of Antiquities.*

30d)
When the cattle have been trapped in the forest cover, one finds three trees with a stone in their midst. The tree-tops are tied together with a red string and the following is said:
You tied up what belonged to me,
I tie up what belongs to you.
One should not keep the trees tied longer than three days. If the cow has not come within three days, then the forest master is not responsible.
(Salmi. 1932–38. Maija Juvas 290. –Lutjonen's wife, 60 years).

The most common means of 'binding' or 'trussing up' the forest was with red thread. Anna-Leena Siikala has pointed out that red cloth was commonly used in clothing worn by *tietäjäs* and Eurasian shamans in order to win the favor of the spirits (Siikala 1992: 240). The use of this distinctive color was an important communicative device to signal to the forest that this binding was a special, intentional and ritualistic act.

"Binding" rituals were used to force the forest, water or earth spirit to do other things as well, such as forgive the human supplicant and remove a *nenä* illness, or reveal in a dream whence the *nenä* infection had come and how it was to be cured. We can thus view 'binding' as not only a means of coercing the forest spirit to release trapped animals or humans, but in a wider sense as a means of forcing a desired response from the forest spirit:[153]

31a)

If some illness has infected from the water, and no one has sent it [through sorcery], then in that case the divination-water does not give signs concerning the illness, rather, the water spirit must be trussed up, this is done in such a way that one takes two rowan roots, which are put upright into the current, into the water, and their tops are bound together and a burnt stone from the sauna stove is taken and is rubbed nine times with a wool string and this string is used to suspend the stone freely from the tree tops and it is allowed to be there three nights and then [the water spirit] will surely say in a dream what it is, how one will recover and whence it has infected.

(Archangel Karelia (Pirttilahti). 1889. H. Meriläinen II 872. –Nikolai Kallio, 61 years).

31b)

Binding the water, forest and cemetery

If the direction whence the infection has come is not revealed either in dreams nor by divination, then go to river rapids which run northward and bind the forest at three places along the river and then go to an anthill and once again bind the forest master's testicles, two rowan trees opposite each other and say the following spell:

jos et metsän	If you do not,
kultanen kuningas,	forest's golden king,
metsän valtikka väkövä,	Forest's mighty ruler,
vaan tänä yönä näytä vikoasi,	reveal this night your harm,
niin panen 3 kuuksi kiini	then I will bind three spruces
a jos vaan näytät vikasi	and if you reveal your harm
tänä yönä,	this night, then in the morning
niin aamulla lasken.	I will release you.

Then you go to the cemetery (*kalma*) and bind the cemetery (*kalma*), and say the same spell. Then you go to sleep and dream what it is, and go and give it greetings (this is considered very important).

(SKVR II:773. Lupasalmi. 1884. –Jehkimä Putune, 65 years, heard from Jeylo Bohodannof, parentheses in original).

Rituals to release livestock and children trapped in the forest cover, like *proškenja* rituals, express a series of assumptions concerning the rights and obligations of humans and forest spirits. Although the disappearance of a cow or horse in the forest cover was usually perceived to be an 'unjust' act on the part of the forest spirit, it could also be the result of humans accidentally binding the forest, cursing or using profanity when letting the cows out to pasture, or failing to perform the proper ritual when letting the cows out for the first time in spring:

32a)

When you let the cows out and curse, the forest covers the cow. When letting the cows out one must not curse.

(Tulomajärvi. 1943. Helmi Helminen 2355. –Marfa Jogorov, 70 years).

32b)

The forest starts to 'cover' if, when binding a fence one happens to bind two live trees. When one cuts the twigs which bind them and releases the

forest, then the forest, too, immediately ceases to 'cover'. Gauroi [= name of a certain *tietäjä*] was of the opinion that the forest in fact never 'covers' in other circumstances, only when it is tied to some fence.
(Tulomajärvi. 1943. Helmi Helminen 2352. –Gauroi Agejev, 81 years).

32c)
Iroi Kiekkinen told how her farm's cattle had been near home in the forest. They could not be found, no matter how people searched for them. "[The cows] were there for five nights, and nearly dead; they had gone round and round a single tree, their curdled milk in the black dirt." Her godmother said that they had been in the forest cover. The reason was that "my brother had been drunk and did not allow us to walk around the cattle when they were let out to pasture in the spring".
(Uhtua. 1929. Lyyli Kokkonen. KKTK-KKA).

Usually, however, by trapping the farm animal, the forest was seen to have taken something it had no right to, and consequently humans were allowed to harass and pressure the forest through 'binding', 'lynching' and 'closing' it. This was believed to force the forest to release the trapped animal. On the other hand, since the disappearance might have been caused by a malicious person versed in magic, the one who bound the forest was not 'allowed', according to this series of assumptions, to keep the forest bound or closed indefinitely, but was obligated to release it within three days, whether the animal had returned or not. If the human did not honor this obligation, the forest had the right to infect the person who bound the forest with *nenä* illness or cause insanity.

Offerings to saints in the village chapel

The threat of the forest wilderness was also dealt with collectively in two different types of rites oriented toward local saints, either the patron saint of the village, or other saints represented in the holy icons displayed in the village chapel (*tsasouna*). The first of these rites were sacrificial festivals (*uhrijuhlat*) in which a ram or bull was sacrificed as part of a village's *praasniekka* celebration and the meat eaten together by all members of community (or in some cases only *male* members of the community), as well as guests and outsiders who happened to be present. Some of these festivals may have their historical origins in the Byzantine era (Sarmela 1981:234), and by the 19th century sacrificial festivals were held on saints' days throughout Orthodox Karelia (Haavio 1949:159–160). The best-known festivals were held on the islands of Mantsinsaari and Lunkulansaari in the parish of Salmi in Ladoga Karelia, and in Venehjärvi village in Archangel Karelia. The festival on Mantsinsaari Island in which a bull was sacrificed in honor of St. Elijah took place on the Sunday on or after August 1. The festival on Lunkulansaari Island in which a ram was sacrificed took place on the Sunday on or after July 11. This festival was not dedicated to any particular saint, meaning that the official Church had not managed to

Sacrificial feast in Venehjärvi, 1894. Photo: I.K. Inha. Finnish Literature Society.

appropriate it for an officially-recognized devotional purpose (see Ailio 1897; Jääskeläinen 1912; Haavio 1949). In Venehjärvi, a ram was sacrificed each year on the day of Dormition (*bogoroditsa* or *emänpäivä,* August 15) in honor of St. Nicholas (*Miikkula,* Inha 1910 :359–362).

These sacrificial festivals represented a multilayered ritual event open to numerous interpretations and performed for a variety of purposes, but it is clear that at least one purpose was to draw a boundary between the human community and the threatening wilderness. This is suggested by legends telling of the original events which served as the catalyst for the first celebration of the festival, namely, attacks by forest predators on farm animals (and in one case, an attack by a strange, bloodsucking creature from the forest).[154] Informants further explained that the ritual sacrifice was continued each year so that the forest predators would not attack the cows and sheep during the coming year,[155] and that when, one year, the ritual had not been performed on Mantsisaari Island, dire consequences had followed as a result: a wolf had come to the island where the sheep were grazing and had wreaked much havoc.[156] Based on these legends and folk beliefs, Riitta Tilvis (1989:77,87) has argued that these ritual sacrifices represented *crisis rituals* rather than calendrical rituals.

Other types of offerings were given to local saints as well, usually on the saints' own particular day of celebration, but also at other times, in response to illness (especially sudden pain), or in return for supernatural protection already given. The offerings, which included livestock, butter, wool, agricultural produce, tapers and money, were brought to the village chapel

*St. Elijah's (*Ilja's*) festival day, Salmi, 1939. Photo: Eino Toiviainen. Finnish Literature Society.*

and were either distributed to the poor or donated to the chapel itself. If the offering was the fulfillment of a sacred promise or vow already given to the saint, this act of giving was known as *jeäksintä*, the same term used to refer to holy vows to undertake pilgrimage journeys (see pages 68–69, 160–164). Although offerings to village chapels were motivated by a wide range of causes, an important one was the danger posed to cattle by forest predators. In this case, the offerings were usually directed at St. George, the saint seen to be responsible for restraining or "keeping in chains" the bears and wolves of the forest (see pages 128–131). As one collector noted regarding the practice of *jeäksintä* in Ladoga Karelia, "the informant's mother had promised a heifer to St. George when the cattle were let out to pasture in spring so that St. George would protect the cattle".[157]

Summer: a time of temporary truce with the forest

Because forests were seen to contain resources and 'growth' values (see Anttonen 1996:77–78,95) utilized by both the human realm and wilderness realm, the overlapping areas shared by humans and the wilderness had to be divided up *temporally*, that is, "temporally segregated" (cf. Zerubavel 1981:103) in a sort of time-sharing arrangement. Rules regarding the use of forested pasture land, for instance, were seasonal in nature, only in effect during a specified period during the summer, and had to be renegotiated each year by human and wilderness representatives.

According to the seasonal arrangement by which forests and fields were shared by humans and the wilderness, humans and their cattle had the right to exploit resources in the forest environment during late spring, summer, and early autumn, a period seen to extend from St. George's Day in the spring (*Kevät-Jyrki*, April 23) to the Day of Intercession (*Pokrova*, October 1) or St. George's Day in the autumn (*Syys-Jyrki*, September 30, days differ according to locality). The forest and forest 'cattle' (=bears and wolves), on the other hand, had the right to use this area in the late autumn, winter and early spring. This meant that after *Pokrova*, a number of human subsistence activities pertaining to pastures and fields were forbidden, including cattle-grazing and plowing:

33)
Only after Pokrova was one allowed to begin the autumn slaughter. On Pokrova the cattle were put in the cowshed. Cowherds worked until Pokrova. Between Pokrova and Autumn-George one could still keep the cows in the pasture during the day, but not after Autumn-George, not even during the day. One could not specify one exact day because the procedure had to be carried out in an auspicious wind.
(Porajärvi. 1943. H. Helminen 1415).

Seasonal taboos regulated an entire array of activities related to the use of natural resources: for instance, the forest nature itself was seen to be poisonous, full of dangerous *väki*, during the winter months until Whitsuntide (*Stroitsa* or *Troitsa*, 50 days after Easter), so that in Olonets and Ladoga Karelia there existed a taboo on picking flowers and cutting twigs too early in spring:[158] "In the spring, one is not allowed to pick flowers before Whitsuntide. If one picks them earlier, one's hand starts to hurt";[159] "When the flowers bloom in spring, one is not allowed to pick them before Whitsuntide. Whoever did, his/her hand began to hurt."[160] One informant from Ladoga Karelia reported the following belief regarding the cutting of birch branches for use as bath whisks:

34)
The birch was baptized on Whitsuntide (*Stroitsa*)
Already in my childhood, mother warned us not to touch the birch in spring. Not a single twig was allowed to be broken off, because the birch was unbaptized. Sometimes, when there came an early summer, the birch was already in leaf by Ascension Day [=40 days after Easter] and Whitsuntide [=50 days after Easter]. But it was not allowed to make a birch whisk. On Whitsuntide the birch was baptized. After that one was allowed to make whisks from it. In former times it was the custom that birch branches were brought into the house on Whitsuntide. I recall how my godmother came to visit us on Whitsuntide, she went to the birch and brought some of it inside. She said that this was the way it was done in the old days. My godmother was very old. She explained that the birch should always be brought into the house on Whitsuntide to commemorate the fact that this day is the day of the birch's baptism.
(Suistamo. 1959. Siiri Oulasmaa E 246:301. – Paraskeeva Makkonen).

The notion of the birch tree having to be baptized before it could be used to make sauna whisks may be an indirect reference to its impure or polluting status prior to Whitsuntide, since in Orthodox Karelian folk tradition newborn infants could be considered unclean and polluting before they were baptized.[161] Further north in Archangel Karelia, the first day on which it was allowed to cut branches or otherwise 'disturb' the forest was later, on Midsummer's Day. On this day, 'Leaf-John's Day', the forest was not to be disturbed, and only after this day did people cut branches for sauna whisks. Before this, a 'sin' (*reähkä*) would come of disturbing the forest (Virtaranta 1978:103).

Work in the fields was also allowed in the summer period but not in the late autumn, as informants from Archangel Karelia pointed out:[162]

35a)
After Pokrova one is not supposed to disturb the ground any more, or to plow the field. One should leave the ground alone, let the earth and forest rest in peace. If one disturbs the ground after [Pokrova], then nothing more will grow there.
(Vuonninen. 1915. Paulaharju 18313).

35b)
One is not allowed to plow the fields after Pokrova. If one does, then northern dock (*Rumex longifolius*) begins to grow on them. A 'sin' comes of it.
(Vuokkiniemi (Kivijärvi).1911. I. Marttini 1289)

In the context of cattle husbandry, the basic assumption of this seasonal arrangement was that the forest spirit, after having received an appropriate gift, would be responsible for the well-being of the cattle in the forest pastures throughout the summer,[163] but that this responsibility ended in the autumn:

36a)
Old folk belief about the forest spirit
In the old days it was believed that the summertime between St. George's Day in spring and St. Nicholas' Day in autumn was the only time that a farm animal could be kept out to pasture, and in the spring the forest spirit, placated with an offering, would protect the farm animals from its own cattle (forest predators) during this period. At other times of the year, that is, during the winter, the forest spirit let its own cattle, the forest predators, move about freely in the forest, and was not responsible during this period for the evil deeds committed by these beasts against farm animals.
(Sortavala. 1938. Juho Hyvärinen 1943. –Hilma Tiainen, b. 1879. Heard from her parents. Parentheses in original).

36b)
On Pokrova the *jumala* [=God, saint, divine being] orders the person him/herself to watch over the cattle: "I watched in the summer, you watch in the winter".
(Vieljärvi. 1943. Maila Saarto 656).

During the summer period, the forest spirit was supposed to muzzle or chain up forest predators or send them far from areas of human habitation and cattle grazing (see also Tarkka 1998:119–120); this can be seen from ritual incantations directed at the forest spirit when cows were let out to graze for the first time in the spring:

37a)

Metsän herra,	Lord of the forest,
Maan kuningas!	King of the earth!
Kun katsoit kartanossa,	As you watched in the manor-house,
Niin hoi'a katajikossa!	So tend in the juniper thicket!
Anna nyt rauha raavahille,	Now give peace to the bovines,
Pane suet suitset suuhun,	Put bridles on the wolves' mouths,
Karhut rautakahlehisin...	Put the bears in iron chains...

(SKVR VII₅:3790. Sortavala. 1886).[164]

37b)

...Sinä metsän	...You, forest's
kultainen kuningas,	golden king,
metsän emoinen emäntä,	forest's matronly mother,
elä käy karjahani,	don't attack my cattle,
elä koske karjahani,	don't touch my cattle,
mene mailla selkosilla,	go to the backwoods lands,
lauko lehoilla elukattomilla.	run to glades free of cattle
Kuin kuulet kellon äänen,	When you hear the sound of the cow-bell,
paina turpas turpehen...	thrust your muzzle into the sod...

(Pentikäinen 1971:255. –Marina Takalo, b. 1890).

Taboos against uttering the 'true' name of the bear also followed a seasonal pattern. Since to use the bear's real name, *karhu* or *kontio*,[165] was to summon it, during the summer when it was most dangerous to human subsistence activities the bear had to be referred to with euphemisms such as forest creature (*metšelävy*), honey-paw (*mezikäbäl*, *mezikämmen*), grandfather (*djiedoi*), or birchbark-shod foot (*virzujalgu*,[166] see also Virtaranta 1978:97; Tarkka 1998:120–121):

38a)
It was said that the forest spirit (*metšänhaldii*) was the bear. One did not call it by name, particularly in the summer. It was angry at the cows that summer, if one did so.
(Korpiselkä. 1933. Martti Haavio 557. –Ahponen's widow, approx. 80 years).

38b)
One is not allowed to mention the name *kontio* after the cattle have been let out to the forest pastures and the crops have been sown. One should say *mettšelävy* (= "forest's creature") or *mezikäbäl* (= "honey-paw"). If one speaks of *kontio*, the bear will eat the cows and destroy the crops in the field...In the autumn after *Pokrova* one was once again allowed to speak of *kontio*.
(Tulomajärvi. 1944. Helmi Helminen 4129).

38c)
After St. George's Day the bear was referred to in speech only as *virzujalgu* (= "birchbark-shod foot"), *djiedoi* (= "grandfather"), *metšän djiedoi* (= "forest's grandfather"), *djiedušku* (= "little grandfather"), or *mezikämmen* (= "honey-paw"). After *Pokrova* it was again fitting to call the bear *kontio*.
(Tulomajärvi. 1943. Helmi Helminen 3267).

The establishment of temporal boundaries between the human realm and the natural realm ensured the joint exploitation, by turns, of the forest resources. I have already mentioned the association of the positive or 'right-hand' image of the sacred with growth and augmentation of things socially important, and the negative, or left-hand image of the sacred with degeneration and exhaustion of growth potential (see Anttonen 1996:77–78, 95; 2000:279). The wilderness exemplified a dualism in this sense, since on the one hand it could be exploited to promote human growth and prosperity, yet on the other hand it threatened to limit growth and human life. During the winter, the *non-growth* aspect (depletion, death) of the wilderness was in ascendance, and during this time, the wilderness and its predators were seen to be in control of the resource-rich zone on the boundary between human community and deep wilderness. This may be why, for example, the earth, trees and flowers were seen to contain a harmful, *väki*-like force if touched too early in the spring. The 'handover' of the resource zone from the wilderness to the human community took place at the start of summer on St. George's Day, and this liminal day was marked with numerous taboos and ritual procedures which had to be carried out in a precise manner so as to not endanger the transfer (e.g. Mansikka 1943:175). For instance, on that day it was not allowed to move about in the forest, break twigs off trees, or overturn stones.[167] According to one informant, it was forbidden to eat meat on St. George's Day, otherwise "the forest would rise up with greater fury in the summer."[168]

The wilderness was a primary site of economic exploitation over which, however, it was impossible for individual peasant farmers to gain the upper hand using traditional tools and methods. Thus *the inevitable presence of the wilderness itself* represented an ongoing crisis, one which motivated the rituals discussed so far in this book. The forest wilderness could not be conquered, tamed or avoided, which meant that the implicit contradictions in the human-wilderness relationship could not be 'solved' but instead had to be *endlessly deferred* through ritual. According to Catherine Bell (1992) in her book *Ritual Theory, Ritual Practice*, rituals do not *solve* problems or contradictions but imply "a resolution without ever defining one" (p.106) by stating the problem or contradiction in new terms and thus deferring or postponing the perceived crisis:

> Moreover, this orchestrated deferral of signification never yields a definitive answer, a final meaning, or a single act—there is no point of arrival but a constant invocation of new terms to continue the validation and coherence of the older terms (ibid).

In the cattle rituals discussed here, the implied resolution was to 'make peace'[169] with the wilderness, to arrive at a kind of truce. But the formulas themselves make it clear that the rituals performed in spring were only a temporary or deferred solution of the sort discussed by Bell – the truce would collapse when the winter came and humans no longer needed to negotiate over the use of the forest pastures and fields. In Archangel Karelia, this idea receives its most dramatic expression in ritual formulas spoken

123

when letting the cows out for the first time in spring. [170] Performers spoke of waging war with the forest in the winter, but at the start of the summer addressed it with phrases such as "let us swear our brotherhood (*vannokas myö veljeksyttä*)", "let us make a summer pact (*tekkämäi kesä sovinnot*)" or "let us strike a border peace! (*rajarauhat rapsakkame!*)":[171]

39a)

Ohtoni, metsän omena,	My Ohto, forest apple,
Metsän kuulusa kuningas,	Renowned forest king,
Nyt tiemmä sulosovinnon,	Now we make sweet reconciliation
Kesärauhan rapsoamma.	build a summer peace.
Jos talvet sotoa käymmä,	If winters we wage war,
Lumen aijan luskehimma,	tussle in the time of snow,
Talven aijan tappelemma.	fight in the time of winter.

(SKVR I$_4$:1380. Niskajärvi. 1894. –Hovatta Teronpoika, brother of Varahvontta Lesonen).

39b)

Metsän tytti, mieli neiti,	Girl of the forest, desirable maiden,
Tyynikki, Tapion tyttö,	Tyynikki, Tapio's daughter,
Salakorven vaimo kaunis,	Beautiful wife of the secret wood,
Talven myö sotia käymme,	All through winter we wage war,
Lumen aiat luskajamme,	tussle in the time of snow,
Laaimme kesäisen rauhan.	We make a summer peace.
Teemmekö sulosovinnon,	Will we make sweet reconciliation?
Kesän tullen, suon sulaten,	As summer comes, as the swamp thaws,
Lätäköisen lämmitessä?	As the puddle warms?

(SKVR I$_4$:1440. Vuonninen. 1894).

Christianized nature spirits and forest saints in boundary maintenance

An important aspect of the fuzzy taxonomies of Orthodox Karelian folk religion is that the wilderness was addressed and treated as 'Christian', while holy men and women honored by the official church were sometimes treated as 'wilderness' figures. Although the intermingling of these two semantic fields appears at first glance to be the result of folk confusion and ignorance, I suggest that they were instead strategies by which ritual performers simultaneously 1) privileged the distinction between the human community and the wilderness, and 2) ensured an agreement on common principles from which to conduct two-way mutual ritual communication and thus negotiations across this boundary.

Syncretization in folk religion is not a unidirectional process of assimilation and fusion but is the outcome of a dynamic combination of processes moving in several directions at once. Nor are these processes necessarily random: they can be strategic adaptations to particular needs and conditions of the ritual context. An example of this from Orthodox Karelia is the way in which the dichotomy Christian versus non-Christian could serve to gloss the oppositions *good versus evil* or *pure versus impure*. On the other hand, the designation 'Christian' might be used instead to denote the status of a supernatural or divine being as "somebody like us". Where the wilderness was located with respect to Christianity depended on the ritual context. On the one hand, there existed a tendency to express the impurity of the forest through the demonization of nature spirits: by this I mean the use of Christian demonological images and/or terms to draw distinctions between things which were Christian and therefore protected by the symbols of Christianity (including prayer, rituals of blessing or baptism, wearing a cross, etc.) and those which were not. Such a process of demonization can be seen in the use of the term 'devil' (*piru*) for the forest spirit. It can also be seen in folk beliefs in which persons unprotected by the symbols of Christianity were precisely those who were at risk of being either infected by *nenä* from the forest, water or earth, or of being trapped by the 'forest cover'. In the story below, a girl trapped in the forest cover was freed when a priest blessed the forest:[172]

40a)

Forest-cover

My mother-in-law from Hautavaara farm [told the following]: her stepmother cursed her as a child, the forest "covered" her. People shouted, did not find her, and left. My mother-in-law vanished, the *karu* took her to the forest-cover. One carried her on his back, a second walked alongside , a third walked behind them. Bread was given [to the girl]. The third man, an old man, warned the girl: "Look, my girl, don't eat it!" On Monday she was taken, a week later on Tuesday a priest blessed the forest. Then the forest released the girl near Potkuselkä farm. The girl went up to the house. "Whose girl are you?" "From Hauduvoara [Hautavaara] farm". "Aren't you Dan's daughter Anni?" "I didn't know who accompanied me: one carried me on his back, a second walked alongside, the third walked behind."
    She was trapped by the *karu*. A *jumal* [=saint, god] forbade her to eat. "I didn't eat, and was released."
(Suojärvi. 1933. Martti Haavio 552. –Marppa Tšutsune, 68 years).

40b)

A child wearing a cross around its neck cannot be trapped by the forest cover. The forest "will not take a person wearing a cross."
(Salmi. 1935. Maija Juvas 288).

40c)

Forest-*nenä* infects if you leave without wearing a cross around your neck, or if you don't say the prayer "Bless me Lord".
(Riipuškala. 1942. Lauri Laiho 6401. –Anastasia Ignatjev, 62 years).

40d)

If a child falls ill at home before baptism or on the way to the baptism, then it can be infected by any sort of "extra" [=*väki* force] from the water, earth, or forest...
(Suojärvi. 1931. Nasti Lesonen (Lesojeff) b) 257. –Outotja V. Murto).

40e)

An unbaptized child must not be left in the room [in which one is performing magic to drive out vermin and pests]. The forest spirit will torment it, all unbaptized beings belong to his numbers. The snake is one of the forest spirit's servants and belongs to its cattle.

(SKVR I$_4$:1964. Tiirov. 1888. –Teppana Karjalaine, heard from H. Kylmänen in Muhos).

In folk beliefs, therefore, the wilderness could be conceived of as a 'non-Christian' or 'anti-Christian' entity. And yet the issue of whether the wilderness was 'Christian' or not could be strategically manipulated to suit the purpose at hand: in ritual *communication* with the wilderness, in which it was crucial to establish common ground rules and ethics, we see first of all a tendency for the wilderness to be treated as Christian. Second, in a reverse strategy, Christian-derived sacred agents such as St. George, Jesus or the Virgin Mary were reinterpreted as 'wilderness figures', as occupying roles which also belonged to forest and water spirits. I argue here that this blurring of categories was no mere accident of folk misinterpretation but rather, that its logic can be found in the primacy of the human/wilderness boundary within folk religious ritual.

In the first type of syncretic tendency discussed here, human social organization and value systems served as a model for the denizens of the 'other world'. The process by which nature spirits were 'Christianized' is suggested first of all in incantation references to nature spirits using the Christian epithets usually reserved for prayers to the saints or holy hermits: for instance, "Pure forest, provider (*Puhas metšä kormulitša syöttäi*)",[173] and "Water, righteous one (*Vesi pruavetnoine*)".[174] In Olonets, moreover, even the bear, the most important representative of the forest wilderness, was described in two incantation examples as having been baptised at some point in the mythical past:

41)

Miss' on Ohto ristittünä,	Where was Ohto[175] baptized,
Karva-jalga kastettuna?	The furred-foot immersed?
Tuossa Jordanan jovessa,	There, in the river of Jordan,
Pühän virran püördiessä,	in the eddies of the holy current
Mie kummina olova.	And I was the godparent.

(SKVR II: 983. Lupasalmi. 1871).[176]

In addition, ritual incantations referred to the denizens of the "other side" using Christian-derived titles. *Proškenja* incantations might begin with *"Water master, water mistress, water's golden king..."* and continue by listing a number of other occupational and social categories modelled on human social life. What is interesting is that these incantations also addressed nature spirits as "servants of the church", "bishops", "priests", "assistant priests", "deacons", "vergers", "sextons", "godparents", "the baptized and the unbaptized"[177], and two informants even addressed the entire community of water spirits as "spiritually upright Christian folk (*oigie hengis kristikansoa*)"[178] and "people of the true [i.e. Orthodox] faith (*pravoslaudoid*

126

rahvahad). [179] In a ritual to free livestock from the 'forest cover' described below, the forest spirits were also referred to as "good men of the true [i. e. Orthodox] faith (*hyväd miehed pravoslavnad*)":

42)
The informant knows how to release an animal from the forest cover...As the sun is rising, one must go into the forest to some road. There the informant stands with his hands behind his back and shouts loudly three times in the same direction, toward the forest, bowing...

Hyväd miehed pravoslavnad,	Good men of the true faith,
tsarid i staritsad,	Czars and czarinas,
polkovnikad i polpolkovnikad,	colonels and lieutenant-colonels,
papid i papadjad,	priests and priests' wives,
olettek ottud mustan živataizen.	have you taken a black cow.
No ka pästkad,	well, release it back
kuspäi otit,	to whence you took it,
sihe i togad tagaze,	bring it back to that place,
mina teil souptan	[or] I will close
kaik putid i dorogad...	all of your roads and paths...

(Soutjärvi. 1943. Sylvi Sääski 3257. –Matrona Belusov, b. 1879).

Nature spirits were also urged to forgive the supplicant on the basis of a shared (Christian) moral universe. The ritual performer would do this, for instance, by reminding the nature spirit that "there is no such thing as an unforgivable sin"[180], or by threatening to take the matter up at the "At the final hearing held by the *son of Mary*", where the nature spirit would have to answer for its lack of mercy on the "last Judgement Day".[181]

Karelians referred to themselves and other community members as *ristikanza* (Christians, lit. 'people of the cross'), and this term seems to have been in most cases considered equivalent to 'human being'. Sacred agents were thus modeled after Orthodox Karelian society and its total identification with the *idea* of being Christian. On the level of basic religious notions used in real-time problem solving (see Barrett 1999), the act of Christianizing supernatural agents may have simply been a way of making them more intuitively anthropomorphic, more human-like. Orthodox Karelian folk world view brought the communities of the forest, water, etc. closer to the world of the human (Christian) community by giving them Christian characteristics. Attributing elements of 'Christianity' to the 'other side' was a way of assuring a common ground for negotiations: both communities were thus conceptualized as being familiar with the norms and concepts of justice, sin, forgiveness and mercy emphasized in Christian teachings. The spirits of forest, water, and wind were urged to acknowledge and follow Christian norms and rules of behavior, and humans used Christian concepts to convince nature spirits to maintain harmony and play fair.

On the other hand, Christianizing the wilderness did not alter the main structure of categories in Karelian ritual thought nor affect the "otherworldly" status of the nature spirits. This is because, in the cultural thought underlying the rituals, the most salient distinction still lay between this world and the

127

other side (forest wilderness). In the ritual communication carried out within the *sacred boundaries* complex, Christianity was not a *category* used to classify or organize the relations between this world and the other side, but was rather an *attribute* to forge strategic and situation-specific equivalences between two spheres plotted as opposites. In other words, the 'boundary' in the sacred boundaries complex did not lie between the realms of Christian versus non-Christian (=pagan/evil), but between the human world and the 'other side' (wilderness, abode of the dead). In this context, Christianity could be an attribute of *all* sentient beings capable of agency, communication, and moral conscience, whether supernatural or human. In the rituals taking place within the *sacred boundaries* complex, there were no participants who were expressly 'un-Christian' or evil supernatural beings, and no category which would oppose and therefore define 'Christian' as closer to purity, more central. That distinction, as we shall see, was emphasized within the *sacred centres* complex, which served the function of dividing the world into more and less purely Christian spheres and persons.

At the same time that the wilderness spirits in these rituals showed a tendency toward being 'Christianized', Christian figures in the incantations were recast in the roles of nature spirits. This can be seen in cases in which saints and forest spirits were asked to perform similar sorts of functions. For example, both Christian figures and forest spirits were asked, through ritual formulas, to protect and herd the cattle during the summer.[182] In Orthodox Karelian folk culture, a distinction was made between nature and culture, but *not* between Christian and non-Christian, when the ritual performer asked an entire range of sacred agents, including the bear, the 'forest mistress', the 'lord of the forest', St. Blaise, Ss. Laurus and Florus, St. George, the Virgin Mary and Jesus to watch over the cattle in both the human and forest realms: in the cattle shed (referred to euphemistically as the manor house, chamber, the 'roofed' place) in winter, and the forest pastures (juniper thicket, heath, pinewoods, 'roofless' place) in the summer:[183]

> 43a)
> When I was a girl I was a serving maid, and in the spring when the cows were let out to the forest for the first time, the people said the following incantation:
>
> | | |
> |---|---|
> | Metsänherra maankuningas | Forest-lord, earth-king |
> | kun sä kaitset kartanossa | as you tended them in the manor house |
> | kaitse katajikossa. | so tend them in the juniper thicket. |
> | Anna rauha raavahille, | Give peace to the bovines, |
> | pane sudet suitsipäähän | put a muzzle on the wolves |
> | karhut rauta kahlehisin! | the bears in iron chains! |
>
> (Ilomantsi. 1939. Einar Peimi KT 241:108. –Hilda Hämäläinen, farm mistress, b. 1889).

43b)

Pyhä Ulassie, kormelitsa!	St. Blaise, provider!
Katso kaikista pahoista,	Watch out for all evils,
Varjele vahinkoloista.	Preserve from harm.
Likasuoh sortumasta,	From landslides into filthy swamps,
Lätäkköih läpehtymästä!	From drowning in ponds!
Kun nähnet tuhon tulovan,	When you see destruction coming,
Hätäpäivän peälle soavan,	Distress beginning to descend,
Niin sie siivillä sivalla,	Flap with your wings that fly,
Lentävillä leuvahuta!	Take flight with your wings!
Kuin katsoit katollisessa,	As you watched in the roofed place,
Niin kato katottomassa,	So watch in the roofless,
Varo varpahuonehessa!	Beware in the chamber of twigs!
Työnnän lehmäni leholla,	I drive my cows to the glade,
Hatasarvet hoavikolla.	My frail-horned ones to the pinewoods.

(SKVR I$_4$: 1370. Akonlahti. 1894. –Outi Juplantytär Nykäni).[184]

43c)

Mielikki, metsän emäntä,	Mielikki, mistress of the forest,
Salakorten kaunis vaimo,	Beautiful wife of the woodlands,
Sie ole syömättä lihava,	You are fat without eating,
Pesemättä puhtukainen,	Clean without washing,
Valkoni valelomatta.	White without rinsing.
Katso miun karjoani,	Watch over my cattle,
Miun sontasääriäni,	My dung-legged ones,
Kuin katšoit katollisessa,	As you watched them in the roofed place,
Niin katso katottomassa,	So watch them in the roofless,
Sivutuulet tuulomah,	Make the winds pass by them,
Sivu satamaan satiet!	Make the rains skirt 'round them.

(SKVR I$_4$:1384. Kenttijärvi. 1894. –Outi).[185]

43d)

Pyhä Jyrki, syöttäjäni,	St. George, my provider,
Tules karja katsomahan!	Come and watch over the cattle!
Kuin katsoit katoxen alla,	As you watched them under the roof,
Niin katso katajikossa,	So watch them in the juniper thicket
Kuin hoiat huonehessa,	As you tend them in the chamber,
Niin hoia hongikossa,	So tend them in the pinewoods,
Lehen puussa liehuessa,	While the leaves flutter in the trees,
Ruohon maassa roikahuess,	While the grasses wave on the ground
Kusiaisen kulkiessa,	As the ants march,
Maan matosen matkatessa.	As the earthworm travels.

(SKVR VII$_5$:3796. Suistamo. 1846).[186]

The distinctions made in these rites were not between Christian and non-Christian, since the sacred agents called upon for assistance came from the ranks of both saints and nature spirits, with no indication that one was favored over the other. Instead, the key categories were nature (the forest realm) and culture (the human realm). This can be seen from the obligatory poetic epithets for the cattle shed and forest pastures, which drew a clear distinction between the former as a cultural, man-made space and the latter as a 'natural' space.

Jesus, the forest mistress and St. George were also asked to separate the human's cattle from the forest cattle, so that the forest cattle (i.e. bears and wolves) would go to the forest realm, and the human cattle would come home: [187]

44a)

Kuvo, Iesus, kulta kangas,	Weave, Jesus, a golden cloth,
Pane, Iesus, vaskivaippa	Put, Jesus, a copper cloak
Kahen karjan maan välille,	Between the lands of two cattle herds
Jossa ohto yötä olisi,	Where the bear would be at night,
Päivät päällä puuhoasi.	Would be busy by day.

(SKVR I$_4$:1402. Vuokkiniemi. 1825).

44b)

Mehtola on metinen neiti,	Mehtola is a honeyed maiden,
Salo kaaren kaunis vaimo!	Lovely wife of the woodland arch!
Karjani kaha erota,	Divide my cattle in two,
Kotihin kotonen karja,	Home's cattle homeward,
Metsän karja Metsolahan,	Forest's cattle to the forest realm,
Illan tullen, yön pimiten!	As evening falls, as night darkens!

(SKVR I$_4$:1361. Akonlahti)

In numerous incantation examples, St. George, the Virgin Mary, the forest spirit, and the mistress of *Pohjola*, the mythical realm of the North,[188] were all asked to 'tie up' or 'chain up *their* dogs', in other words wolves and bears, so that these predators would not attack the grazing cattle:[189]

45a)

Pyhä Jyrki kormilitsa,	St. George, provider,
Linna rautanen rakenna,	Build an iron fortress,
Valli vaskinen valele	Pour a copper rampart,
Kahen puolen karjastani,	On both sides of my cattle,
Kahen puolen kartanosta!	On both sides of the manor-house!
Kytke hurttas, haukkas kiini,	Tie up your hound and falcon,
Sata seipähäsen,	To a hundred stakes,
Pane susi suitsi suihin,	Put the wolf's mouth in a bridle,
Karhut rautakahlehisin!	Put the bear in iron chains!

(SKVR II:974. Tulemajärvi. 1845).

45b)

Neitsyt Maaria emoni,	Virgin Mary, matron mine,
Rakas äiti armollini,	Beloved mother merciful,
Mie (on) lasen lehmiäni,	I have let out my cows,
Sie (on) kyte koirias(i),	You must tie up your dogs,
Rautakahlehih rakenna!	Put them in iron chains!

(SKVR I$_4$:1420. Kylänniemi. 1894. –Martta Remsujeff).

45c)

Porto Pohjolan emäntä,	Harlot mistress of Pohjola,
Kielläs pois on koiriasi,	Restrain your dogs,
Kahlehi penikkiäsi,	Chain up your pups,
Rautasihin rahkehisin,	in iron traces,

Kytkysihin kultasihin.   with golden tethers.
(SKVR I$_4$:1414. Vuonninen. 1908. –Mikko Kossini).[190]

Certain saints were identified with the forest in other ways as well. In one incantation in which the supplicant bows to and addresses an anthill,[191] St. George is referred to as "George of the forest" (*Metsän emäntä, metsän isäntä, metsän Yrjö...*).[192] Two other examples identify the forest as belonging to Christian saints, as in the incantation phrase "When we drive the cows into St. Nicholas', St. George's and St. Blaise's forest" (*pyhän Mikkulan, pyhän Jyrin ja pyhän Valassin soimeh*)[193] and in the incantation below:

46)

Pyhä Jyrgi kormilitsa,	St. George, provider,
pane hurttas kiini,	tie up your hounds,
raudaizih rahkehih,	in iron traces,
vaskizih valjahuksih,	in copper harnesses,
hobiaisih ohjaksih,	in silver reins
Pyhän Jyrrin tarhal kesäkse	In St. George's orchard for the summer,
Pyhän Illan soimel	In St. Elijah's forest
ristikansan ziivatta.	is the cow of the Christian.

(Vieljärvi. 1943. Maila Saarto 549. –Sandra Miikkonova, 80 years).

The central Christian figure associated with the wilderness in these ritual formulas was St. George (see Mansikka 1943:197). This is probably best explained first by his status as a dragon-slayer, generalized to 'master over all dangerous predators', and second by a coincidence in the Orthodox Karelian calendar of saints' days, in which the festival days of two *different* saints named George happened to fall near the beginning and end of the cattle's summer grazing season: that of Great-Martyr George the Victorious on April 23 (known as 'Spring-George'), and that of Hieromartyr George, Bishop of Armenia on September 30, (known as 'Autumn-George'). In traditional thought, these two saints named George became fused into a single St. George who was conveniently associated with the entire period during which the cows would spend their days grazing in the forest pastures, as can be seen from the following ritual description:

47)

On *Spring-George* the cows were encircled with a holy icon. Scythes and axes were put on the lintel of the cowshed. Children went round the house ringing bells. When the cows were driven into the forest, the following was recited:
"Saint George, watch over and guard from all mishaps!
As you watched in the manor-house so watch in the juniper thicket!"
On *Autumn-George* the cows were taken into the cowshed and tethered.
(Suistamo. 1933. M. Haavio b) 671. –Maloi Karppanen, o.s. Soframoff, 80 years. Emphasis mine)

Another holy man who figures in these syncretisms in an interesting way was the holy hermit and founder of a small monastery in Olonets Karelia,

St. Adrian of Andrusov (known in the vernacular as *Andrei Andrejevits*, *Ondrei Ondreijevits*, or *Ondri Ondreitš*).[194] He was addressed as the water spirit responsible for *nenä*-illness in five examples of *proškenja* incantations, (see examples 48a-c) and as the forest spirit responsible for livestock trapped in the 'forest cover' in one known example (example 48d).[195] Adrian of Andrusov's association with the wilderness can perhaps be traced back to legends which tell of the holy hermit having lived a life of seclusion in the forest, a life which began when a bear guided him to the hermit cell of St. Alexander of Svir, founder of The Monastery of the Holy Trinity (Piiroinen 1979:32, in Laitila 1995:91–92). The other name referred to in the last two examples below, Vasiljouna/Vassilevna, may be connected to the Orthodox saint Basilissa.[196]

48a)

Vein izändy olet sinä	You are the master of the water,
vanhin Andrei Andrejevits,	the eldest, Andrei Andrejevits,
velleksiz vanhin,	the eldest of brothers,
prosti tämän voimattoman	forgive this feeble one's
pahat työt, pahat sanat.	evil deeds, evil words!

(Tulemajärvi>Salmi. 1932–38. Maija Juvas 265. –Katri Markström, 56 years).

48b)

Veis proshkenjan pyydö	Asking forgiveness from the water
Vesi kuldaine	Water, golden
kuningas Vasiljouna,	king Vasiljouna,
Vesi kuldaine	Water, golden
kuningas Ondrijouna,	king Ondrijouna,
Proshti!	Forgive me!

(SKVR II:934. Vuatšoila. 1901. –Petra Ivanov Potshi, 63 years).

48c)

Vein isäntä	Master of the water,
Ondrei Ondreijevits,	Ondrei Ondreijevits,
vein emäntä Vassilevna,	mistress of the water, Vassilevna,
vein plateutsat,	water's newborns,
vein suuret sutjat,	water's great judges,
vein kaunehet kasakat,	water's beautiful peasant men,
vein kaunehet piijat...	water's beautiful maidens...

(Suojärvi. 1931. Nasti Lesonen 258. –Outotja V. Murto).

48d)

Ondri Ondreitš,	Ondri Ondreitš,
Onofri Onofritš...	Onofri Onofritš...[197]
...Gesli et pästä,	...If you do not release it,
minä teiledei tegen	I will make
roudaisen pihan	an iron fence,
i kivisen seinan.	and a wall of stone around you.
Teide putit i dorogad	I will close your paths
mina soubtan	and roads
itšein tsivatan putin aveitan.	and open a path for my cow.

(Soutjärvi. 1962. J. Perttola 42. –Anna Klopova, b. 1874).

The appearance of saints and holy hermits in the roles of nature spirits was not due to a decline in the belief in nature spirits in the early 20th century, since it is clear from the available material that knowledge of nature spirits was alive and well as late as the 1930s and 1940s in Orthodox Karelia. Rather, I posit that these syncretisms in communicative rituals indicate certain structural tendencies in the Orthodox Karelian folk religious belief system. In this particular version of the Karelian folk religious worldview, we see a tendency toward *one primary* dichotomy between humans and otherworldly beings. The conceptual dichotomy between self/farm/community on the one hand and the forest environment on the other, as well as the constant threat posed by the wilderness, required that humans carry on an endless, negotiatory dialogue with it. Since it is possible to negotiate only with sentient agents, it appears that many sorts of supernatural agents in Karelian folk belief were recruited to patrol the boundary between human culture and forest wilderness. Even things that were not originally agents at all, such as holy icons depicting legendary or Biblical events, were anthropomorphized in order to swell the ranks of sacred boundary agents. The Christian saints most often evoked in incantation rituals such as St. George, St. Blaise and the Virgin Mary were *not* needed on the 'inside', at the center of 'culture' and the human community (and when Christian sacred agents *were* needed at the 'center', they were different Christian agents: God, monks, and holy hermits). Instead, saints were needed to *mediate the boundaries between 'inside' and 'outside',* and they were eminently suited for this task since they already shared the agreed-upon moral universe of Christianity with humans, a basic point of departure from which negotiations could proceed.

The complex society of the "other side": forest as mirror for the human community

Ritual communication with the forest wilderness necessitated that the forest and its denizens be treated as Christian. In this ritual communication, the wilderness community was therefore to some extent treated as a projection of, *or model of*, the human (Christian) community. This modelling process, however, could work in both directions. In this section I examine the ways in which the community of nature spirits may also have served as a *model for* the human community (cf. Geertz 1973:23), as a constructed mirror-image in which the forest was attributed those characteristics which the human community wished to see in itself but lacked. An exemplary social universe characterized by stability, hierarchy and longevity was projected onto the supernatural wilderness in order that it might provide an expression of the community's idealized view of itself. The role of the forest as a backdrop against which society could view various reflections of itself has already been explored by Lotte Tarkka (1998:135), who states that

> ...legitimations of the social order can be found in the metarepresentations of the social domain projected onto the spheres of both nature and the

other world – i.e. in the multiple projections of cultural order onto interpretations of the unknown or unfamiliar.

In the verbal incantations recited during *proškenja* rituals, the denizens of the earth, water, wind and forest were given names. These were only rarely personal names, nor were they necessarily titles of respect or authority, instead they were labels denoting social rank, with higher level authorities such as kings, priests and judges, and lower-ranking strata such as workers and servants. Ritual epithets spanned the entire spectrum of *age* and *gender*: "the great and the small", "the young and the old", men, women, maidens, youths, and babies. Kinship terms were also commonly used, including references to daughters, sons, children, sisters, brothers, grandfathers, grandmothers, daughters-in-law, grandchildren, godfathers and godmothers. From the top of the social ladder to the bottom, social statuses and roles occupied by nature spirits included emperors, "emperors of emperors", czars and czarinas, kings, lords, bishops, colonels, priests, priests' wives, assistant priests, deacons, vergers, servants of the church, judges, constables, sextons, peasants, faithful servants, salaried serving-maids, vassals, purchased slaves, and drudges. Miscellaneous occupations included childminders and conjurers.

Often, the entire community of nature spirits was addressed in the couplet: "The (forest's) great patrilineal clan, the (forest's) bright matrilineal clan (*Metsän suuri sukukunta / Metsän helie heimokunta*)",[198] or with the phrase: "Greetings to all your people! (*Terve, kaikki kansakunta!*)".[199] Forgiveness was requested from the kin community of nature spirits "to the eighth stock, to the ninth generation (*kaheksah kandah saah / yheksäh polveh saah*)",[200] in other words, all nature spirits whose kin connections went back nine generations back, so as to cover all possible members of the 'Other' community:

49)
Water-*nenä*
(Read three times, do not bathe)

Terve vein isännälle,	Greetings to the waters' masters,
terve vein emännille,	greetings to the waters' mistresses,
lapsille suurille,	to their children, great,
pienille, keskkertasil,	small and middling,
Vein isännät, vein emännät,	Waters' masters, waters' mistresses,
lapset suuret,	children, great,
pienet, keskkertaset,	small and middling,
piiat, kasakat,	serving maids, farmhands,
papit, d'iekat,	priests, parish clerks,
niekkunat, ponommarit,	priest's assistants, sextons
vein kuningahat,	the waters' kings,
vein keisarit, keisarin keisarit	the waters' emperors, the emperor's emperors,
ja vein valdakunda kaikki,	and the whole of the waters' empire,
prostikkua, antakkua anteeks,	forgive me, absolve me,
heitäkkyä selkieks	leave me in peace
siks ilmoist igiä,	for all eternity,

rauhoa ja tervehyttä.   in peace and in health.
(Suojärvi. 1966. Senni Timonen KT 374:602. –Aleksi Rakki, magic-user and farmer, b. 1896).

As we know from folk narratives and incantations, one purpose in listing all the members of the 'Other' community was to ensure that all were present when the supplicant asked forgiveness. The reason that long lists of epithets for nature spirits were recited during a *proškenja* ritual was so that all members of the nature spirit community would be present to hear the supplicant's request for forgiveness, so that the individual perpetrator of the *nenä* illness would not be able to continue to hold a grudge:

50)
The inhabitant of a certain village in Olonets Karelia had a skin disease, which the village healer (*tietoiniekka*), having divined its cause, identified as originating from the water. Then this healer went with his patient in the heart of the night to an open hole in the ice and demanded the presence of all of the water's folk , its masters and mistresses, priests, sons, and deacons. When the water's folk had arrived at the ice hole, the healer asked them: "are all of your folk now here?" They assured him that everyone was present, but the healer insisted that someone was still missing. Finally the water's folk admitted that one half-blind and crippled inhabitant had indeed remained at home but that they had not considered it necessary to bring him along. The healer said that nevertheless, everyone had to be present and then the blind and lame one was also sent for. It was in fact precisely this one who had sent the illness into the person, for the patient had at one time urinated into the spring and the urine had put out the eye of the one-eyed water spirit. Then the inquiry was made as to who was responsible for the loss of his leg, but he said that "he had done it to himself" and he blamed no one for it. When the usual *proškenjas* had been made to the water, then the person recovered.
(Olonets. 1936. Eino Toiviainen 182. –Oudotja Ruskoi, 80 years).

To name something is to organize it, control it, to evoke from it a new set of meanings. As Helmuth Berking points out (1999:78) "…every (god's) name is also the origin of an imaginary world that would remain invisible without it." The 'other side' (*tuonpuoleinen*), the other world, could just as easily have been evoked by naming one or two nature spirits, for example 'forest master' and 'forest mistress'. Why was an entire *community* of nature spirits necessary for the enactment of reciprocal relations with the wilderness? Through the epithets for social ranks attributed to nature spirits, depictions of the other world in *proškenja* rituals were able to focus on *two* aspects: the first was the *size* and *social composition* of the 'Other' community, which was diverse, well-ordered, multi-layered and hierarchical. The second was the 'Other' community's *permanence* through time and across generations. I suggest that through the ritual construction of a large, stratified, enduring society in the other world, people first of all linked themselves and their interlocutors, the nature spirits, to larger structures of authority in which "kings", "emperors", "czars", etc. played a role. They did this in order to bolster their own claims and remind nature spirits of their 'social' responsibilities. At the same time, they created an ordered cosmos which reflected the image of an ideal society. This ideal image compensated for the reality of life in backwoods Karelia, and for the community's perception of its own potential for disintegration, of the tentative boundaries which separated it from the ever-encroaching wilderness.

In many parts of in rural Orthodox Karelia, daily life was characterized by isolation and poverty. Villages were usually laid out along waterways (primarily along rivers in Olonets Karelia, lakes in Archangel Karelia, and Lake Ladoga in Ladoga Karelia), and while farms in a single village could be located quite close to each other, the villages themselves were usually small and distant from each other, separated by broad expanses of trackless wilderness (Kaukiainen 1998:125). In many cases, even individual farms and cottages were scattered at great distances from each other and isolated in the wilderness. The average population density throughout Orthodox Karelia, for instance, was quite low: only 1–5 persons per square kilometre, and in Archangel Karelia and northeastern parts of Ladoga Karelia, it was closer to one person per square kilometre (Hämynen ibid: 153–154).

Farms and communities were potentially transient fixtures in the social landscape: due to harsh agricultural conditions, fortunes regularly rose and fell, farms were founded and failed. Up until the last quarter of the 19th century, famines and epidemics regularly ravaged the countryside, sometimes wiping out entire households and weakening further small communities' already precarious sense of order and permanency. While not wishing to overlook the socially integrative functions of annual village festivals (*praasniekkas*), weddings, cooperative work ventures and networks of visiting (see e.g. Sarmela 1969, Sauhke 1971), it must be pointed out that living close to the edges of the wilderness also had negative implications for social cohesion: persons engaged in the multiple forms of livelihood demanded by the harsh backwoods conditions spent long periods of time isolated from others, in hunting, fishing and cattle-herding. This may have led to difficulties in social interaction (cf. Ylikangas 1996), promoting further isolation and increasing the threat of social breakdown.

The communities of Karelian ritual participants, therefore, bore little resemblance to the imagined communities of nature spirits and the dead. The latter reflected instead a composite of the ideal kin-based community and the peasant's eye view of the more socially stratified Finnish and Russian centers of power: towns and cities. Could this cohesive and enduring picture of a complex society have been an image with which persons and communities living at the edge of the wilderness wished to identify? Could it be that such a constructed self-image made these backwoods dwellers feel themselves part of a larger, more intricate social arrangement and therefore more securely encultured, more 'human'? Tarkka (1998:131) has, for example, pointed to the social stigma attached to a strong association with the forest in 19th and early 20th century Archangel Karelia. Here, the closer one lived to nature, the less 'human' or 'cultured' one was seen to be:

Barbarity associated with the forest also functioned as a criterion in the stereotypical distinctions made among neighboring villages. "Foresters" inhabited the "forest villages", which lacked the level of civilization found in the heartland villages or "village-villages". According to proverb, a girl would rather marry the trees of a parish village than the men of a "forest village": even a small forest growing in a proper village was more cultured than a village settlement situated in the middle of the forest.

The construction of a self-aware, anthropomorphic 'other' community as a personification of the wilderness may have offered the possibility for creating a new field of dialogue through which to redefine human society, and through society, the self: Connerton, for instance, (1989:12) points out that

> [s]ocieties are self-interpreting communities...among the most powerful of these self-interpretations are the images of themselves as continuously existing that societies create and preserve. For an individual's consciousness of time is to a large degree an awareness of society's continuity, or more exactly of the image of that continuity which the society creates.

Orthodox Karelian kin-based communities emphasized their own permanence not only through *proškenja* rites, but also through ritual communication directed at the *dead* – those community members whose departure from the ranks of the living to the "other side" posed the greatest threat to a sense of social continuity. Like the *proškenja* rites discussed above which addressed whole kin communities of nature spirits "to the ninth generation", ritual formulas for summoning the dead to memorial feasts (see next section) invited nine generations of the dead to come and eat with the living. In so doing, they re-established the connections between community members separated by time and reconstituted a fundamental "eating community" (see Falk 1994), one of the most basic of social groupings in traditional societies.

In the field of dialogue created through *proškenja* rituals and other ritual communication aimed at the supernatural denizens of the "other side", the human community redefined itself by endowing the "other side" with the qualities it wished to see in itself, simultaneously lending a measure of sanctity to its own existence. In other words, community members were able to reify the 'ideal' human community and keep it fixed in their own awareness by incorporating it into the 'mirror' image of the 'Other' community. The persons who appear to have been primarily responsible for this were, once again, the ritual specialists of the community, the *tietäjäs* and healers who were versed in the proper *proškenja* incantations by which nature spirits were addressed. As we saw in the case of the *proškenja* rite itself, healers and *tietäjäs* did more than simply describe the other world, communicate with it and effect cures, but were also responsible for constructing patients' conceptions of the boundaries of self and society, as well as an understanding of what constituted society as opposed to the threatening 'Other' which lay beyond society's boundaries.

The poor and the dead: communal
cohesion and disorder in the margins

Incorporating the dead into the community of the living

Viewed from the perspective of Orthodox Karelian rituals of communication with sacred agents, it was not only the *wilderness* which threatened the order and equilibrium of human life. Processes constantly at work within the community itself, particularly the death of community members, also required boundary maintenance. The cohesive functioning of any small community is always disturbed when one or more of its members die. In Orthodox Karelian communities, where individuals' roles, statuses and sense of self were organized according to kin ties, the loss of a kin member was simultaneously the loss of a link in the chain which specified how each member was connected to everyone else. As Pentikäinen (1969:94) points out in his study of traditional Finnish concepts regarding death, "for the individual, death means his destiny in the afterlife, while for the community it is a factor which shakes cohesion and organization. Every personal death changes the communal structure..."

In the case of Orthodox Karelia, the community's sense of its fragility and impermanence necessitated that the dead continue to be counted among its numbers. For both individual families and the community as a whole, treating the dead as members of the group strengthened both the group's cohesion and its sense of its own continuity, as was pointed out by Harva in his book *Suomalaisten muinaisusko* (The Ancient Beliefs of the Finns, 1948):

> The actual object of devotion was, however, not the dead in general but the deceased belonging to and honored by each family and kin group, the continuation of whose work and activities, as well as the fulfillment of whose wishes, was the sacred responsibility of the descendants. This tradition was the basis for the entire social life of the folk in former times. The dead were appealed in all phases of the individual's and kin group's life. The dead guarded morality, judged practices and upheld organized society (p. 510–511).

Ritual communication with the dead took place through several types of ritual activities: the first type of ritual activity, *pominominen*, has already been mentioned above (see pages 66–69, 79–81). Another form of ritual devotion was *muistajaiset*, commemorative ritual meals occurring at particular intervals (three days, six weeks, six months, one year etc.), to which were invited not only the living members of the kin group or community but also the dead, and at which both the living and the dead were expected to eat.[201] It was believed that for the first six weeks (*kuusinetälihine* or *kuusnetäliset*) after death, the deceased remained among the living, visiting the places he or she had known during life. After six weeks, a memorial meal was held in order to help relocate the deceased permanently to the world of the dead. Only after this period was the dead person referred to using a new term: *pokoiniekka* (literally "one at peace", Utriainen 1992). The third type of ritual, *piirut*, was known primarily in Ladoga Karelia and was similar to *muistajaiset*. The term *piirut* referred to a ritual meal which did not fall on a particular anniversary but was organized by relatives in fulfillment of a promise or vow made to the dead person (usually one's father or mother) while he or she was still living (Harva 1932:479; Haavio 1934, 1937:431). In any given parish, this type of memorial ritual might take place only once in a decade, but was for this reason a highly memorable event, recounted in narratives handed down from generation to generation.[202]

Ties binding the family to its dead, therefore, did not end with death and burial, but collective interaction among community members continued even after death. The kin community was seen to be made up of the living *plus* the dead: it was sometimes referred to as consisting of nine generations of the dead going back in time, as well as nine generations of the living, that is, those living relatives who could trace a common ancestor as far back as nine generations. According to Martta Kähmi from Ladoga Karelia, nine generations of the *living* were invited to the *piirut* celebration,[203] and the number of generations of the *dead* invited to the *piirut* were also nine: lamenting women at the cemetery called out: "Come, departed master and mistress! Bring with you your relatives to the ninth generation!" (Harva 1932:480). At memorial meals for deceased kin members in Archangel Karelia, those whose names could no longer be recalled were referred to as *pokoiniekkas*, and were honored in the following formula (Utriainen 1992:161):

> Pominoi, Hospod pokoiniekkoi,
> yheksäst polvest yheksäh polveh,
> muistetut tai muistamattomat,
> tietyt tai tietämättömät…

> Lord have mercy on the ones at peace,
> From the ninth generation to the ninth generation,
> those remembered and forgotten,
> known and unknown…
> (Vuonninen. 1932. Samuli Paulaharju b)18218. –Anni Lehtonen).

Lamenters at a young girl's grave, city of Aunus, 1941. Photo: Sakari Pälsi. National Board of Antiquities.

The system of reciprocal rituals directed at the dead helped maintain a sense of connection between the living and the dead by perpetuating social interaction with the deceased person. In the context of *muistajaiset* and *piirut*, for example, after the dead were invited to attend the memorial meal using ritual lamentation,[204] they entered the house by way of long cloths hung from outside the windows.[205] They were believed to eat alongside the living: beside each table setting intended for a living person was an empty plate for the dead person,[206] and in some cases the dead person was thought to eat with the same spoon and drink from the same cup as the living guest – these had to remain right side up so that the deceased could use them.[207] The fact that the dead were physically present at the ritual could be demonstrated, for example, if the next morning there was a depression in the pillow provided for them to sleep on. According to one account from Ladoga Karelia, "there once came so many of these invisible *piirut* guests that the stool at the dining table collapsed".[208]

As with other reciprocal relationships with sacred agents, not only were the living expected to fulfill ritualized obligations toward the dead, but the dead were also expected to assist the living in various ways, including promoting the farm's cattle- and fishing-luck[209] (example 51a), assisting in childbirth (example 51b), aiding a son going off to war,[210] helping with the spring sowing[211] (example 51c), and helping with the summer work on the farm (example 51d):

51a)
When one is fishing and mentions the dead, as in
"Give us much fish, departed ones,
and then we will remember you
on the day of memoriam
and give you fish and and offerings,"
then one receives a lot of fish when one lowers the nets or weir into the
water. The dead person whom you miss the most or who is closest to your
heart is mentioned first.
(Vuonninen. 1932. Samuli Paulaharju 18235. –Anni Lehtonen, b. 1868).

51b)
A pregnant wife may certainly ask help even from the dead. She might
say:

Toattoseni tuonelasta,	Father mine from Tuonela,
moamoseni moaemästä,	mother mine from mother earth,
auta milma	help me
kun miul' on mieli	because I have a desire
loatie lapsie...	to have a child...

(Vuonninen. 1932. Samuli Paulaharju 18783. –Anni Lehtonen).

51c)
When one begins to sow the field, one asks one's dead father for help.
"Father bless me as I sow". One's father was also asked for advice.
(Salmi. 1932–38. Maija Juvas 177. –Lutjonen's wife).

51d)
On Whitsuntide, when people visit the cemeteries, they ask their dead
relatives for help with the summer farm work. Whoever has a deceased
husband, asks her husband to help, whoever has a son, asks her son. 'Come
help (tule abuh)', they say.
(Tulemajärvi. 1944. Helmi Helminen 4138).

Not only were ritual obligations and assistance between the living and the
dead two-directional, but actual *communication* between them, too, worked
both ways. In the same way as with nature spirits, the living communicated
with the dead through incantation prayers and ritual offerings, and the dead
were seen to communicate with the living through *dreams*.[212] In these dreams,
the dead might ask for special foods they hoped their living relatives would
bring to the cemetery on the holy day of "Memorial Saturday" (*muistinsuovattu*, example 52a). The dead could also inform the living of the ways
in which they had already assisted that person (example 52b). The dead
could reproach the living for neglecting their duties towards them: for
example not being home on the night before *muistinsuovattu* when the dead
visited the homes of their living kin and expected to receive food and warmth
from them (example 52c, see also Järvinen & Timonen 1992; Stark et. al.
1996):

52a)
During the night before *muistinsuovatta* people saw dreams. The dead
announced what kinds of foods they wanted [the living person to bring to

the grave the next day]. The living saw, for example, that their own relatives in the other air were hungry, since they didn't always feel like always eating the same pasties or pies. Every now and then they wanted something special, for example, blueberry pies instead of ones filled with peas. The gifts were left at the graveyard. Even if it were only bread made with chaff, one was supposed to take even that to the cemetery on *muistinsuovatta*. "When a dead person leaves this place", he is asked for provisions in the other air. If he has nothing to share with the others, the chickens peck at the dead person there.
(Porajärvi. 1942. Helmi Helminen 2060).

52b)
Now when these wars started, one man from Suona village went to the cemetery upon leaving for war. He said to his father at the grave: "come help me, dead father". In a dream the father [later] told him in what all situations he had helped his son. The soldier ended up in the Finnish army through Germany and spoke of this when visiting Suona village in the summer of 1943.
(Tulomajärvi. 1943. Helmi Helminen 3872. –Jevdokia Kohlojev, b. 1874).

52c)
On *muistinsuovatta* the dead persons [*pogoinikat*, lit. 'ones at peace'] walk the earth...They come to their former home to spend the night, and sleep on the baking oven.[213] Outi told the following: "Olesa's son was in Robohoila...(he was afraid to be alone on the night before *muistinsuovatta*). I was invited there for the night, and Olesa's wife went away." "In a dream", when Outi slept in the cottage of her son, she saw her own cottage fill with dead people! "They came, came, and filled the cottage, there were both young and old". They asked: "Hasn't food (*vero*) been prepared for us?"
  Outi explained the dream: I wasn't in my own home on the night before *muistinsuovatta* and during that time the deceased came to an empty house, did not receive their food, did not receive any warmth.
(Tulemajärvi. 1943. Helmi Helminen 3455. Parentheses in original).

Memorial rites and the maintenance of socio-economic equilibrium

Rituals performed for the dead served to not only temporarily erase the differences between the living and the dead but also to alleviate, at least for a short time, socio-economic differences among members of the community. Food brought to the cemetery for the dead and offerings of food given at *piirut* celebrations were nearly always redistributed to the poor and crippled who had gathered, uninvited, in large groups in the cemetery or near the house where the memorial rituals were held. After rural population growth in 19th-century Karelia began to outstrip the carrying-capacity of the land, there was no way for the community itself to resolve the contradiction between the peasant ideal of communal equality and the 19th-century reality of a growing gap between landowning farmers and the landless itinerant population. A ritualized deferral to bring the real and ideal closer together was thus the only way of dealing with the increasing problem of the landless and homeless poor. In this deferral, rituals ostensibly directed at the dead became channels for the temporary redistribution of resources to the living. As Martti Haavio describes for a *piirut* occasion: "At the end of the hymn, all of the food was moved to another table, or was given to the poor and the infirm, who had gathered in large groups near the hosting farmhouse" (1937:429). An informant from Olonets Karelia described how at a memorial meal (*muistiset*) "each guest brought a large loaf of bread with them, and these were put together in a storehouse and distributed to the sick and the crippled."[214] Other descriptions of similar practices are as follows:

> 53a)
> When we were in Salmi, I had the chance to observe Orthodox customs. For example...the poor are given donations and alms on behalf of the dead person. There are also proper cemetery days, when people go to church, taking with them bundles of provisions, and beggars go too. In the center of each bundle's contents, either bread or sweetbread, a candle is placed and lit. The bundles are put on the floor of the church. The priest blesses them with holy incense. Then everyone goes to the cemetery, the priests too, for there are several. The beggars follow behind. The priests go to the gravesites to pray. Then the provisions are distributed to the beggars, and the people themselves eat, too. Also crumbs are given to the birds. In former times the intent was to leave food for the dead. To one's best friend was given the bread where the candle had been burning.
> (Salmi. 1961. Elsa Jaatinen TK 26:183)

> 53b)
> ...When the dead person was taken to the grave, then at the same time was taken all of the food which was at the funeral. This was intended to be the dead person's provisions and at the cemetery it was distributed to the poor, who were sometimes waiting in large groups for it. Also on memorial days when one went to the cemetery, food was divided among the waiting poor.
> (Salmi. 1958–9. Elsa Pukonen 247 (b. 1899). –Tatjana Suuronen nee Kirmonen, farm mistress, born 1908).

> 53c)
> ...In Salmi it has been, and in Suojärvi still is, the custom to give food that has been on the table to the poor when bringing new nourishment for the dead person to the table. But in addition to the food on the table, the dead person is also offered other nourishment. In the icon corner, under the holy icon, *proskuna*, that is, wheat bread, pasties or sprouts which have been blessed, are kept for the dead person. This is put in its place at the same time that food is placed on the table. Usually also this food is distributed to the poor.
> (Lehmusto 1937:420).

Even the food offerings given to the dead in order to cure cemetery-*nenä* (see pages 79–81) were subsequently distributed to the poor:

54)
Cemetery-*nenä* is cured in such a way that one makes three times nine pasties. These are given to beggars. Then one visits the grave from which the *nenä* was received in order to ask forgiveness.
(Salmi. 1946. Otto Harju 4010. –Maria Kuosmanen, b. 1899).

As in the *pominominen* rituals discussed earlier (both for the dead and those trapped in the 'forest cover'), here again we see the sharing or providing of *food* as a way of incorporating marginalized members of the community (those beyond communal boundaries or on its periphery) back into the group, even if only temporarily. The most visible occasion on which the community strove to incorporate the poor into its ranks through the sharing of food was when its boundaries opened to include the other 'outsiders', the dead. The poor may have been viewed as 'standing in' for the dead, serving as their representatives, since the distribution of food and clothing to the poor was explained in some cases as a form of giving to the dead. According to Kaarle Krohn (1915:47), beggars were considered to be the representatives of the dead person "and were even referred to in the context of their appearance at the cemetery as the 'non-existent (*olemattomat*)'..." According to Lauri Pelkonen's (1965:370) account of a ritual custom in Suojärvi parish,

55)
...the delicacies brought for the dead were always given, down to the last crumb, to the poor. They were the "provisions of the dead person (*pogoiniekka*)". In the same way, [discarded clothing] was also donated. Such was the idea that whatever was given to the poor, the dead would receive the same thing in the 'other air'. If food was given, the dead person would know no hunger, if clothing was given, he or she would feel no chill.

The same idea was also expressed by other informants in describing *yönistujaiset*, the wake held through the night for the dead person:[215]

56)
In the evening, supper is eaten. One end of the table is set (at the other end of the table lies the dead person). The dead person (*pokoinnik*) has a teacup beside him or her the whole time. It is poured out on the ground and given to the beggars who always come to the wake and it is filled again and again. To the beggar is said: "When you take this, bow, bow, our Anni needs it." It is said over and over to the beggar to bow down. "Drink it, it seems that (the dead person) will not come to drink, may the cup go to our dear departed."
(Tulemajärvi. 1932–38. Maija Juvas 63. –Katri Markström. Parentheses in original).

Rituals and festivals connected with the dead were linked to the maintenance of socio-economic equality in other respects as well. Descriptions of these memorial rituals repeatedly emphasized that it was the *wealthiest* families who distributed the most food and clothing to the poor, and who hosted the largest memorial rituals, known in Olonets as *muistaiset* (as opposed to the

Memorial ritual (muistajaiset*) in Äglājärvi village. 1937. Photo: Yrjö von Grönhagen. Finnish Literature Society.*

lounalliset held on a smaller scale). According to informants, "*muistaiset* could only be held on the richest farms", since those invited were not only relatives but also members of any households containing persons who remembered the dead person at all, and this could amount to well over 300 persons, all of whom were given as much food and drink as they could consume. [216] This more extravagant scale of ritual devotion can be seen as a form of conspicuous consumption which functioned to level socio-economic differences within the community. Such expenditure was linked to the notion of 'limited good' and the ideal of communal equality. This ritual redistribution of wealth in Orthodox Karelian communities appears to have fulfilled a function similar to that of the system described by Foster (1965:305) for Mexico in which wealthy peasants sponsored costly fiestas for the community. In the fiesta complex, "[a] person who improves his position is encouraged (...) to restore the balance through conspicuous consumption in the form of ritual extravagance (...) These practices are a redistributive mechanism which permits a person or family that potentially threatens community stability to gracefully restore the status quo, thereby returning itself to a state of respectability."

A death in the family was used as an opportunity to narrow the socio-economic gap in more direct and personal ways as well, as described in the following account: [217]

57)
Upon the death of a daughter, rich families sometimes donate her dowry cow to the poor. The cow is secretly taken at night to the cottage of some poor person. A note is attached to the bell cord on the cow's neck which

says that the cow is given as a gift ("to you and to God"). Not even the dead person's name is mentioned, but naturally it is easy to guess from which farm the gift was brought.

...After the death of their son, some rich families have given a horse to some poor person. "Let us give a horse so that the dead person can ride a horse too," the family says to one another. The horse is taken secretly, the recipient is not even told the dead person's name. The recipients go to church to bow on behalf of the benefactors and the dead person, for naturally they soon find out whose horse it was.
(Tulemajärvi. 1932–38. Maija Juvas 81–82. –Katri Markström).

In some cases, the dead person was reported to have appeared in a dream and requested that his/her clothing be given away to the poor. In this case, the dead were seen as *actively* working to uphold the ideal of social redistribution of resources:

58)
Whatever clothing the dead person has owned, these are given at least in part to the poor. It is said that the dead person sometimes appears to his/her relatives in a dream to say that all of his/her clothing should be given to those who ask for it. When giving the clothing one says: "This means you must pray for a whole year (on behalf of the dead person), one must not forget to pray, take it only if you intend to pray, take them but you must bow down and mention Vasya's name: "Give this suit to Vasya, who needs it" (=perhaps Jesus in heaven will give the suit to Vasya).
(Tulemajärvi. 1932–38. Maija Juvas 80. –Katri Markström. Parentheses in original).

The poor were thus given food, drink, clothing and other gifts, and were expected in return to pray for the well-being of the deceased. As one female informant from Olonets Karelia observed in the 1930s: "the dead person's provisions, all the food brought to him, are taken to the grave, and there distributed to beggars, to whom is always said: 'Bow down and mention (the dead person's) name'".[218] The bowing required of the poor was similar to the bowing required of illness victims wishing to communicate with sacred agents in the 'other world'. At issue was a symbolic gesture signifying the opening of a channel of communication across a boundary which was usually seen to be closed.

As in the case of Christian saints cast in the roles of nature spirits, here again we see the recruitment of agents to stand in for or function as sacred boundary agents. Whereas in human-wilderness relations, boundary agents were recruited from the ranks of Christian figures (Mary, Jesus, St. George, etc.), in the case of funeral customs and memorial feasts, these boundary agents were the beggars and village poor who were either reconstrued as the dead themselves, or were obligated through the receipt of gifts to perform *boundary-work*, that is, to carry on ritual negotiations with the 'other side' by means of prayer on behalf of the deceased, to communicate across the boundary between the world of the living and the world of the dead.

The nature/culture dichotomy in communal self-definition

Rituals of reciprocity aimed at nature spirits, saints and the dead point to the problematic relationship between the human world of everyday life, farm and community, and the realms existing at the margins of the human world which were seen to be threatening and dangerous. Such realms were simultaneously physical places in this world (forest, cemetery) and supernatural realms of the imagination, other worlds wherein dwelled entire communities of sacred agents. The concerns expressed in *proškenja* rituals and rites to protect cattle *do not support* an image of the Orthodox Karelian peasant in harmony with forest nature. Harmony was an ideal never fully achieved amidst the tensions and difficulties of the human-wilderness relationship. These tensions were derived from *competition* over scarce resources, a situation which was temporarily alleviated, but not permanently resolved, through exchange and ritual activities aimed at equilibrium and equity between peasants and the forest.

Although various sacred agents were addressed in the context of *proškenja* rituals, I suggest that all in their own way represented the wilderness, the natural environment beyond the human community. The prototypical *nenä* illnesses addressed within *proškenja* rituals, those from forest, water, and wind, were all connected to the natural environment. *Nenä* illnesses caused by the dead in cemeteries can also be viewed as coming from the "wilderness" because cemeteries in Orthodox culture were often located in sacred groves or on a forested island or peninsula, and were generally left untouched, abandoned to the forces of nature. The close association between forest and cemeteries in rural Orthodox Karelia can be seen in photographs from the late 19th century and first half of the 20th. In them, many cemeteries are located within dense groves of tall spruces or pines, and give the appearance of miniature forests standing alone in the village fields, in other words small, contained pieces of wilderness separate from the forest proper.

According to Harva (1932:476), the oldest cemeteries in Karelia were known as 'spruce groves' (*kuusikkos*) because they were located in the forest. As Iivar Kemppinen (1967:36) explains, "trees were never felled [in the cemetery], so that Karelian cemeteries, among others, are still today islands of forest in which grow enormous firs and primeval pines." Kemppinen

(1967:45-46), in fact, considers it possible that in pre-Christian times, Karelian graveyards grew up around the custom of burying persons and families under large trees which came to be regarded as sacred. As they died, other members of the kin group were later buried beneath trees in the vicinity of these sacred trees, and the entire area became known as a sacred grove. In such a grove, sacrificial rituals were held and offerings given, and the grove was demarcated from the surrounding areas as a sort of 'island' of the dead. Only after the Christian church insisted that the deceased be buried in the churchyard (which, however, could be conveniently situated next to the sacred grove), did this practice begin to change.

The connection between the cemetery and the forest in folk world view can be seen in a description related by one informant from Olonets Karelia:

> 59)
> In the "spruce groves" one did not even break off branches in former times…one did not break off branches in the spruce groves because one received cemetery-*nenä*, if one thought, "what will come of it?"
> (Tulomajärvi. 1943. Helmi Helminen 3864. –Jevdokia Kohlojev, b. 1874).

Some informants, in fact, presented sacred agents connected to the dead and the forest as belonging to a single category: *nenä*-illnesses deriving from the forest, water and cemetery (and sometimes wind) could be described as 'brothers':[219] according to informants, "if one of them infects, they all infect",[220] "if an illness infects from the water then all of the *nenäs* are together (water, forest, cemetery)",[221] and "when there is one, they must all be asked forgiveness".[222]

In a territorial sense, the edge of the forest marked the limits of the known, socially-organized human environment, the world belonging to "this side". This can be seen not only in folklore (see Tarkka 1994:93) but also from historical linguistic data, as Anttonen points out:

> Linguists have demonstrated that forest [*metsä*] has long signified not so much "a plant community whose primary vegetation consists of trees", but rather *limit, edge, side*. According to this interpretation, 'forest' in the Finnish-Sami linguistic area has meant "a boundary in which, moving inland from the shoreline, the coastal area ends and the interior begins" (Anttonen 1996:117, quote from Vilppula 1990:287).

That the boundary between human habitation and the wilderness was of primary concern in *proškenja* and divination rites is supported by the fact that *nenä* illnesses were never seen to derive from *cultural* places (i.e. places where living members of the community worked and resided) such as houses, barns, or mills. While sacred things within the home (fire, holy icons) might infect if not shown the proper respect (turning one's back on the fire or dowsing it with dirty water, accidentally splashing a holy icon with water),[223] these objects were never seen to infect merely because the human took fright or 'thought' about the possibility of infection, as in the case of forest-*nenä*, water-*nenä* and cemetery-*nenä*.

A cemetery in Vuokkiniemi district, Archangel Karelia, 1915. Photo: Samuli Paulaharju. Finnish Literature Society.

Moreover, all of the items given as offerings in *proškenja* rituals to nature spirits show a strong emphasis on *culturally-valued objects* and *human workmanship*: nothing was given to sacred agents which had not first been worked, shaped or processed by humans in some fashion, and many of the offerings were objects which might have been bought from a travelling peddlar or a local tradesman. Items reported as suitable offerings included alcohol, tea, coffee, tobacco, bread, small pasties, rice, salt, hulled barley, silver or copper coins, an earring, mercury, tin, pieces of flint, an old knife, a needle, a sewing pin, wool, silk thread, linen fibers, clothing, a red piece of cloth, red wool thread, a wooden spoon, wood chips, buttons made of bone, an old whetstone, pieces of glass wrapped in two pieces of cloth, and burned bricks. To the dead was usually given food: pasties, bread, or sprouts.

The items given in *proškenja* offerings were those that the nature spirit or dead person was assumed to desire: according to one informant from Olonets, for instance, "the water loves tobacco (*dubakan vezi ljuubiu*)".[224] In a large number of incantation texts, sacred agents linked to the wilderness were represented as having 'stolen' the human patient's health or essence: humans urged the sacred agent to take away its own 'evil' or 'brown blood'[225], and give back the human's own 'good'[226] 'better'[227], 'white blood'[228], 'health'.[229] In some cases the supplicant even tried to mislead the sacred agent, saying "take back your own good (or gold), give me back my own evil".[230] One collector explained this as a way of persuading the forest spirits to take away the illness and give back health, "and in that way to exchange back what belongs to each!"[231]

Because the sacred agent had to be lured or cajoled into exchanging back the human's essence or health, and because the items offered to placate the sacred agent were human-made, products of culture, it can be surmised that sacred agents were considered eager to possess things belonging to the world of humans, including both human 'health' and man-made products. The fact that this distinction was continually made in *proškenja* rituals between the human-made products of culture on the one hand, and the 'Other' community which lacked and therefore desired them on the other, suggests that *a fundamental divide between culture and nature was what really separated the human and the supernatural* in this ritual context.

In the rituals examined here, the dichotomy between 'self' and 'Other' is expressed as a series of ever-expanding circles like rings in a pool of water, proceeding outward from the embodied self, locus of consciousness, and embracing home/farm, community, as well as the human-made culture represented in human dwellings and handcrafted offerings (cf. Tarkka 1994:93; 1998:134). 'Forest', 'nature' and 'wilderness' are opposed to all of these in the ritual communication and associated folk belief examined in this study. From the perspective of cultural classification and symbolic pollution, the forest wilderness in Orthodox Karelia was dangerous because it was viewed as the definitive "Other" for both the human body and human community. In fact, the wilderness itself was seen to be the 'other world' or 'other side'. Based on an intensive study of folk beliefs surrounding the 'forest cover' (*metsänpeitto*), Uno Holmberg (later Harva, 1923:27) suggested that "the mysterious curtain" of the forest which hid the trapped victim from searchers was in folk belief precisely the same boundary which separated 'this world' from the 'other side'. This is borne out by folk names for the forest spirit meaning "other side", which included *teine puol* in Olonets Karelia, [232] and *toisipuolehiní* in Archangel Karelia (see Virtaranta 1958:76).

Rituals of communication with the forest *used in hunting* represent a different tradition than the rituals of communication used by peasants and pastoralists discussed here, yet they show certain similarities. Both types of ritual addressed the boundary between forest nature and the human sphere, and they were in both cases characterized by communication and gift-giving between human and forest and guided by moral codes of behavior (Tarkka 1994). Beyond this, however, rituals performed in the contexts of hunting versus cattle-husbandry, for instance, show distinct differences. Because hunters regularly undertook journeys deep into the forest from which they then returned home, they were engaged in particular rites of passage and ritual purification which were not undertaken by those occupied in farming or herding (cf. ibid.). In rituals connected to hunting, because the hunter was intentionally entering the territory of the "other side", categories of nature and culture could become intertwined and the hunter could change places with his prey/predator (Tarkka 1994:68). This intermingling of categories could not, however, occur in situations outside the sphere of hunting without dire consequences. In fact, the most important difference between ritual communication carried out with the forest during hunting and at other times was the *motivation* of the rite. Hunters undertook ritual

The cemetery of Niskajärvi village, Archangel Karelia, 1915. Photo: Samuli Paulaharju. Finnish Literature Society.

conversation with the forest in order to obtain a good catch. Others initiated ritual communication with the forest in order to deal with *the disorder* caused by it.

The forest realm was seen as fundamentally dangerous to those things belonging to the human world. There was no way for forest predators to co-exist peacefully with grazing livestock, nor for the dynamistic forces of forest, water, wind, etc. to enter the human body without producing illness. Territorial boundary markers such as forest vegetation often become margins or boundaries used in the ordering of social experience. If, as Mary Douglas (1991:56) has argued, such boundaries are treated by society as dangerous and polluting, then it is understandable that those boundaries which did not remain in their proper place, but constantly *threatened to invade the human community*, would have been perceived as very dangerous indeed.

Neither the wilderness nor the sphere of the dead were static domains, but were instead characterized by *movement* (Utriainen 1992; Tarkka 1994, 1998). *Nenä* illnesses were described as actively "escaping" from the forest,[233] "throwing" themselves across the boundary of the human body.[234] Forest predators did not merely lie in wait for livestock in the forest but crossed the boundary between forest and farm to attack the cattle in the cowshed, and the forest itself was in the continual process of reclaiming, through the regrowth of forest vegetation, the fields wrested from it through burn-beat methods of land clearing. Inherent in the fear of forest movement, according to Tarkka, was that the two fundamentally different realms of human and forest would mix, and by extension, that the human's own self-definition as separate from his/her environment would collapse: "the social and corporeal self was in danger of melting into the other" (Tarkka 1998:134).

The crisis which motivated the rituals carried out in the non-hunting contexts discussed here was *the inevitable presence of the wilderness itself*: the forest was a primary site of economic exploitation, over which it was, however, impossible for peasant farmers using traditional tools and methods to gain the upper hand. Anxieties over the possibility of the wilderness environment penetrating the human body were reproduced on the bodies of community members through *nenä* illness. A body infected with *nenä* illness was a body whose awareness of the boundaries between self and other had become fuzzy: the aim of the *proškenja* ritual was to remap the boundaries between self and other onto the body (and thus onto the patient's perception). The cultural interpretation of *nenä* illness as the exchange of the human's own 'essence' and anxieties over the boundaries of the self were at the same time a case of collective anxieties writ small. On the level of social order, such collective anxieties included concerns over 1) the potential breakdown of the human community, and 2) the dissolution of the boundaries which separated the community from the non-human, natural environment.

Ritual communication dealt with these potential crises in several ways. Divination rituals transformed the undifferentiated chaos of the harmful natural and supernatural environment into clear-cut categories by identifying specific dangerous 'others', enabling persons to seek culturally-specified solutions to various types of disorder (illness, loss of cattle), and to guard the boundaries of the body/self against infection or penetration by these forces. Both divination rites and *proškenja* rituals presented the forest nature as the most important and dangerous 'other' with regard to the patient's body/self. In some *proškenja* rituals, the unknown forest wilderness was made more 'knowable', more easily negotiated with, by 'Christianizing' it, by endowing nature spirits with Christian attributes and thus creating a common moral basis for negotiations between humans and the forest. *Proškenja* rituals went further to reinforce each individual sufferer's awareness of the boundaries between this world (human culture) and the other world (forest wilderness, the dead), so that these boundaries could be mapped onto the sufferer's own body image. The cultural message behind divination and *proškenja* rites was that body boundaries were weak and vulnerable in the face of outside forces. Each person was responsible for guarding these boundaries of the self, and boundaries which were breached in individual consciousness when persons let down their guard by "thinking", "taking fright" or "falling down", had to be repaired by the ritual specialist.

In the Introduction to this study, I discuss the sacred as a concept deriving from a culture's efforts to separate things with a positive growth value from those things depleted of growth potential. Both the dead and the wilderness in Orthodox Karelia had a dualistic character in this regard: the dead who were still actively remembered, who retained their identities as social persons under certain circumstances, were incorporated into the community *at certain intervals* and were seen to be vital for its well-being. This dimension of death was indexed by using the terms *vainaja* or *pokoiniekka* to refer to the dead person. On the other hand, the dead were also characterized by a simultaneous loss of capacity to produce growth for society's benefit. This

Graveyards were often located in the forest and abandoned to the forces of nature, which eventually covered all visible traces of them. Photo: Väinö Salminen. Finnish Literature Society.

darker, tabooed side of death was indexed using the term *kalma*, which referred to the dangerous aspect of the dead: their dynamistic, infectious force. It is in this *kalma* aspect that the dead, especially the forgotten dead who had lost their individual identities, were seen to have merged with nature to become part of the wilderness environment. Ritual practices aimed at the dead mediated between these two aspects, in other words, between purity and impurity. In particular, they specified a *temporally*-ordered arrangement to distinguish between the two. The dead were reincorporated into the community only on certain ritual holidays or anniversaries reserved for that purpose, while on other days, unexpected visits from the dead were seen as *hauntings*, a rupture in the cosmic and social order to be prevented at all costs.[235] Such a temporal partitioning took into account both the growth aspects (purity) and the non-growth aspects (impurity) which characterized the dead.

153

This same pure-impure dichotomy applied to forest nature as well. Because fields and forests were seen to contain resources and 'growth' values utilized by both humans and the wilderness, to have drawn a spatial boundary which made the forest permanently on the 'other side' would have created difficulties at the level of the symbolic Order when necessity forced the actual exploitation by humans of forest resources: fish, game animals, fur-bearing animals, fodder for cattle, wood for fuel and building materials, and so forth. Since humans had to routinely enter and use the forest, particularly the zone of the forest closest to human habitation, this jointly shared area had to be divided up *temporally* in a sort of time-sharing arrangement so that cattle and forest predators would not be in the same forest zone at the same time. This arrangement attempted to maximize the growth value of the wilderness while minimizing its dangers.

The purity of the sacred in the sacred boundaries complex was always a *relative* purity, specific to a given place or time and shifting with each ritual context. What the sacred boundaries complex did *not* address were cultural ideals or concepts of *absolute* purity. This was the function of the *sacred centers* complex, to which I now turn.

Sacred centers – Cultural ideals and pilgrimage to monasteries

The pilgrimage vow and sacred ideals

Part I of this study dealt with exchange relations between Orthodox peasants and pastoralists on the one hand, and the dead, nature spirits and saints on the other. I have suggested in the foregoing that these exchange relations formed a local sacred system (*sacred boundaries*) which sought to ritually address and alleviate important crises facing the community: the threat of the wilderness, socio-economic inequality, and death. If the dilemmas experienced by individuals and communities were addressed through this ritual complex, why then, did these same peasants and pastoralists undertake lengthy, arduous pilgrimages to distant monasteries and chapels? What did the ordinary pilgrim find at the pilgrimage goal which did not exist in the local sphere of everyday folk religion?

Our only access to the experiences and perceptions of ordinary pilgrims is through the medium of language: in this case, the late 19th- and early 20th- century narratives which were recorded and collected as written folklore texts. And while these narrators often recounted their own firsthand experiences and impressions, the cultural significance they gave to these experiences was derived from what they heard from others on their pilgrimages, from returning pilgrims, or from fellow villagers and family members interested in pilgrimage. Present-day anthropologists such as Jill Dubisch in Orthodox Greece have noted that it is commonplace for pilgrims to exchange legends, stories and anecdotes at the pilgrimage site itself:

> ...At the same time there is also a large oral tradition, consisting of pilgrims' own experiences and those relayed to them by word of mouth, a large part of which is not found in the literature of the church. The recounting of such stories (as well as tales of unusual vows or other dramatic incidents) is a common type of exchange among pilgrims, especially at major festival times when the crowds are large and people are more likely to fall into conversation with each other (Dubisch 1990:126).

This "web of tales, legends, history and miracle stories that spins out from the sacred center" makes up what Alan Morinis (1992:22) has called the "informational field" (as opposed to the "social field") of the pilgrimage center (ibid: 18). This informational field, which was bound up with pilgrims' expectations and interpretations of their experiences, can thus provide the researcher with important insights into the cultural meanings of devotional journeys and pilgrimage sites.

Scholars of pilgrimage have pointed out that sacred centers such as monasteries can be seen as *cultural capitals* which develop and project a magnified image of accepted ideals in the culture. They represent a higher, purer or more ideal version of what the pilgrim already values and seeks within his/her culture. The 'sacred' aspect of pilgrimage sites thus "arises from the collective investment in the *ideals* that are enshrined [in them]."[236] Just what these ideals were in Orthodox Karelia will be explored in the pages which follow. But it is the fact that the sacred center performed a different function from the sacred boundaries complex, namely that it represented a concentration of purity rather than negotiated a boundary between purity and impurity, which explains the monastery's sacred, even supernatural power of attraction in the eyes of rural pilgrims. While local rites for communicating with the dead, saints and nature spirits defined the boundaries separating the known, human community from the 'other side', the monastery was a sacred center which presented cultural ideals in a form that was more perfect, more pure, and more difficult to attain than those manifested in the cultural milieu of everyday life on the farm or in the village.

Some monasteries fit the image of a sacred center better than others. For instance, Solovki was twice described in folk narratives as 'the sacred city', an appellation not applied to other monasteries.[237] Valamo was also conceived of as a cultural capital, a repository of sacrality in many forms. This could be emphasized through links to other, distant sacred places. One narrator, for example, mentioned the concrete mapping of image structures deriving from the Biblical Holy Land onto the Valamo landscape:

> 1)
> At the so-called New Jerusalem of Valamo monastery I have heard that there is a piece of Jesus Christ's coffin, which a certain German monk brought to Valamo after having visited Jerusalem, a long time ago. The same monk then built Valamo's New Jerusalem [Church] to be just like the real main church in Jerusalem, but on a smaller scale.
> (Salmi. 1936. Pekka Pohjanvalo 134).

It should be pointed out that in accounts given by Karelian informants, sacred centers were not always depicted as distant pilgrimage goals. Most of the narratives and anecdotes recorded on the topic of pilgrimage and monasteries come from Ladoga Karelia, home of Valamo and Konevits monasteries. In these accounts, both Solovki and the Monastery of the Holy Trinity were the subject of lengthy journey descriptions and narratives describing pilgrimage motives, obligations and folk advice. Konevits, on the other hand, was the subject of neither journey descriptions nor information about pilgrimages, while Valamo received only one brief mention as a pilgrimage goal, this information coming from more distant Olonets Karelia rather than Ladoga Karelia.[238] What this suggests is that the perspective of a sacred center *as a pilgrimage goal* depended on distance: Solovki and the Monastery of the Holy Trinity were located further from the homes of the majority of the Ladoga Karelian narrators and thus were more readily perceived as objects of pilgrimage, sacred *goals*.

Valamo, on the other hand, played a different role in the lives of the Ladogan Karelian narrators: it was a center of power which exerted significant economic, political and historical influence on the surrounding region. An institution the size of Valamo – with over a thousand monks, novices and workers by 1913, extensive holdings of agricultural land, fishing rights, salt boileries and generous financial support from the merchant class of St. Petersburg (Kohonen 1983:35, 39) – impacted the lives of those living near it in numerous concrete ways (see Kilpeläinen 2000). It is therefore no surprise that Valamo was depicted in folk narratives from a variety of perspectives, including some which were anti-clerical in attitude.[239]

Historical aspects of Valamo are suggested by references to its greatness arising from small origins[240] and how it was nearly destroyed by kings or pirates.[241] Various stories tell of the activities of monks and priests at different periods who prayed to avert danger, who gave money to the poor or who taught Christian values to the populace.[242] The economic side of Valamo was expressed in references to people buying cows from the monastery[243] or rich pilgrims bestowing large sums of money to it.[244] Here and there we see other references to the role of Valamo in people's daily lives such as narratives from workers or residents on the island.[245] As we might expect, the only corresponding historical and economic references to Solovki come from Archangel Karelia, its home region.[246]

In Orthodox Karelian discourse, pilgrimage narratives served to continually distinguish between purity (things culturally valued) and the impurities which threatened individual and community (illness, sin). This can be seen from the fact that mental illness and disease were depicted as impurities to be cast away from the sacred center. Numerous accounts mention miraculous healings and exorcisms of evil spirits at the monasteries which were carried out by monastery founders and monks, or occurred when persons kissed the monastery icons or walked beneath the tomb of St. Alexander of Svir at the Monastery of the Holy Trinity:[247]

2a)
Strange stories circulated regarding how such and such person had recovered after they had been to Orusjärvi monastery on a *jääksintä* visit and had fervently begged the aforementioned saint to turn his gaze toward them and pray for a cure from the Heavenly Father.
(Salmi. 1941. Raja-Karjalan Sivistysliitto (Manuel Saarinen) 5. –Filip Feudorinso Rovio, b. 1869).

2b)
In former times it was told how the sick were brought to Valamo monastery to be healed through the power of the spirit of God, so that the ailing person was brought to the church and placed in front of an icon of the Son of God. And the priests prayed to him to heal the sick person, and a certain Paavo Paavilainen, who had been a novice at Valamo monastery in his youth told the informant of having seen this actual event approx. 40 years ago.

Once, an elderly woman was brought from St. Petersburg to the monastery and behaved as if possessed by an evil spirit, shrieking and tearing out her hair, nor did she want to go inside the church. The woman was taken inside the church by force, brought in front of the icon of the Savior and made through coersion to embrace the icon of the Savior, and when the woman had done this, she fell onto her back as if half dead in front of the Savior's icon. And the high priests prayed to the Savior to cure her illness.

The woman lay in a stupor on the floor for a long time. And her chest rose and fell with incredible force, and steam like a green gas was seen to come from her mouth. And the woman rose from the floor looking sound, she no longer shrieked nor tore out her hair, rather, she had suddenly regained her health. The woman was believed to have been possessed by a so-called evil spirit, and this spirit had departed from her. So the priests had explained and this eyewitness Paavilainen still believes it to be a certainty even though he is not religious in his views.

(Sortavala. 1936. Juho Hyvärinen 783. –Matti Pulli, b. 1882).

The healing power of the monastery could also be transferred to the bodies of pilgrims who drank its water: there existed a belief that visitors to Solovki monastery who drank from a saltwater pond could subsequently heal other persons by spitting on the afflicted body part:

3a)
At Solovki (*Solovetski*) there is a saltwater pond. People go to drink water from that pond. Whoever has drunk this water has the ability to heal through spitting (...) On whatever day one had drunk the water, it was said that on that day one should spit [in order to heal another person].
(Salmi. 1934–1936. Martti Pelkonen 602. –Malannu Ivaanouna Aalto).

3b)
If a child's jaw is hurting from *tulenlendoi* [=name of supernatural illness caused by fire], a person who has visited Solovki monastery (*Solouhkoih*) can spit on it, and it will heal.
(Salmi. 1940. Martta Pelkonen 367. –Oudottu Feudorantytär Torgouttšu).

Illness was thus a major motivation for pilgrimage. It is interesting to note that the illnesses which motivated pilgrimage were usually different from those which motivated *proškenja* rituals. While *proškenja* rituals were responses to mysterious pain, swelling, dizziness or fatigue, pilgrimage was a response to more crippling or classifiable ailments such as epilepsy, progressive blindness, deafness, the paralysis or crippling of the limbs, and mental illness (which could be interpreted as demonic possession, see also Tilvis 1989:48).

It is clear that some pilgrims made journeys to the sacred center in order to seek a cure there. For example, a substitute pilgrim could make the pilgrimage journey in order to pray for a cure for someone too ill to travel: "when a person was seriously ill and was not capable of going themselves to the monastery, to Valamo or Solovki, then another went in their stead to those sacred places to pray for a cure."[248] In the form of transaction known as *jeäksintä*, however, the potential pilgrim made a promise that he or she

160

Karelians returning from Valamo monastery, 1909. Photo: T.H. Järvi. National Board of Antiquities.

would make a pilgrimage journey *only after* a recovery took place at home (see Kilpeläinen 2000:46).[249] As an informant from Ladoga Karelia explains:

4)
At thirty years of age my eyes became ill, I didn't see God's light, and in those times a neighbor woman also got a swelling disease. And so we decided to make a *jeäksintä* vow (*myö duumaitsimmö, jotta jiäikseitsen*): we would go to Solovki (*Solovetski*) on foot, which is a distance of about 800 versts. We vowed to God that we would visit Solovki on foot, if we recovered in a week's time. Towards the end of the week I began to see again—and my eyes were soon completely healthy, and the neighbor woman recovered as well. Then we left on our promised journey. At the beginning of the trip there weren't any others who were going there, but at the place called Poventsa there were already about 500 persons. Finally we arrived at Solovki monastery, and it was grand—more beautiful and bigger than Valamo, we prayed there every day for two weeks.
(Impilahti. 1938. Mikko Jaakkola PK 29:5258).

In addition, children and even horses which had fallen ill were pledged to monasteries in order that their illnesses might be cured.[250] According to an informant from Kostamus, Archangel Karelia, a common practice was to 'promise' or dedicate a sick child to Solovki monastery for a period of time ranging from days to years (see Virtaranta 1978:246; Kilpeläinen 2000) – if the child recovered, then once having reached adulthood, he or she

161

would make the journey to the monastery and stay there for the promised duration to perform volunteer labour:

5a)
[Collector's note:] In former times it was the custom to make a holy vow to take a child for a specified amount of time to Valamo monastery, so that the illness which had befallen the child would be cured.

"In the old days we called it *jiäksintä*. A child was taken for maybe three years to Valamo. One made the sign of the cross: '*Jumal* [=god, saint, holy icon], give health to him/her in exchange for three years of service!' Whoever was going deaf, whosoever eyes were going bad, then one made the sign of the cross: '*Jumal*, let the ears hear, the eyes see, this much time will work be done at Valamo.'"
(Salmi. 1940. Martta Pelkonen 270. –Tatjana "Hötti").

5b)
...parents believed in the healing power of God and said that if the child recovers, the child would be (at the monastery) for a year or even two, both parents promised. And then when the child was old enough, they took him there, and the child was there without pay, received only food and clothing.
(Simo Peiponen, HYUL 71–54, in Kilpeläinen 2000:243. Parentheses in original).

5c)
I was ill and mother had gone (to Valamo) on a vow (*jiäksinä*). Mother had visited there and then made the promise. Mother came home and said that now I should go there to work for the summer, would I go? I said that I would, one of the neighbor girls was going as well, so why shouldn't I go? We were there for the whole summer until autumn.
(Maria Airaskainen, HYUL 71–12, in Kilpeläinen 2000:243. Parentheses in original).

5d)
When a child was promised to a monastery because a miracle cure had occurred in their case, this was called *jiäksentä*. From then on it was said of the child "this child has been *jiäkseity*". Boy children were promised to Valamo, girl children to Lintula convent.
(Suistamo. 1959. Siiri Oulasmaa E 241:132.-Anna Votkin (formerly Kalevainen), 68 years).

A sick person could also promise that a relative would go and perform unpaid labour in the monastery if he/she recovered:[251]

6)
Jiäksiminen was when someone was gravely ill...and they made (a promise) that if God cures me, I'll send my child or my sister or brother to the monastery to make it up to you or do work, if I recover.
(Maria Airaksinen, HYUL 71–12, in Kilpeläinen 2000:243. Parentheses in original).

The *jeäksintä* vow was made to God, Jesus, or a monastery founder.[252] In cases where persons made a vow through their local chapel to undertake a trip to a distant monastery, the saint they addressed (by speaking to the holy icon representing her) was usually the Virgin Mary. In the *jeäksintä* vow, as in any transaction, there were costs which could be measured in terms of time, energy, and even money.[253] Hannu Kilpeläinen (2000:245–246) points out that in many cases those who made the *jeäksintä* vow went to Valamo monastery to volunteer their labour for a period of time, but if they did not go in order to work, what was emphasized in their recollected narratives was the difficulty or length of the journey. Pilgrims living in Ladoga Karelia often made pilgrimages to the more distant monasteries of Solovki and the Monastery of the Holy Trinity. For instance, the pilgrimage from Soutjärvi in Olonets to the Monastery of the Holy Trinity took approx. 5 days by foot, and the pilgrimage from Soutjärvi to Solovki monastery took two weeks by boat (3–4 days spent at the monastery).[254] The distance from the parish of Salmi in Ladoga Karelia (from which the greatest number of pilgrimage descriptions was recorded) to Solovki monastery was approximately 750 kilometres, and from Salmi to the Monastery of the Holy Trinity, over 100 kilometres (Tilvis 1989:98–99). On longer journeys such as these, people usually travelled by foot, as two informants describe:

7a)
...[t]hey made vows to undertake a long journey from Mantsisaari Island, women went to Olonets (to the Monastery of the Holy Trinity (*Stroitsa*)) and Solovki (*Solovetski*) monastery, and a long way further from Olonets. And they went there on foot. The journey took many weeks, and in the end on bare feet, since shoes naturally wore out before then...They went in groups, went where they had promised to go.
(Salmi. Mikko Peipponen, HYUL 71–163, in Kilpeläinen 2000:245–246. Parentheses in original).

7b)
One had to make the entire trip to those sacred places by foot, all of the land stages by foot. One was allowed to make the water journeys, which had to be made when going to Valamo and Solovki (*Solovetski*), by boat. There wasn't any other choice, since the monasteries could only be reached by water.
(Suistamo. 1959. Siiri Oulasmaa E 246:213–214.–Paraskeeva Makkonen).

Children and farm animals were also dedicated to monasteries and village chapels in order to ensure their future protection from harm and illness. As Pentikäinen (1971:154) describes in the case of Marina Takalo:

Takalo once visited Majoalahti village, having made a vow to the chapel there during the illness of her son Risto. As Takalo understood it, it was precisely this visit to the chapel and this fulfillment of the vow that was responsible for the fact that Risto never fell ill for 22 years thereafter and, among other things, was the only one of the Takalo children to avoid the smallpox epidemic that raged in Oulanka in the 1920s.

People also visited or promised to visit a particular chapel or monastery for reasons other than illness. A pregnant woman could go to ask that her labour would be without difficulty,[255] a man might promise to make the journey if a son was born to his wife,[256] or even, as related by Marina Takalo (b. 1890), a promise could be made to undertake a pilgrimage on the condition that a legal dispute be settled in one's favor.[257] In the description below, one reason for making a *jeäksintä* journey was so that young men and women could win the hearts of those they desired:

8)
In general, those who made longer journeys were pilgrims. They came to pray and bring offerings whenever illness befell one of their family members. Mothers made *jääksiimöinti* (a promise) on behalf of small children. Young maidens did the same on behalf of the young man they loved. Young men who did the same were more rare, but both [young men and women] were found who undertook pilgrimages in order to release their darling either from illness or from the clutches of an alluring rival suitor.
(Salmi. 1941. Raja-Karjalan Sivistysliitto (Manuel Saarinen) 5. –Filip Feudorinso Rovio, b. 1869, parentheses in original).

Having committed a sin was also a reason for making a pilgrimage, but rather than a disruption in one's personal *spiritual relationship with God*, sin was conceived of more in *social* terms, as a wrongful act against other persons or the norms of the community (see Stark 1995).[258] While a person could make a *jeäksintä* vow to atone for a minor sin, legends and stories tell how the unrepentant or those who had committed major sins *were not even allowed access to the monastery*: such "impure" persons had no place at the sacred center.

The sacred center was not easily reached. For example, Valamo and Solovki were islands, and this gave the impression of isolation, as well as requiring the pilgrim to journey by water, often in boats and weather which did not guarantee safe arrival, as Elias Lönnrot vividly recalls in his description of his trip to Valamo in 1828 (1985:138–141). In Lönnrot's description of the boat passage to Valamo, we see the liminal aspect of the journey—the distance between shore and island was such that pilgrims could not sight their goal immediately upon setting sail: after leaving the shore they had to spend time on the open water with no land in sight. But when the monastery island came into view and the boat was docked, one was met with the impressive sight of the many silver-capped domes of the monastery towers (ibid:124–125).

The difficulty of passage to the monastery emphasized the sacred center's image as a place set apart. Because the sacred center represented moral purity, the journey to it was seen as means of testing the purity of each traveller, and of excluding those who did not meet the monastery's exacting standards. Since access was almost always described in terms of crossing water, what we find in the folk narratives is the motif of a floating rock or boat which stayed afloat if carrying passengers without sin, but which began to sink if carrying 'sinful' passengers. For example, monastery founders who gained access to the sacred site by sailing on a flat rock were described as "holy": "[the founder was] a holy man if the rock carried him",[259] "They were said to be so holy that they sailed on a flat rock to the island...",[260] "[They] were so holy that they were even able to row on a flat rock".[261]

In other narratives, however, the founders of Solovki monastery fall short of this ideal, putting them at risk of not reaching the sacred center:

9a)
In former times the old people said that Sroitzza, Valmoi and Solohkoi were brothers. They rowed to Solovki (*Solohkoi*) on a stone raft...Roizza didn't want to live on an island. He said that it's not good to live here, and left...When he left on the stone raft it began to sink so that the water was up to his knees, because he had made a great sin by not wanting to live there. He came back and founded the Monastery of the Holy Trinity (*Stroitsa*)...
(Suistamo. 1936. M. Kähmi 16).

9b)
There were two brothers, the elder's name was Isossim and the younger Savatij. They went across the White Sea on a rock. The younger brother began to wonder, why doesn't the rock sink? Then it began to sink into the water a little. The older brother said: 'What are you thinking, empty-head, of course we'll reach the shore'...[262]
(Porajärvi. 1936. L. Laiho 4022).

The issue of *moral gatekeeping* at the monastery was also expressed in two narratives of a boat which began to sink or go in circles if carrying a 'sinful' passenger to Solovki:

10a)
Anyone who might have stolen a plow or harrow from another person couldn't go to the monastery. In the middle was a body of water called the White Pond. The boat wouldn't take the person, just went in circles or stopped, finally it was necessary to return to the shore. Each person openly told the priest what his or her sins were. Then somebody confessed to the priest: 'I have taken another's plow secretly', or any man who had been with a woman who was not his wife, these were not allowed back on the boat, they had to leave, they didn't reach the monastery.
(Salmi. 1935–40. M. Pelkonen 268. –Tatjana "Hötti", 69 years).

10b)
...Thieves, arsonists and murderers were not carried by the Solovki (*Solovetski*) boat. The boat would begin to sink. Then whoever had done something wrong was made to swear the truth, people were taken off the boat one by one, and one by one they were put back on. Whoever had done something wrong had to confess it, they had to say it, and then they were not allowed to board the boat. The boat could continue the trip when the sinner had left. There was a woman named Hersoi from Pielisjärvi. When she was a girl she had given birth to a child and had killed it. Then, when she went to Solovki it was suddenly discovered. The boat wouldn't take her to Solovki, it began to sink. She had to confess then and there, and she

was turned away, and came home. She didn't get to visit Solovki, she had to go home. There were a lot of people there. From the villages, you see, people came in big groups. It was a long, long time ago. Only our parents remembered it.
(Salmi. 1935–40. Martta Pelkonen 366. – Outti Feudorantytär Torgouttšu).

In yet another story, the informant's grandmother had visited Solovki as a young girl, but "the captain did not allow the grandmother's companion on the boat because she had done naughty things with men" (Tilvis 1989:100). These narratives put the monastery on a plane of moral gatekeeping higher than that of the surrounding culture: unconfessed murderers (as well as thieves and adulterers) could not be readily distinguished from their neighbors in the course of everyday village life—but *within the sacred space* of the monastery they were automatically subjected to a re-examination which separated the guilty from the innocent, demanding a greater accountability with regard to Christian cultural ideals. This idea of moral inspection and exclusivity represented in the folk narratives was instrumental in creating an image of the monastery as a sacred center with higher cultural standards, embodying 'perfection' as opposed to the 'imperfection' of more mundane spaces.

Tales from Valamo also refer to a similar 'weeding out' process and difficulty of entry, again connected to Christian moral ideals. One narrative describes how when the "last archbishop" of Valamo was dying, he only let the "pure of heart" come to receive his blessings (example 11a). In another story, not everyone was allowed into the monastery church of St. Nicholas when it was opened to the public once per year on the 6th of August. "Mikkula" would not allow anyone to enter who was not a "pure Christian" – the sinner would become dizzy and start to tremble, and would have to leave before ever entering the church (example 11b):

11a)
The first priests at Valamo were very godly... People visited [the last archbishop] in order to be blessed, except that not everyone was allowed in to see him. He looked at the visitors and didn't let everyone in. He knew about each visitor, what kind of person he or she was. To the poor he gave money, saying, "Go, may you be blessed by Christ!"—Even the poor he allowed in to see him, if only the heart was pure.
(Salmi. 1935–40. Martta Pelkonen 269).

11b)
Collector: Which of the churches in Valamo was built first?
Informant: The church of St. Nicholas (*Mikkula*) was built first, it is the smallest, it was not allowed to expand. Only once, at the time of *Spuasampäivä* [August 6] are people allowed into that church, only, not everyone can go. St. Nicholas does not let them. Whoever is not a pure Christian begins to get dizzy and tremble, whoever is 'dirty' is not allowed in. They begin to tremble. [One of the informant's companions at the time she was visiting the church] became dizzy, left, and did not get in. One has to have a pure heart and be a cleansed person...
(Salmi. 1935. Martta Pelkonen 108. –Tatjana "Hötti", nee Jaronen).

Some pilgrimage narratives emphasized the gender exclusivity of the monastery by telling how only men were allowed to enter these sites or view them. In some cases these restrictions seem to have been enforced physically, while in other cases they were enforced through narratives which warned of curses, supernatural punishments, and the like. In either case, the aura of exclusivity appears to have been psychologically real:[263]

> 12)
> About four versts from my home was the monastery of St. Adrian of Andrusov (*Antrei Antonski*), it was founded because one holy man, St. Adrian of Andrusov, had been killed and buried there, but the body wouldn't stay underground, instead it rose to the surface no matter how many times it was buried, and so finally a monastery was built, and his bones were put in a casket under glass, and he was considered holy. Men were able to look at it, but not even a single woman: it brought a curse to a woman if she looked at it—*but I looked*, and there behind the glass were teeth, hands and feet, and all the bones.
> (Salmi. 1937. Ulla Mannonen 4716).

A cult of traces

From the point of view of folk narrators, monasteries were places to *observe traces* of God, the saints or the monastery founders, to honor and remember them. A widespread belief among ordinary Karelians held that in the past, Jesus and other holy men and women had walked the earth and left traces of their passing: footprints where they had stepped, and imprints of their bodies in the rock on which they slept. These beliefs may be linked to the notion that in a distant, primordial past, the bedrock was still soft, "soft as bread", retaining the imprint of human feet when walked upon (Krohn 1917: 73–74), as in the following local legends from the Karelian Isthmus:

> 13a)
> When I was young I heard it always said that at the beginning of the world the stones and cliffs were as soft as porridge, and that when people walked on them imprints remained, on the beach of Haltiasaari Island there is a large rock, and on that rock are the Savior's footprints, just as if the bare feet of a large man had been walking there. They are said to have been made when the Savior walked upon the earth and the stone was soft. Then when the stone hardened, the imprints remained.
> (Koivisto. 1937. Ulla Mannonen 2078. –Konsta Rousku, 70 years).

> 13b)
> My late mother always told the story of how, when the Savior walked the earth in former times, the stones became soft, here on Haltiasaari Island there are such stones, in which can clearly be seen the prints of the Savior's toes, on the stone where he walked.
> (Koivisto. 1936. Ulla Mannonen 617. –Anna Katrina Hohman, 67 years).

Much of the folk interest in pilgrimage in Orthodox Karelia can be regarded as a cult of traces. The acts of sacred persons were seen to have been rendered concrete through being imprinted onto the topography, 'set in stone' so to speak, for pilgrims to see and touch. Informants' recollections of such traces can be seen below:

14a)
I've heard that the old people said that Jesus himself visited Valamo. There in the rock one can see the footprints of holy Jesus. They have been preserved there as an eternal reminder of when Jesus visited Valamo.
(Suistamo. Siiri Oulasmaa a) 6209. 1961. –Ivan Ladovaara (Plattonen), 78 years).

14b)
At Valamo was a picture of St. Nicholas (*Miikkula*), he looked like a holy man. On Pyhityssuare Island [=Pyhäsaari] was St. Nicholas' church. The traces of where his head, feet and elbows had been when he lived as a hermit in the rock cleft were all there. I heard that St. Nicholas was a holy man. Women were allowed to enter the church only during the religious festival.
(Salmi. 1957. Silja Rummukainen a)16. –Maria Titov, 50 years).

14c)
...Those stones on which the founders of [Konevits] monastery sailed to the island can be seen in the monastery yard. They are about 1/2 meter long and on each of them there are two big hollows, just where a person's knees would fit. It seems that the men were on the stone for so long that their knees pressed into the stone.
(Pyhäjärvi V.l. (Karelian Isthmus). 1935–36. Yrjö Kinnari KRK 126:256. –Heikki Kuranen)

14d)
...It was still on the shore of the monastery, the stone upon which the holy hermits who had founded the monastery, Sosima and Savvati, travelled sixty versts across the sea to the island.
(Impilahti. 1938. Mikko Jaakkola PK 29:5258).

14e)
...And when more people, forty men, came to [join the founder at the monastery], this holy hermit had fed them all by grounding the flour alone with a hand-held grinding stone, baking the bread alone, enough for all the people, and still having time to do other work. And there are still the imprints where his knees wore into the rock from praying. And he also had time to sleep, since there is the imprint of his head, shoulders, hips and heels, all worn into his stone bed. All of these could be seen at the hermit cottage. The narrator saw them with her own eyes when visiting, and had heard the story.
(Impilahti. Sanni Tiensuu a)102. 1936. – Maria Mäntylä, b. 1882).

Magnificent wealth versus ascetic poverty

The sacred center offered Orthodox pilgrims not only a concentration of cultural ideals relating to 'purity' and traces of the past presence of holy hermits and monastery founders, but also a showcase where other cultural ideals were 'displayed' both visually and through the informational field. Pilgrims went to monasteries in order to see the physical traces they had heard of in monastery legends, but they also went to see and feel and hear the *extremes* of cultural values made tangible. They travelled far to behold all the wondrous things which one could not see in everyday life and which, by their very magnificence, proved that the sacred center was more special, more powerful, more exclusive:

> 15)
> The [monastery] churches were very beautiful. The icons were as tall as a man, candles were lit and bells were rung...
> (Vieljärvi. 1947. Artturi Railonsala 3397. –Anni Agafonov, b. 1870).

The treasures of Valamo, for example, included delicately crafted candelabras and censers, gold Eucharistic vessels, gilded silver hand crosses and silver candle stands which were displayed in a highly visible manner to pilgrims and visitors. Church interiors were lavish with richly decorated altars, iconostases and doors, and prime examples of this splendor were the magnificent gilded sarcophagi of Sergius and Herman in the lower church (Lainio & Kohonen 1983).

A good description of the splendor of Valamo as it appeared to an outside observer can be found from the travel journal of Elias Lönnrot, in which he describes the monastery church interior as it appeared to him for the first time in 1828:

> The afternoon mass had now begun, and I went to the church. My awe was great when I saw all of the beauty which opened up in front of me. The walls were completely covered with pictures, and these had gold- and silver-plated frames. In the same way the columns and ceiling arches were gilded and silvered. Here and there jewels sparkled in gold and silver settings. Wherever the eye roamed, it saw only gold and silver as well as the aforementioned paintings which depicted events from the Old and New Testaments and displayed the likenesses of famous saints (Lönnrot 1985: 132–33).

The mystique of monastery wealth is also depiced in numerous tales of hidden monastery treasure (icons, church bells, candlesticks and chalices) walled up inside a monk's cell, submerged in a lake, or buried in a pit of unknown location:[264]

> 16a)
> One old man named Hilkku had told the narrator (...) that he had lived the major part of his life at Valamo monastery, and that he had heard from the old monks at the monastery that in former times the treasures of Valamo

were hidden inside a monk's cell, which had been walled-up and made unnoticeable from the outside, and there the treasures are still today, nor do the present monks know in which place or in which building this treasure room is located.
(Valamo. 1936. Pekka Pohjanvalo 133. – Jaakko Ahokas, 75 years).

16b)
In ancient times at the beginning of Christianity there was a monastery on this hill. This monastery was called 'Kelja monastery', from which has come the name Kelivaara. This monastery was built by two holy men, but it is no longer known who they were or when they founded it... During peace times the monastery grew larger and richer and there were great treasures there: icons of God and the holy hermits, church bells of great value, candlesticks and chalices for communion...[At the arrival of enemy soldiers] the monks hurriedly put all of the riches of the monastery into a large sack and dug a great hole in the earth, burying the riches in the hole...After having covered up the hole the head monk read an incantation, but it is not known what kind, and then 'locked' it with a talisman, with which they could retrieve the treasure from the ground in times of peace...
(Impilahti. 1935. Juho Kuronen KRK 143:1).

The ideals showcased for the folk pilgrim by the sacred center could be contradictory, however, for *poverty* and *simplicity* were also part of the image of the monasteries. These ideals were most clearly expressed in the tradition of holy hermits who inhabited solitary hermits' huts in remote locations such as on the islands surrounding the main monasteries, or holy hermits who began their religious calling as monks but later left the monastery to live a solitary existence in the wilderness. Asceticism and the renunciation of worldly wealth are ideals which also show up in folk *legends* and *narratives* concerning monastery founders and holy hermits who survived on nothing more than bread and water:[265]

17a)
...They went to the island [Valamo] and there they made themselves a cave in the earth. There they prayed to the Creator. They didn't have any food there, no water, not even fire. They were just there in the cave in the earth. Nobody there came to visit them, nor did anyone know that there was somebody there. They dedicated themselves to God's will there and the Holy Spirit went to give them food. That's how they survived. And they didn't want anything more than water and bread, and some salt...
(Aunus > Salmi. 1938. J. Hautala and L. Simonsuuri SKSÄ A 133, in Järvinen 1981:119).

17b)
...In the beginning their food was berries from the forest, their bed the bare earth and their pillow a stone. Finally some fishermen found them and brought them some seeds to plant grain. Sergei and Herman began to cultivate a little land. They ground the grain with hand mills. The Russian Karelian refugee said that these stories really happened.
(Suojärvi. 1936. J. Koivunen KT 128:8).

17c)

Adrian of Andrusov (*Antrei Antrayski*) was a hermit, a holy man, who lived in the woods, tortured himself with fasting and dedicated his life to worshipping God...
(Salmi. 1936. Ulla Manonen 1135).

In one legend text, a figure known in Karelia as *Oleks Boozei* (referring to St. Alexis, a saint who gave up a life of wealth in 4th-century Rome), appears as the founder of "Soluskoi" (=Solovki) monastery. This text recounts how Oleks Boozei gave to the poor all the 'best foods' brought to him and was content to eat food of poor quality and drink dirty washing water. In the same text, Oleks Boozei leaves behind a life of wealth and sails on a stone raft to a distant shore, where he meets two holy hermits:

17d)

...Having reached the dwelling place of the holy hermits, Oleks tried to join them, but the holy hermits told him that they followed a dietary regimen in which they did not even eat fish. When they badly wanted to eat fish, they chewed on pieces of wood shaved from the wall, but otherwise they ate only bread, water and salt. Nonetheless, Oleksei told them that they had one form of nourishment too many, and that in order to be real holy hermits, they should eat only two kinds of food. Then the men began to think hard what they would give up, water? But one can't get by without water, one needs water more often than bread. But if one gives up bread, one soon dies of hunger. Nor can one get by without salt, reflected the holy hermits, and in such contemplation three years went by...
(Suistamo and Salmi. 1936. Eino Toiviainen 175).

Another belief legend from Olonets Karelia emphasizes how monastery figures who did not lead holy or ascetic lives had no place at the sacred center. In this story, the abbot of an unnamed monastery summons a wise old hermit (who rides a bear and performs miracles) in order to criticize him for eating meat. In the course of his visit, the hermit demonstrates that the abbot too, eats meat, that he has fathered a child, blamed another, and has bribed the child's mother to cover his misdeed. The abbot is dismissed and the position offered to the hermit who refuses it and returns to the forest.[266]

The dual sacred – Comparing the two sacred complexes

Competition, renunciation and territoriality: two complexes, different ethics

Of the various ideals held by the rural populace of Orthodox Karelia in the late 19th and early 20th centuries, two which are of central importance for the present analysis have been identified by Teuvo Laitila (1995). The first, exchange (*vaihto*), characterized the relationship between Christian saints and the human farming community. The second, renunciation (*luopuminen*), characterized the activities of monasteries and holy hermits. Renunciation involved "the respect for nature and restraint from destruction and exploitation of nature which was associated with the tradition of reclusion in the wilderness and was largely unconscious" (ibid:88). Laitila continues:

> In spiritual struggle, the ideal was renunciation or frugality. For this reason the 'good', what the holy hermit could exchange with nature, was for him limited to only what was absolutely necessary, the goal was to function so that even from a 'limited good', some surplus would remain. The holy hermit renounced worldly things in order to accumulate spiritual riches. For this reason, competition did not arise over the riches of nature (Laitila 1995:89).

The value of these observations for the present study is that Laitila identifies an important way in which the ideals attributed to monasteries (*sacred centres*) differed from those upheld in the relationship between human community, local saints and the wilderness (*sacred boundaries*). The peasant-wilderness relationship in the sacred boundaries complex was one of tension and competition over scarce resources. Because of this, it was also closely interwoven with the 'image of limited good' in which one party's gain was seen as another's loss, and in which a careful equilibrium in resource distribution was the only way to avoid disparity and crisis. On the other hand, it appears that the human-monastery relationship functioned *outside* this model of resource competition and 'limited good'. Both the *asceticism* practiced at the monastery and its *extravagant riches* represented a rejection of the image of 'limited good'. Ascetic monks rejected even their own share of this 'good' when they lived in abject poverty and chose to consume the minimal amount of resources required for survival, giving up even the few comforts of peasant life that were within reach of all able-bodied rural folk.

Monastery ascetics were not in competition with peasants or the wilderness nature for resources, and therefore did not exist in the same context of tensions between reciprocity and exploitation as did the farming and herding community.

This contrast between these two types of community – peasant versus monastic – can be seen, for example, in stories of the simple, ascetic lifestyle of self-denial practiced by holy hermits and monastery founders on the one hand, and on the other, folk beliefs and anecdotes regarding local saints venerated by peasants who were thought to have a fondness for rich foods such as flour, milk and butter. The latter paint a picture of these saints as greedy, wanting *more* than their fair share. For example, one informant from Salmi told how the miller of her village had claimed (in jest?) that St. Nicholas (*Mikkula*) himself had stolen grain, since it could be seen from his icon that he had bits of flour on his beard.[267] According to an article in the periodical *Laatokka* from 1929, Saint Blaise was called "Milk Blaise" because, according to legend, he was too fond of milk and butter and was for that reason so fat (Tilvis 1989:72). Such images, I suggest, arose from tensions inherent in the annual exchanges between peasants and saints, in which peasants were compelled to give saints the agricultural products of their labours (especially wool and butter) in order to receive prosperity and protection from them.

Monasteries which displayed their conspicuous wealth, on the other hand, were clearly not striving for the economic equilibrium that limited the socio-economic ambitions of peasant farmers. The idea that the monastery lay outside the communal system of 'limited good' is also supported by the fact that the wealth of Valamo monastery was described in local legends as having been provided by rich pilgrims or Czars living in more distant parts of Russia rather than accumulated at the expense of the surrounding peasant community. In other words, the monastery's surplus riches were *acquired from 'outside' the closed system of the peasant community,* rather than subtracted from the peasant's own share of limited good (cf. Foster 1965:306–309):

> 1a)
> ...and when other Czars came [to the throne], they started to favor monasteries and gave them donations, so that they grew rich...
> (Archangel Karelia (Makslahti). 1937. Ulla Mannonen 4798. –Aki Melik, 50 years, from Kemi).

> 1b)
> ...Their reputation as holy men began to spread, and rich pilgrims from faraway places began to visit them and left money with the holy men, thereby receiving forgiveness for their sins. And thus did the monastery begin to grow from insignificant beginnings and gradually broadened into a magnificent institution.
> (Sortavala. 1935. Juho Hyvärinen KRK 141:203).

Several folk informants, in fact, pointed out that it was namely Russian pilgrims from outside Karelia who sent large donations to Valamo monastery upon returning home. By contrast, Karelian pilgrims from nearby Salmi parish gave only small gifts: "We were a poor people, we had nothing more than small gifts to give". Such gifts included especially homemade textiles: table cloths, silk scarves and ceremonial towels to decorate the monastery churches and chapels (Tilvis 1989:68).

The fact that monastery founders and holy hermits were seen to have *functioned outside the system of exchange and competition with the wilderness* can also be seen from legends which depict encounters between monks or holy hermits and the forest wilderness. These encounters were described as peaceful, lacking the inherent tension and threat of danger found in peasant-wilderness relations. While legends stress the fact that the wilderness was always present on the edges of the sacred center, the monastery and its holy hermits did not need to engage in threats or negotiations with it. A hermit at Valamo monastery named Nikon († 1822), for instance, was said to have spent years in a cave full of snakes, living in harmony with them (Laitila 1995:91). A legend recorded from Olonets Karelia tells how a holy child, Arsha, grew up to be the Abbot and forced a wild bear to be a servant of the monastery,[268] while another from the same parish recounts how an elderly holy hermit living in the forest wilderness was able to summon a bear which came peacefully and allowed itself to be ridden.[269] Laitila (1995:91–92) also addresses this topic:

> This apocalyptic peace is also encountered in the forests of Russia and Karelia. It is said of the holy hermit Adrian of Andrusov, who apparently lived at the turn of the 16th and 17th centuries, that his life as a recluse began when a bear guided him to the cottage of St. Alexander of Svir. According to the bibliography of Eleasar, who was a hermit monk living in Solovki at the beginning of the 1600s, "forest animals and seabirds were his daily friends". The same is said of certain holy hermits of Valamo at the beginning of the 1900s.

Icons, illness and healing

We have seen in the foregoing how sacred *boundary* agents occupying local forests, cemeteries and chapels were proprietary agents considered to be easily angered. The dead in the cemetery and the spirits of forest, water and earth defended their territory by infecting with *nenä* illness those who either violated their boundaries or who did not show them proper respect. It is significant that sacred agents associated with monasteries (ascetics, founders, God and Jesus), on the other hand, did not 'own' or 'occupy' space, time, or any other privileges which they defended with penalties. Because they had no boundaries which could be violated in the same way as those of nature spirits and the dead, they had no need to infect with *nenä* illnesses. No taboos existed ensuring proper behavior towards these sacred monastery agents, no times when it was dangerous to walk past a monastery site. Instead of infecting with illness, monastery agents were responsible for the *healing* of illness. We can, in fact, regard the activities of wilderness agents and monastery agents as occupying two opposite ends of a continuum with respect to illness and healing: at one end of the continuum, wilderness agents were capable of infecting with supernatural illness, they were thought to be easily angered and therefore had to placated through the giving of gifts. At the other end of the continuum, monastery agents were seen not to cause illness but rather to cure it, they were not seen to become angry, and were therefore not given offerings.

When we consider that the divine figures of Christianity (Christ, the Virgin Mary and the saints) were believed in Orthodox Karelian folk religion to exist concretely in the holy icons which represented them, we can see the aforementioned continuum expressed in the folk beliefs surrounding *holy icons*. A curious attribute of Orthodox icons located in homes and local village chapels was the fact that they, like the forest, water, wind, and so forth, were thought to infect with *nenä* illness (*obrazanenä*):

2)
Obrazanenä
=Illness caused by a holy icon (from offending a holy icon). For example, "I had a toothache, went to the *tietäjä*. Oleši's wife put water in a ladle and lowered stones into it, and looked at the water – a white foam rose, rose, from the stones, then the woman said: 'the anger of the holy icons has come down on you, you have splashed water while combing your hair, the *nenä* from the holy icons (*obrazannenit*) has been created now. '[I went to the icon and said]: 'St. Nicholas, merciful one, if I have done something stupid, turned the wrong way, forgive Sasha, a servant of God, a Christian, take away the pain at once, the aches this day, put the pains under a pain-stone, the aches under a pillar; come to eat and drink with me. (A piece of unleavened bread is on top of the icon while praying). Then I ate the bread at the foot of the icon.'Oleši's wife cured my *obrazannenä*.When the dead are angry, then the foam goes along this way, but when an icon is angry, then the foam rises upwards.".
(Säämäjärvi. 1928–9. E.V. Ahtia. Karelian Lexical Archives. Parentheses in original)

As an article entitled "Vestiges of magic belief in Border Karelia" appearing in the periodical *Laatokka* in 1906 explains:

Those old holy icons, how capricious they are. They have the power to cause pain in the stomach or head, to a wound or elsewhere, but they are especially apt to cause toothache. And the respect with which they are treated is mingled with fear. When one suspects that a holy icon has become angry (*niipustunut*), then one goes to make *proškenja* (ask for forgiveness)…If doctors must work hard to cure a deeply rooted disease, then neither does one easily recover from the torments of a holy icon (Tilvis 1989:53, parentheses in original).

Anni Lehtonen from Archangel Karelia explained to folklore collector Samuli Paulaharju that "the holy icons (*jumalit*) infect if you walk past them and do not make the sign of the cross, and think: 'perhaps I will be infected from them'. If you go to church after giving birth before six weeks have

The chapel (tsasouna) *and iconostasis of Hautavaara village, Suojärvi, 1934. Kuva: T. Itkonen. National Board of Antiquities.*

passed, then you will also be infected. If a holy icon is in a chilly room, then take it away. One must not leave a holy icon in a cold room. One sees in a dream, if holy icons have infected."[270] Another informant from Ladoga Karelia explained: "if the holy icons have been angered, one must light a taper and make the sign of the cross and say 'Savior in Heaven forgive me' (if the icon depicts some other saint than the Savior, one says the name of the saint when asking forgiveness)."[271]

If the prototypical agents of *nenä* infection in Orthodox Karelian tradition were the forest nature and the dead, then what explains the fact that holy icons were also seen to have the capacity to cause *nenä* illness? Here it may be useful to survey the properties attributed to holy icons in three primary locations: local chapels, famous chapels and monasteries. Icons located in ordinary village chapels never cured illnesses – they *only* infected (see example 3 below). Holy icons located in monasteries, by contrast, had potential *healing* powers, but never infected with *nenä* illness. Famous shrines which had started out as local chapels but by the late 19th century had become well-known pilgrimage sites such as those at Orusjärvi, Palojärvi or Kinnermäki can be seen as occupying a symbolic location midway between the local community (sacred boundaries complex) and the monastery (sacred centers complex). Icons located in these shrines could both infect *and* heal (examples 4a–b). Some icons specialized in curing toothaches, others healed eye diseases, etc.:

3)

"Something extra" [=dynamistic force] could easily come from a holy icon (*obraza*). For example if one walked past the chapel in Suonaa village without making the sign of the cross, the holy icon immediately became angry. In order to make amends, one had to take food and clothing, for example a scarf or an embroidered towel (*käsipaikka*).

If the illness has come from an icon, the asking of forgiveness always took place early in the morning in front of the icon...

(Tulomajärvi. 1943. Helmi Helminen 2386–7. –Solomanida Petrov, b. 1862).

4a)

The chapel in Palojärvi village is on an island, and St. Sreitenny the Provider cures people of toothache. He is good for the teeth. When one is slightly infected (*nenävyybi*) then one makes a vow to him (*jiäksitäh*), pays him a visit. One lights a taper, as expensive as one can afford, and he is placated. Then one recites: "St. Sreitenny, provider, help me, release me, save me!" There are also other icons there too. One is St. Nicholas, then there is St. Elijah, and then the Virgin Mary, then there is the "tooth-saint" (*hammazjumal*), I don't recall his name, he is in the entryway, above the chapel door, on top of the lintel...

There was a funeral at Palojärvi cemetery inside the chapel (*tšasouna*). A female relative of the narrator (probably her brother's wife) was in the cemetery. Because there were so many people, she could not enter the chapel. The "tšasounu" became angry and caused her tooth to ache. The patient recovered after making a holy vow to visit the chapel and fulfilling her promise.[272]

(Salmi. 1935. Martta Pelkonen 362–363. –Outti or Oudottu Feurdorantytär Torgouttšu, nee Lammas. Parentheses in original).

4b)

The village chapel of the "Ancient Mother of Christ" is the *tšasouna* in Kinnermäki village, Vieljärvi parish. An icon made its way there in a soldier's pack. At the intersection of three roads there was a spruce grove, like there is now. People put the icon on a cross there in the crossroads. Although it was taken elsewhere, the icon always returned to the crossroads. A chapel was built which could not be destroyed...people take embroidered towels (*käšpaikat*), wool, etc. to the Kinnermäki chapel. Even today people take these offerings. Eye diseases are cured when people visit Kinnermäki chapel.

(Tulomajärvi. 1944. Helmi Helminen 2235. –Jevdokia Kohlojev, b. 1874).

To summarize, while holy icons in the local village chapel infected with illness, icons in the monasteries did not. I suggest that if we were to plot out the geographical domains of local folk religious rites (sacred boundaries complex) alongside the monasteries' spheres of influence and activity (sacred centers complex), then where these two domains overlapped would be the very boundary between icons which infected and those which healed. The more closely an icon was associated with the notion of the sacred center, the more pronounced its role in healing, signifying the purity (health) of the center as opposed to the impurity (illness, pollution) of the more local periphery. The closer it was to local farms and communities struggling to delineate symbolic boundaries, the more capacity it was thought to have for causing *nenä* illness. These differences are summarized in the table below:

	holy icons infect with nenä-illness	holy icons cure illness
icons in local village chapel	YES	NO
icons in famous chapels	YES	YES
icons in monasteries	NO	YES

Not only holy icons themselves, but also the village chapels (*tsasounas*) which housed these icons were seen to be capable of infecting with *nenä-illness*. In some cases, the village chapel could be seen as the physical representation of a saint or a holy icon reinterpreted as a saint (see example 5a, below), but in some cases the chapel itself was personified without any explicit reference to a Christian figure (example 4a, 5b):

5a)
The village chapel was build in honor of St. Kasan [The Kazan icon of the Mother of God], and it was also the name of a holy festival day....On that day the villagers went to the chapel in the morning in a festive mood, and they took gifts with them for Kasan which were then given to the poor, in that way Kasan was venerated. It was believed that if one did not venerate Kasan then it could become angry and offended, some sort of mishap could occur or an illness, and if that happened, then one went immediately to a *tietäjä* to divine whether the village chapel had taken offence or not. If the *tietäjä* said that yes, it has taken offence, then they went right away to the chapel to light a candle and gifts were brought so that the saint would be appeased and the person would recover...In the same way if someone fell ill then the older people said that now it has become angry, there's nothing else to do but go quickly to the village chapel and summon the saint and light a taper and take a gift of wool or something else when asking for forgiveness, and probably the saint will be appeased by that. I heard about, and even saw with my own eyes when one female cousin had a toothache which gave her no peace, and so her grandmother told her to walk past the chapel and "make the sign of the cross, for the boy saint is angry and will not leave until you have asked for forgiveness"...
(Suojärvi. 1941. Viktor Hankka 88).

5b)
There was a village chapel (*tšasouna*) in Hutakka village, people brought money to it. Some small boys had their eye on the money and took it. One small boy took the money home and told his mother "I took it from the *tšasouna*." His mother said, "take it back, you will fall ill", but the boy did not obey her, and he became so ill with boils and scabs that he nearly died. The money was taken back to the *tšasouna* and the boy recovered and is still alive to this day.
(Suistamo. 1939. Jouko Hautala 986. – Mikko Majuri, approx. 65 years).

A cemetery, village chapel and site of sacrificial festivals in former times on Mantsinsaari Island, Ladoga Karelia. Finnish Literature Society.

One text told of a village chapel becoming angry and afflicting its human caretaker after the caretaker kept it locked following a theft of money from the offering box. The informant explained that it was not the theft itself which aroused the chapel's anger, but the fact it had been closed to the public when it was supposed to have remained always open.[273] In another example from Ladoga Karelia, a boy was said to have ignored the warnings of other boys and picked raspberries from inside the fence surrounding the village chapel, after which his arms and legs cramped up: "an infection had come from the *tsasouna*."[274]

Infection from local chapels may be explained in part by the fact that village chapels were usually built on or next to the site of a former sacred grove, a cemetery, or a pre-Christian sacred object such as a sacrificial stone:[275]

> 6)
> When Arsenii Konets [=St. Arsenius of Konevits] founded a monastery on Kono Island [=Konevitsa Island], the first thing he did was purge the island of evil spirits, among other things. Over there on "Horse Rock" there lived at that time a demon …on the rock was built a shrine, a *tsasouna*. (Sortavala. 1938. Juho Saikkonen KT 136:94).

Erecting a church or chapel on the site of a pre-Christian object of devotion to appropriate it for Christianity has been a strategy utilized throughout Christian Europe (Nolan & Nolan 1992:291–335; Kilpeläinen 2000:125). Lukkarinen (1918:68) described this process in Archangel Karelia:

> This is one method typical of the Russian priesthood (...) when it did not dare to condemn an earlier religious practice of the populace outright, nor scorn its pagan holy places, it devised a clever compromise. It allowed all of these to remain otherwise as before, but gave them Christian names and added to them their own symbols and insignias. Thus have these valuable objects of research been rescued and preserved for science up to the present day.

From the Church's point of view, the site was now 'sanitized' while still retaining its specialness, its sacrality in the eyes of the laity. In other words, village chapels in Orthodox Karelia continued to signal a particular location in the landscape that was supposed to remain recognizeable as 'special' or 'different'.

At one level, therefore, I suggest that notions regarding the infecting *väki* force of the both the local *tsasouna* and its icons were derived from associations with former sacred groves and/or graveyards, which themselves were earlier markers of boundaries between 'this world' and the 'other side'. Christian chapels built on these sites would have then 'absorbed' the symbolic non-growth value associated with the wilderness and cemetery, as well as the taboos against offending them or trespassing on their territory. It is significant that in descriptions of healing icons in better-known chapels, on the other hand, informants sometimes stated that the chapel marked *not* the site of a cemetery or sacred grove but the final resting place chosen by a 'wandering icon' (example 4b above).

Since both sacred boundary agents and sacred monastery agents were clearly "place-bound" agents, why is it that only sacred *boundary* agents (in this case represented in local holy icons) reacted with anger to violation of their territory, and defended that territory through *nenä* infection? Ultimately, I suggest, the infecting *väki* force of sacred boundary agents derived from their role in alerting, warning or signalling threats to the boundaries that were vital to cultural classification. The fact that sacred boundary agents operated within the limited scope of boundary zones while sacred monastery agents fulfilled a broader moral function is best illustrated through a closer look at sacred agents access to strategic information, in other words, how much these agents were thought to know in advance about the exchange situation and the human participants involved.

Sacred agents and access to strategic information

Scholars in the cognitive study of religion have pointed out that humans are cognitively equipped to posit not only agents but socially-relevant agents on the basis of very little evidence, and that these supernatural agents are represented as 'interested parties' in moral choices. 'Social relevance' here refers to the information that humans need in order to engage productively and meaningfully in social interaction, and ultimately to benefit from that interaction. According to Pascal Boyer (forthcoming), such information includes that which is needed to monitor social exchange, for instance finding out who is co-operating with whom, under what circumstances, as well as punishing cheaters and avoiding people who fail to punish cheaters in order to understand other people's actions and motives, build and maintain social hierarchies, construct coalitions and so forth.

From the individual's perspective, socially-relevant information is *strategic* information, and as a rule, given our embodied state and limited information-processing capacity, humans have only partial access to such information. Supernatural agents important for religious belief, on the other hand, are implicitly construed as *perfect access agents* who can be everywhere at once and know everything, including human intentions and thoughts (Boyer 2000). Thus divine agents are beings which have full access to important information regarding human-human and human-divine interaction, even if such attributes are never verbalized, whereas humans, who are not all-seeing, cannot read the minds of other humans, and cannot be in more than one place at one time, have only partial access.

This point has particular bearing on the division of labour between sacred agents in the sacred *boundaries* complex and those in the sacred *centers* complex. The characterization of sacred agents as having full access to strategic information is applicable only to sacred monastery agents (God, Jesus, monastery founders). These supernatural agents were believed to know whether a pilgrim's heart was 'pure' or housed some hidden sin, with sinners being subsequently prevented from entering the monastery. Sacred boundary agents, on the other hand, do not seem to have operated in the same way. There is nothing in the Orthodox Karelian material to suggest that nature spirits, the dead or local saints ever had *full* access to strategic information. On the contrary, there is much to suggest that these agents were construed as having only limited access to important knowledge regarding human-divine relations.

According to informants' descriptions, nature spirits, the dead, and local saints had knowledge only of their own limited sphere of influence, of disturbances within or violations of that sphere's boundary. Sacred boundary agents were not interested in whether a person led a sinful life, but rather whether that person had behaved properly when in the boundary zone or had responded to the sacred agent with the appropriate ritual greeting or offering. The focus, therefore, was not on the inner moral purity of the human supplicant, but on his or her outward behavior. Sacred boundary agents appear to have needed certain signals from humans to tell them that rituals of interaction and communication were about to begin. Among these signals were verbal forms of greeting and address, as well as bowing. Without them, sacred boundary agents were thought to not recognize an attempt at ritual communication.

Sacred boundary agents were addressed through elaborate rituals of communication in which pains were taken to supply them with all relevant information. For instance, it is clear from descriptions that performers of *proškenja* rites felt it necessary to inform the dead person or nature spirit of the reason for performing the rite, or why the forest was being bound. Persons who bound the forest in Archangel Karelia, for instance, could stage a ritual dialogue for the forest spirit's benefit (see also Part I, example 29b):

7)
...When binding, one person asks the other: "what are you doing?" He says: "I am hanging the forest spirit's (*piru*) son." The questioner goes away a short distance, then comes again and asks: "what are you doing?" The one who carries out [the binding] says: "I am hanging the forest spirit's son, since it will not give back my cow." The same is done a third time and then the [bound saplings] are left where they are...
(SKVR I₄:1474. Kiisjoki. 1888. – Mikittä Kontulaine).[276]

Furthermore, in *proškenja* rites the terms of agreement had to be spelled out verbally: gifts were not simply left for sacred agents, rather, sacred agents were told specifically that the gifts were intended for *them*, and were further told what the giver expected in return: health. In order to communicate with sacred boundary agents, the performer of the rite had to go to the site of the infection itself or stand at the boundary between the farm and forest: a likely explanation is that otherwise the sacred boundary agent would not have understood that the channels of communication were being opened between "this world" and the "other side". The healer also had to bring to the ritual site either the patient him/herself or an article of the patient's clothing so that the nature spirit or dead person could identify the suffering party correctly and recall the incident in question. Finally, a witness needed to be present so the place spirits or the dead could trust that the supplicant was speaking in good faith and would henceforth uphold the agreement not to disturb the sacred agent in the future.[277] For instance, in a formula addressed to the forest spirit during a *proškenja* rite, the speaker could say: "if you don't otherwise believe me, over there is a witness" (the witness stood further back).[278] This "witness" could be another person or, if none were available, an object resembling a person "standing upright" (see pp.102–105) such as a walking stick, sometimes with a hat placed on top.[279] This last detail suggests that that the symbolic gesture of a witness "standing up straight" was significant, even if the sacred agent was not necessarily expected to know the difference between a living human and its look-alike substitute.

It is also interesting that not all of the nature spirits in a 'community' of such beings were expected to have access to the same strategic knowledge: only one nature spirit in the "other" community might possess relevant knowledge of the *nenä* infection in question, for instance, while the rest were expected to know nothing of it (see Part I, example 50).

When we contrast this ritual behavior with communication between humans and sacred monastery agents, it is clear that in the latter case, pilgrims had no need for the same elaborate measures : indeed most descriptions of *jeäksintä* make no specific mention of such communication at all. Ritualized greetings and a formal statement of the terms of the agreement, such as are found in *proškenja* incantations, were not used when making a *jeäksintä* vow or embarking on a pilgrimage, nor were any symbolic gestures or gifts needed. *Jeäksintä* vows required no "witnesses" to the promise being made.

Boyer (forthcoming) suggests that one function of supernatural agents in religion is to help express or represent vague moral feelings, intuitions or principles. These feelings arise from our cognitive makeup as social organisms, but regarding them as the viewpoint of supernatural agents, "what the ancestors think I did", or "how God feels about what I did" helps people to represent these principles to themselves more easily, at the same time allowing them to generate new inferences about them. The supernatural agents fulfilling this function would, Boyer explains, need to have full access to strategic information. Although religion is obviously a much more complex universe of meaning than the brief outline of Boyer's argumentation presented here would suggest, the concept of access to strategic information is useful because it draws attention to the different ways in which sacred agents can be construed and raises questions concerning the social and cultural functions of these agents.

Clearly, sacred boundary agents in Orthodox Karelian folk belief were not seen to have full access to strategic information regarding their relations with humans. In fact, they appear to have had no information at all beyond the fact that the boundary between their territory (the 'other world') and human territory was under threat, or had been violated. Their cognitive and cultural function, therefore, seems to have been different from that of sacred monastery agents. Rather than representing moral values concerning "purity" or "sinfulness", their function was to raise the alarm whenever cognitive boundaries vital to the cultural Order were threatened. Instead of guarding concepts of morality, they guarded the margins of classification which underlay society's conception of itself.

Sacred time, place, and bodily movement

In addition to the differences outlined above, the two sacred complexes hypothesized in this study also diverged in how they utilized and represented *time* and *space*. In the *sacred boundaries* complex, *time* was represented as repetitive and cyclic rather than anchored in any point in the past. In this ritual complex, the agreements which legitimized the social contract with the wilderness (and thus ensured social continuity) were *recreated* at *intervals*. In the annual cycle of the peasant and pastoralist, two different kinds of ritualized time, summer and winter, alternated with each other. The sacred times with respect to these seasons were the liminal days which marked the boundaries between them, for example St. George's Day (*Jyrki*) and The Day of the Intercession (*Pokrova*). Similarly, in relations with the dead, ritual days for reintegrating the dead back into the community (memorial feasts, holidays for honoring the dead) alternated with everyday time in which strict boundaries were maintained between the dead and the living. Because time was continuously remade, there was no ritually significant past, no mythic origins or collective memory of important events relevant to the boundary between community and wilderness. The saints who watched over the cattle and helped the grain to grow were generally not believed to have left physical traces indicating a past presence on the

186

cultural landscape, traces which could be seen and touched. Ritual knowledge necessary for the continuation of the human-wilderness ritual relationship was located *not in collective memory of specific events* but in the interpretations of ritual specialists who continually restyled and interpreted this knowledge through divination and *proškenja* rituals.

In contrast to this, much of the Karelian folk interest in *pilgrimage* can be regarded as a cult of traces, as was discussed in Part II. These traces referred back to the monasteries' mythic beginnings. The practice of visiting such concrete traces in the landscape surrounding the monastery or sacred site was usually tied to belief legends which circulated throughout the communities of Orthodox Karelia (such as example 8 below) and were told to pilgrims at the sacred site, who then conveyed the tales to others upon returning home:

> 8)
> The story tells that the founders of Valamo monastery, Sergei and Herman, had sailed to Valamo archipelago on a rock and then founded the monastery there, and I have heard that the rock is somewhere preserved for the public to see, somewhere on an island called 'Pyhäsaari' at Valamo.
> (Salmi. 1935–6. Pekka Pohjanvalo KRK 151:143. –Miina Ahokas, 65 years).

Narratives regarding sacred 'traces' are important because they had the potential to affect how the pilgrim perceived and experienced the sacred site: they influenced what the pilgrim considered noteworthy, and what was passed over unnoticed (see Stark 1995; Bowman 1991). When persons moved about the monastery landscape, going from place to place, their activities were guided by what they had heard concerning the histories and features of various sites. This link between legend and action is exemplified, for example, in the following account:

> 9)
> Near the city of Aunus is the Monastery of the Holy Trinity (*Stroitsa*): "Jesus built the monastery" it is said. Nearby there are chapels built on the places where Jesus sat down to rest. When the narrator was young and left with a few others to Stroitsa monastery, their parents advised them: "Don't sit to rest anywhere else on the journey—you should sit only on those stones where Jesus sat", which were in the vicinity of the crosses and chapels.
> (Tulemajärvi. 1938. Maija Juvas 240).

According to James Preston (1992:41), sacred traces are "the phenomenon of an invisible reality made visible in the world." People transform and make culturally intelligible the spaces they occupy, both through motion (tracing patterns through walking, for instance) and by ascribing meaning (giving names to and telling stories about various points in the landscape). Imbuing spaces with memory and emotion, fragments of knowledge that evoke spirits of the past is one way for ordinary persons to appropriate these spaces, modifying the visual impression which the official institution seeks to create and thus subverting official power (see De Certeau 1984:108; Motz

1998:342). "Haunted places", as Michel De Certeau (1984:108) points out, "are the only ones people can live in". In Orthodox Karelian folk discourse on monasteries, the memories affixed to the landscape by the unschooled laity were *mythical* memories regarding founders and hermits thought to have lived in some 'original' time, while *official* tales and legends surrounding the monasteries and published in the Finnish Orthodox periodical *Aamun Koitto*, for example, dealt with *historical* figures and events which reinforced the political legitimacy and authority of the monastery (see Stark 1995, 1997).

Although thousands of lay pilgrims each year attended the annual festivals which followed the official Church calendar, according to their own narratives the *time which appears to have held the most ritual significance for them* was not cyclic or seasonal but was rather (1) anchored in the ancient, mythical past, and (2) organized around personal illness. This can be seen from the informational field surrounding pilgrimage. The common past shared by pilgrims and the monastery was located in the physical environment, in holy icons or physical traces which were *collectively* interpreted and restyled through the narratives, legends and anecdotes (see Stark 1995). The sacred center represented social continuity in terms of a 'beginning' time which was depicted in legends and folk beliefs concerning the supernatural events surrounding the monastery founders. Sacred time in *both* the sacred boundaries and sacred centers complexes enhanced the perception of social continuity, but in different ways. In the former complex, this perception of social continuity was heightened through cyclic and ritual re-creation, and in the latter, through collective participation in the remembering of events which took place in a mythical, primordial 'beginning' time.

Notions of *space* were also different in the two sacred complexes. Space in the *sacred boundaries* complex was neither concrete nor fixed: the ritual referent was not a specific place but a *conceptual* boundary drawn between the human world and the wilderness. While it is true that some sites, particularly cemeteries, holy icons, and specific wells were seen as likely sources of contagion and therefore served as points of reference in the human-wilderness boundary, no informant ever made mention of the same place or object having infected twice with *nenä* illness. Sites of infection and therefore ritual arenas changed with each ritual enactment. While 'place' was an important criterion for the performance of *proškenja* rituals because the ritual had to be conducted at the same location in which the infection originally occurred, this specific place was significant *only for the duration of the crisis*: afterwards, there was no need for the individual, much less the community, to recall it.

The space linked to the *sacred centers* complex, on the other hand, was organized by *concrete* sites and *physical* traces associated with God, Jesus, and the mythologized holy men associated with the monastery. Not only was the site of the monastery itself *permanent*, but the places which contained traces of the former sacred presence of monastery figures *remained stable*, and thus provided points around which collective memory and identity could be organized (see also Stark 1995).

The village chapel or tšasouna in Äglädärvi village, 1936. Photo: Yrjö von Grönhagen. Finnish Literature Society.

Yet pilgrims did not necessarily organize their relationship with the sacred center exclusively around the spaces considered most important by the monastery officialdom. For instance, the magnificent double cenotaph of Sergius and Herman at Valamo monastery which formed a central symbolic and ideological space for educated pilgrims and church workers seems to have been for folk pilgrims curiously devoid of ritual, mythic or symbolic significance, and remained only a mysterious site of impersonal, magical power (Stark 1995). As is typical of popular religion, the sacred place was, moreover, not monolithic but fragmented. Rather than concentrated only within the monastery buildings, it was scattered piecemeal across the landscape, in the minor churches, chapels, and particularly the traces of holy hermits which were both mentioned in folk legends and could be seen and touched in real life. Founders, saints, and Christ were not worshipped in a single central space but at a proliferation of different locations in the sacred topography. It is also significant that there was not a simple one-to-one correspondence between person and sacred place: sacred persons were associated with more than one site, and sites themselves were crisscrossed with the legendary (and sometimes concrete) footprints of a number of sacred persons. Most of these sites and traces were never mentioned in official stories concerning pilgrims' experiences and recollections, for example those published in the Finnish Orthodox periodical *Aamun Koitto* which regularly featured stories and pilgrimage accounts regarding Valamo monastery.

In this study I have defined the sacred as a zone or point in which purity (order, cohesion, growth) confronts impurity (disorder, depletion, danger, anomaly, cf. Anttonen 1996:154–155). Both sacred complexes dealt with this encounter, and each offered different solutions for conceiving of it and dealing with it. In the sacred boundaries complex, the lived reality of purity and impurity, space and time was organized around the boundary between 'this side' and 'the other side', while the sacred centers complex organized these dimensions around a 'center' and its 'peripheries'. In both of these complexes, the ritual movement of bodies and the telling of narratives were important mechanisms of this organization. We can observe that the informational field linked to the boundary between the wilderness and the human sphere in the *sacred boundaries complex* was a 'ritual field', one meant to activate, through bodily movement, the idea of locality. The informational field surrounding sacred centers, on the other hand, was a 'narrative field', one intended to fix meaning to the idea of locality and create a semantic map of it (cf. De Certeau 1984:118–122). In the former, the ritual movement of bodies created significant *places* from semantically empty *space*, while in the latter the reverse held true: ritual movement was activated by places already made significant through stories and legends.

What this means is that when the performers of *proškenja* rites went to the site of infection, their bodies traced patterns in the surrounding topography which were preserved in the body's repertoire as "mnemonic systems" (Connerton 1989:57). These mnemonic systems, in turn, created and recreated a series of criss-crossing trails demarcating the boundary between farm and wilderness, self and other. This was also true of persons who negotiated with the forest spirit and left offerings on the day that cows were let out to pasture for the first time in spring, and of persons who 'bound' the forest in order to release a lost cow from the forest cover. These patterns and trails were not designated beforehand by narrative, nor described afterward by them. Narratives mentioned the custom of such ritual mapping of the mental landscape, but did not specify sites or routes. However, when pilgrims traced out paths to the sacred center or to sacred sites in the landscape, their paths were guided and constrained by the earlier paths already traced through narratives, by the cognitive 'maps' set out in advance by stories and legends. The purpose of pilgrimage was not to continually generate new paths and patterns in the cultural topography, but to seek out the old ones and the cultural values they inhered, simultaneously reinforcing them. Pilgrims acted out and embodied the distinction between pure and impure every time they sought healing or absolution from a monastery or famous chapel, but just as importantly, they also created this distinction every time they listened to, or told in turn, a narrative which told how only the 'pure of heart' gained entry to the sacred center.

Conclusion: the sacred divided

Representations of the sacred are derived from social experience, and they are therefore actively adapted to the diverse challenges and conditions of that experience. In this book I have presented the model of a two-fold sacred: of two distinct but complementary ritual complexes existing within the same cultural system. A closer look at this system reveals that the differences between the two types of ritual activity carried out in the *sacred boundaries complex* and the *sacred centers complex* addressed different types of crises and offered different solutions to them. In short, they mediated between purity and impurity in different but equally important ways. "Purity" in the present discussion has referred to those things contributing to individual and social order, cohesion and growth. "Impurity", on the other hand, has been used to indicate disorder, depletion, danger, and anomaly, in other words those things threatening social integrity and continuity (see Anttonen 1996:154–155).

Within the local sphere of peasant and pastoralist activity, impurity was to be found in forest nature, which represented a threat to the agrarian populace attempting to safeguard their livestock against bears, wolves, and the forest-cover, and themselves against supranormal illness from *väki*-forces. It was also an attribute of the dead, whose loss from the ranks of the living disrupted the kin-based community, and whose return in the form of 'hauntings' could mean disorder and chaos. The dead also contained within them the dangerous force of death itself, *kalma*. These threats existing in the local sphere were minimized by setting up symbolic boundaries between the farm or community on the one hand, and the forest or dead on the other. The former sphere, that of human life and man-made culture, was designated 'this side', while the threatening realms beyond the boundary (forest, cemetery), were designated the "other side" (*tuonpuoleinen*). Such boundaries were not solid walls but rather 'gates' which allowed some traffic between the two spheres, since the forest nature and the dead were still potentially useful for social continuity, if only contact with them could be ritually controlled.

On the other hand, some types of communal disorder were seen to come *from within the community itself* rather than from outside it, and this included undiscovered crimes against fellow villagers and unexplained illness. Since they came from the 'inside', these threats could not be dealt with by setting up boundaries. They had to be countered instead through the power of a symbolic center outside the community which represented purity and the highest ideals of Orthodox Karelian culture. In traversing the distance from periphery (home farm or village) to center (monastery), it was thought that such disorder or impurities could be brought to light and rectified through exclusion or healing.

The two ritual complexes *shared in common* the fact that (1) both were responses to crisis or disorder in the life of the individual or community, and (2) both involved communication and morally-regulated exchange with sacred agents, that is to say, human-divine relations were manifested as a type of exchange transaction. The exchange nature of popular religion is especially pronounced in communities in which human-human relationships are already characterized by reciprocity, exchange, competition over concrete resources and notions of limited good, as has been the case in rural peasant communities in Europe. In such communities, human-divine relations are modelled from the predominant structures of human interpersonal relations. In Orthodox Karelia, reciprocal relations between humans and sacred agents were formalized in the notion of a 'promise': informants told of having made explicit promises to nature spirits, the dead, saints, God and holy men associated with monasteries. The two complexes of ritual activity were further linked to each other by the fact that ritual participants, specifically using the term *jeäksintä*, made promises to holy persons thought to exist in both local and in distant shrines. Indeed, it is this notion of the promise or vow found in both local rites and pilgrimage to distant monasteries which makes a comparison between the two sacred complexes feasible.

The first aim of this study has therefore been to examine two seemingly autonomous spheres of religious ritual activity, local rites versus long-distance pilgrimage to monasteries, within the same theoretical framework. When we view local rites and pilgrimage within the same framework, it becomes possible to put forward a model in which the differences between the two begin to explain each other. It becomes possible to answer the questions raised at the beginning of this study, such as: why were nature spirits, the dead, and local saints seen to be capable of infecting with *nenä* illness, while the holy men associated with monasteries were not? Similarly, why were holy icons in local village chapels thought to be able to infect with *nenä* illness while holy icons in monasteries were not? Why did the *village chapels themselves* infect with supernatural illness? What does the fact that persons could be infected with *nenä* illness by just 'thinking' about it tell us about the cultural function of this explanatory illness model? Why were the poor of the community given food during rituals meant to commemorate the dead? Why were sacred monastery agents seen to be able to look into a pilgrim's heart and know their innermost secrets while nature spirits and the dead had to be explicitly told nearly everything about the context of the *proškenja* rite addressed to them, including the supplicant's reason for undertaking it?

Table 1. Summary of the differences between the two ritual complexes outlined in this study.

SACRED BOUNDARIES	SACRED CENTERS
◆ **sacres agents are:** nature spirits, Christian saints, the dead	◆ **sacred agents are**: God, holy hermits, monastery founders
◆ **scope of rituals**: local	◆ **scope of rituals**: supralocal
◆ sacred agents are **possessive** of own territory, become angered, **cause illness** and demand gifts	◆ sacred agents **do not possess** own territory, do not become angered, **do not cause illness**, do not demand gitfs
◆ behavioral patters linked to **resource competition and notion of 'limited good'** are extended to cover sacred agents and relations between humans and forest: forest is part of closed resource system	◆ **rejection of competition and 'limited good'** – sacred agents renounce 'own share' or accumulate wealth from *outside* closed system
◆ **impurity or disorder is**: non-growth aspects of forest and the dead: attacks by *nenä* illness, forest predators, forest-cover, death of community members, also poverty of community members	◆ **impurity or disorder is**: crimes committed by one person against another, illness, insanity
◆ **impurity is separated from purity** by drawing a boundary line between forest and farm, living and dead, and summer and winter	◆ **impurity is separated from purity** by banishing it from the center (monastery) to periphery (space outside monastery)
◆ sacred agents have **limited access** to strategic information	◆ sacred agents have **full access** to strategic information
◆ **time** is repetitive, cyclic	◆ **time** as anchored in past events and 'traces' of holy persons in landscape
◆ **space** as fluid, non-fixed, changing	◆ **space** as anchored in physical structures and concrete traces – but also fragmented and scattered
◆ Ultimately, the function of sacred agents was to guard the **boundaries or margins of classification** which underlay society's conception of itself	◆ Ultimately, the function of sacred agents was to guard **cultural ideals and concepts of morality**

In the local setting of farm and village, a basic premise of human-supernatural relations was that wilderness spirits, the dead and even local saints were potentially dangerous and threatening. One reason for this was that these supernatural agents were seen to be in competition with humans for space and resources. All of the aforementioned supernatural agents were seen to desire the resources used or created by humans, whether food, health, livestock, man-made objects, or physical territory. Yet these same supernatural agents could be also be negotiated with through ritual. Exchange between humans and local supernatural agents was the ritual mode by which competition was kept in check.

Relations with monastery agents, on the other hand, operated through different mechanisms because monasteries were not in competition with peasants over resources. Either monastery agents (holy hermits) denied themselves such resources altogether, choosing instead an ascetic lifestyle of near-zero resource consumption, or monasteries received their wealth from distant places, outside of the resource system which ordinary peasants perceived as "closed", beyond the districts adjacent to the monastery itself.

This may explain why sacred boundary agents were thought to infect humans with *nenä* illness but sacred monastery agents were not. Infection was the penalty for violating the territory claimed by the sacred agent (cemeteries, wells, village chapels, a piece of land belonging to an earth spirit), territory which existed in the physical world and could be encountered by humans. Monasteries existed on a different cultural plane, above and beyond the everyday competition for resources, and therefore did not occupy territory that they defended with supernatural attacks of illness.

This, in turn, may be why *holy icons* in local village chapels were seen to be able to infect with *nenä* illness – because these icons represented the local saints who demanded resources and respect from village inhabitants – failure to fulfill these obligations was punishable by *nenä* illness. Icons in monasteries, by contrast, represented monastery figures who did not demand worldly resources from pilgrims, since the monastery, paradoxically, both eschewed worldly goods and received its wealth from pilgrims coming from distant places.

As we have seen in the foregoing, not only holy icons but also entire village chapels (*tsasounas*) infected with *nenä* illness. One explanation for this may be that village chapels were often built on, or next to, sacred pre-Christian sites such as sacred groves or ancient cemeteries (sites seen to contain the 'otherworldly' force of the forest and the dead). The capacity for dynamistic infection inherent in these sacred pre-Christian sites was thus transferred to the village chapel, which would punish with *nenä* illness if its territory or sanctity was violated.

Because the boundaries between farm and forest, and the living and the dead were conceptual rather than physical boundaries, the place where boundary maintenance was needed was above all in human consciousness. But if the boundaries in cognitive awareness began to break down, this boundary breach needed to be expressed on a physical surface so that its repair, its re-inscription, could be made visible and concrete. In Orthodox

Karelian rural-traditional culture, that surface was the human body, and the expression of boundary breakdown was dynamistic *nenä* illness. Infection by *nenä* illness represented the breakdown of important cognitive categories in the human mind: between self and other, and between this world and the other world. Persons approaching a juncture at which human activity overlapped with that of the forest or the dead (at funerals, in handling corpses, hunting or working in the forest, drawing water from wells, etc.) had to remain vigilant against intrusion from the Other, and this even extended to thoughts regarding the Other , or thoughts about the possibility of infection itself.

Nature spirits and the dead were not only dangerous supernatural agents occupying the 'other side', however. They, like humans, were seen to share responsibility for guarding the boundaries between and maintaining the separate status of the different spheres. Thus they were also boundary figures, intermediaries, with whom it was possible to communicate, and to whom it was possible to appeal, to ask for cooperation and assistance. The guarding of cultural and cognitive boundaries was not only performed by carefully guarding the boundaries of the self, it was also carried out in the physical spaces between farm and forest, or village and cemetery. This may be why sacred boundary agents such as nature spirits, the dead and local saints were seen to be supernatural beings with limited access to strategic information about humans and ritual situations– they were single-task agents whose primary duty was to man the boundaries between the world of humans and the world of the supernatural, thereby reducing the possibility for disorder in the human realm. Because local boundary agents were apparently thought not to be able to read the minds of humans, communication with them had to take place through symbolic codes: poetic meter, established epithets and phrases, gestures, and gifts. Only through the symbols utilized in ritual communication was it thought that local sacred agents could be alerted to human needs and intentions.

On the other hand, the broader responsibility of guarding moral purity was given to sacred monastery agents who were seen to have *full access* to strategic information about humans. This may be why monks, holy hermits and monastery founders were reported by pilgrims to be capable of looking into the hearts of ordinary persons, and why boats transporting those who had commited secret sins would not take them as far as the monastery. Such omniscience was necessary in order for monastery agents to determine which pilgrims were to be allowed to reach the sacred pilgrimage goal and which were not.

A third key aspect of the folk religious rituals analyzed in this book was that they were characterized by fuzzy categories and syncretic fusions between official and folk categories. One aim of this study has therefore been to illuminate the nature and function of syncretisms between pre-Christian ethnic belief, popular Orthodoxy, and official Orthodoxy in 19th- and early 20th-century Karelia. The shape taken by these syncretisms was not a random or haphazard one, but one appropriate to a ritual system serving the interests of individual and cultural continuity. This book has been an attempt to answer the following questions, among others: why were Christian holy figures such as St. George and the Virgin Mary mentioned in Kalevala meter incantations as having the same function as nature spirits? Why were the spirits of the forest and water referred to as 'Christians' in ritual incantations?

The points summarized here so far suggest certain hypotheses which might explain these puzzles. The *identities* of the agents recruited to guard and mediate the boundary between "this world" and the "other side" were of less concern than the existence of *some* sentient agent to help maintain this boundary which was so vital to the social and cultural Order. In other words, the need for agents to guard the boundaries between farm and forest and the living and the dead is what explains the seeming lack of coherence in the categorization of sacred agents and their ritual roles.

Given Christianity's emphasis on individual salvation and ethics for interpersonal behavior (charity, mercy, forgiveness, etc.), official doctrine may have suited peasant notions concerning equality and reciprocity, but it was not well prepared to address the pressing concerns of ordinary Karelians concerned with social continuity and the boundary between 'this world' (farm, community) and 'other worlds' (forest, cemetery). Christianity did, however, provide the rural populace with an abundant supply of sacred agents, made familiar to non- or semi-literate laypersons through the visual aids of holy icons. Some of these saints were pressed into service as guardians of the boundaries between farm and forest, their task to control the movements of bears and wolves. In the case of the primary 'forest saint', St. George, his connection to forest predators can be linked to his appearance in icons depicting him as a dragon-slayer. Yet many of the agents recruited to mediate the boundary between this world and the next were not divine or even supernatural agents, they were either anthropomorphized icons depicting Biblical or legendary events or 'supernaturalized' humans, the beggars and poor of the community, reinterpreted as representatives of the dead. The poor, like local saints, were given food and gifts during funerals and memorial feasts in exchange for services rendered as 'boundary-workers': they were expected to pray for, and in some cases stand in for, the dead person.

In considering why nature spirits were given 'Christian' attributes in folk religious incantations and narrative descriptions, a reverse argument can be given by way of explanation. Whereas in the case of 'forest' saints, familiar, anthropomorphic figures were recruited for boundary maintenance and relegated to the imagined landscape of the otherworldly forest, in the case of Christianized nature spirits, shadowy boundary figures already occupying the forested realm were made more familiar, more anthropomorphic, by giving them 'Christian' features. A 'Christian' point of departure for both humans and nature spirits, encompassing a shared ethics and a shared identity, ensured a common ground for ritual negotiations and agreements regarding the healing of illness and the use of resources in shared domains.

Understanding the syncretic aspects of Orthodox Karelian folk religious ritual requires looking at beliefs and practices not only in terms of their form, but with an eye to their function as well. Such a perspective has led me to posit that the incantations and offerings used by Orthodox Karelian peasants to maintain the boundaries of self and society, and the journeys taken by pilgrims to reach the sacred center, were two strategies toward the same goal of managing purity, social order, and social continuity. In the construction and maintenance of any human group's sense of spatial and temporal coherence, the concepts of 'inside/outside' and 'center/periphery' are vital templates for both the separation of purity from impurity, and for the organization of a collective self-image. The rituals examined in this study point to the ways in which the sacred could be expressed through different but complementary mechanisms within the same cultural system, in order for individuals' perceptions of equilibrium and order, and society's sense of cohesion and cultural continuity to be strengthened in the face of the dangers which threatened them: illness, death, and the natural environment.

Appendix 1

Calendar of most common *praasniekka* festivals in traditional Orthodox Karelia (from Sarmela 1981:232).

Kevät-Jyrki ("Spring-George") Holy Glorious Great-martyr and Victory-Bearer and Thaumaturge George, April 23

Kevät-Miikkula ("Spring-Nicholas")Translation of the Relics of St. Nicholas the Thaumaturge from Myra to Bari, May 9

Iivananpäivä ("John's Day") Nativity of John the Baptist, June 24

Pedrunpäivä ("Peter's Day") The Holy, Glorious and All-Praised Leaders of the Apostles Peter and Paul, June 29

Kesä-Miikkula ("Summer-Nicholas"), most likely in honor of St. Nicholas the Thaumaturge, on 1st or 2nd Sunday in July.

Kesä-Valassi ("Summer-Blaise") Holy Equal-to-the-Apostles Great Prince Vladimir, Enlightener of the Russian Land, July 15.

Iljanpäivä ("Elijah's Day") Holy Glorious Prophet Elijah, July 20

Spoasan/spuasanpäivä ("Saviour's Day") The Holy Transfiguration of our Lord, August 6

Emänpäivä ("Day of the Mother of God") The Dormition of our Most Holy Lady the Theotokos and Ever-Virgin Mary, August 15.

Frola Martyrs Florus and Laurus of Illyria, August 18

Kuiva-Iivana ("Dry-John") Beheading of John the Baptist, August 29

Poametti/puametti (Russ. pámjatnij 'Day of Remembrance') for Alexander, Patriarch of Constantinople, Repose of St. Alexander, Abbot of Svir, Translation of the Relics of St. Alexander Nevsky, August 30.

Suuri praasniekka ("Great festival") Nativity of our Most Holy Lady the Theotokos and Ever-Virgin Mary, September 8.

Sviizoi The Exaltation of the Cross, September 14

Syys-Iivana ("Autumn-John") Repose of the Holy Apostle and Evangelist John the Theologian, September 26.

Syys-Jyrki ("Autumn-George") Hieromartyr George, Bishop of Greater Armenia, September 30

Pokrova The Intercession, October 1

Mihaila Archangel Michael, November 8

Tahvana The Apostle and Martyr Stephen, December 26(–27).

Vuasilja The Circumcision of our Lord Jesus Christ, January 1.

Vieristä Epiphany, The Holy Theophany of our Lord, God and Savior Jesus Christ, January 6

Sreitennä Candelmas, Presentation of Christ in the Temple, February 2

Pyhälasku (Shrove Sunday) Sunday before Lent

Voznesenna Ascension Day, 40 days after Easter

Stroitsanpäivä ("Day of the Holy Trinity") Whitsuntide, Pentecost, Descent of the Holy Spirit – Trinity Sunday, 50 days after Easter

Appendix 2

Map of Historical Provinces Comprising Orthodox Karelia.

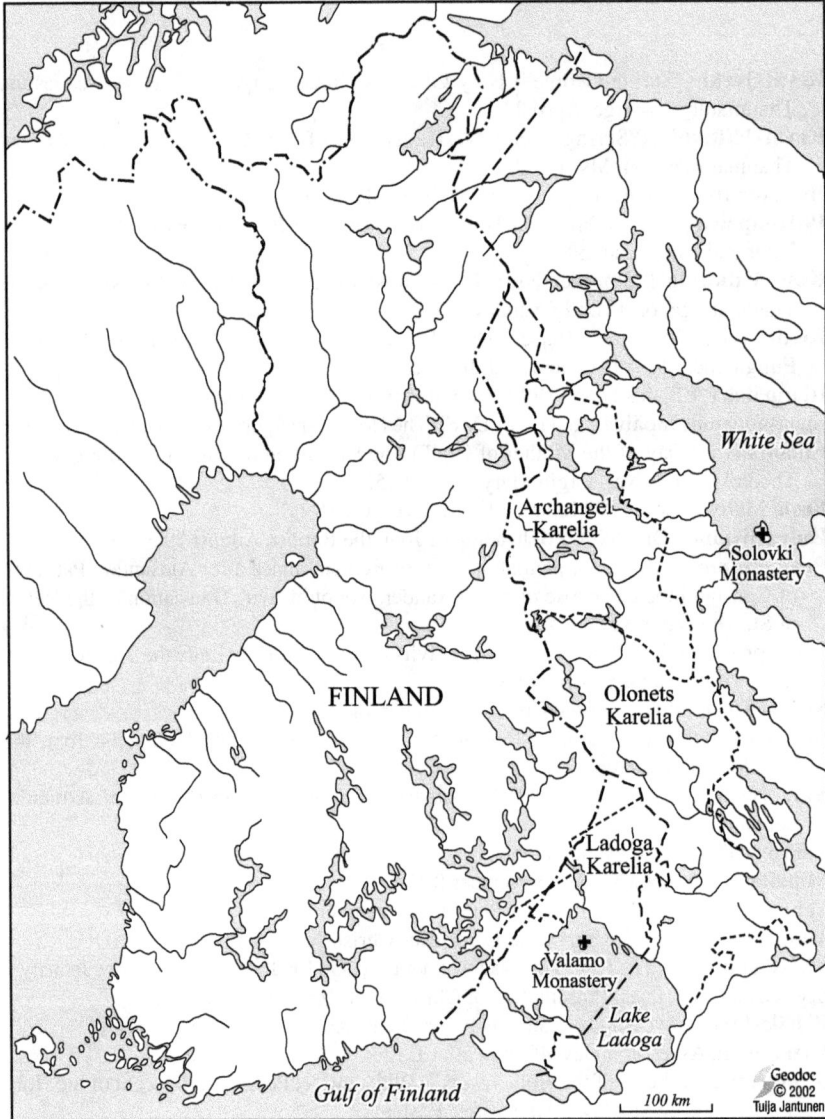

Notes

1 In Finland and Karelia, verbal formulas used in magic rites (*loitsut*) were composed and transmitted in a poetic meter peculiar to the Finnish language and its close relatives: a trochaic tetrameter known as Kalevala meter because it is the same meter used in the folk epic poetry which went into the Finnish national epic, the *Kalevala*, compiled by Elias Lönnrot (1835, 1849). In this meter, one line is composed of eight syllables, with four successive rise and fall positions. The structure of Kalevala meter is characterized by parallelism and alliteration, verse is composed in single lines rather than stanzas, and the placement of syllables is governed by syllable length and stress (Leino 1986). In the opinion of Matti Kuusi (1978:223, in Siikala 1992:34), the basic form of this meter existed already circa 600 B.C. during the period when Liivi and Southern Estonian were branching off from Proto-Finnic, and the Kalevalaic language achieved its strongest position and most highly developed forms in Karelia, where it took root in the 9th century A.D. Kuusi emphasized the unique breadth of the Kalevala meter as the structural template for a wide array of oral-traditional genres by stating: "[t]he language of the Kalevala is not merely a language of art or of ritual. Its use was not restricted to any social community. The language of the Kalevala was developed in Finland, Karelia, Ingria, and among the Votes and Estonians. It has been the dominant language in epic, lyric, magic, and in weddings, bear-killing feasts and annual celebrations. In addition, a significant number of proverbs, riddles, and dialogue in fairy tales and belief legends are cast in Kalevala metre. I know of not a single poetic metre in the world whose usage comes even close to being as widespread as that of Kalevalaic language" (Kuusi 1978:209, in Siikala 1992:32–33).

2 During the period roughly 1890–1970, Finnish and Karelian tradition enthusiasts from the ranks of the rural population undertook the collecting and recording of their own folklore traditions. They wrote down their recollections and interviewed their relatives and neighbors, subsequently sending these texts to the Finnish Literature Society Folklore Archives in Helsinki.

3 See Jääskinen 1981; Kirkinen 1981; Sarmela 1981; Järvinen 1993; Jetsu 1999; Lavonen & Stepanova 1999.

4 For more on syncretism in Karelian folk religious belief, see Järvinen 1993; Kilpeläinen 2000:124–125.

5 The term 'peasants' refers, in the loose anthropological sense set out by Raymond Firth (1951:87), to those of the rural population who laboured within a peasant economy. "By a peasant economy one means a system of small-scale producers, with a simple technology and equipment often relying for their subsistence on what they themselves produce. The primary means of livelihood of the peasant is cultivation of the soil." Firth (1946) also included fishermen as peasants, so that one may assume that agriculture *per se* need not always be the sole economy of peasants, so long as the primary social structures and institutions were organized around agriculture (farms, villages), meaning that they were primarily sedentary, as opposed to the nomadic life of hunting populations, for instance. In the Orthodox Karelian context the definition "labourer in a peasant economy" would therefore refer to farmers, crofters, cottagers and itinerant day-labourers, as well as the craftsmen (blacksmiths, carpenters, etc.) who created the material tools and structures necessary for the continuation of this economy.

6 For more on funerary laments in Karelia, see Mansikka 1924; Honko 1974; Nenola-Kallio 1981; Konkka 1985; Apo 1989; Utriainen 1992, 1998a. For studies of traditional sacred Christian legends from Finland and Karelia, see Järvinen 1981, 1989, 1993. For Marian songs in Orthodox Karelia, see Timonen 1987, 1994.

7 The *tietäjä*, literally "one who knows", was a ritual specialist with the abilities of a seer, healer, sorcerer and ecstatic.

8   In *The Elementary Forms of the Religious Life,* however, Durkheim later noted that
     the supernatural is not a characteristic of the religious. In order to say that something
     is supernatural, it must occur out of the natural order of things, and this idea of a
     necessary order did not, according to him, exist before the birth of the positive
     sciences.

9   See Lawson & McCauley 1990; Guthrie 1993, 1996; Boyer 1996, 2002; Barrett
     1998, 2002; Pyysiäinen 2002.

10   See Järvinen 1981, 1993; Tilvis 1989; Kilpeläinen 2000; Anttonen 1996; Laitila
     1995, 1998; Stark 1995, 1997.

11   See Rivera 1988; Kieckhefer 1989; Badone 1990; Boissevain 1992; Eade and Sallnow
     1991; Morinis 1992.

12   Both during and after the Reformation, the Protestants accused the Catholic Church
     of trying to coerce God through the mechanical use of rituals—i.e. the practice of
     magic (Kieckhefer 1989:15). During the same period, Catholic officialdom itself
     approved of supernatural remedies and protection against demons, etc., but made
     distinctions between 'acceptable' remedies (Church-monopolized) and heretical
     magic, distinctions which were so subtle that the lower-level clergy could not always
     follow them, as demonstrated by the large number of trials against clerics who had
     committed acts of superstition or performed malefical cures, or who had sought
     advice from witches and healers (O'Neil 1984).

13   Having placed popular religion in the context of social obligations and contacts, a
     number of anthropologists have gone further to compare human-saint relations in
     saints' cults to patron-client relationships within Southern European societies
     (Christian 1972; Boissevain 1977; Di Tota 1981). In patron-client relations the patron
     offers jobs and other assistance, usually in return for political or other forms of support
     from his clients. Such relationships are characterized by the client's lack of direct
     access to the centers of power, so that the patron profits from his own position as
     mediator. Within Southern European saint cults, saints are similarly seen as mediators
     between God and the mortals who do not always have direct access to the supreme
     deity.

14   See Badone 1990a; Brettell 1990; Schneider 1990; Riegelhaupt 1973; Di Tota 1981.

15   Mention was made of this concept even earlier by Matti Kuusi (1955) in connection
     with Ostrobothnian magic rites.

16   Keith Thomas (1970) and Jane Schneider (1990) have both discussed the historical
     decline of this popular ethic in early modern agrarian Europe and have suggested
     that the European witchcraft trials of the 17th century were mechanisms by which
     undesirable and "socially redundant" relations of reciprocity and obligation (most
     notably to the poor) were swept away as the rise of capitalistic thinking ushered in a
     new emphasis on individuality and self-responsibility. Both Caroline Brettell (1990)
     and Mia Di Tota (1981), however, have observed the persistence of this same ethic in
     Southern European peasant communities until recent decades.

17   The fact that certain aspects of Orthodox Christianity were deeply rooted in everyday
     life despite the superficiality of popular understanding of Christian doctrine is also
     stressed by Lavonen and Stepanova (1999:31), who point out that while the
     assimilation of Orthodoxy in the lives of Karelians was neither total nor systematic,
     one should not jump to the conclusion that Karelians did not believe in God. Every
     house contained one or more religious icons, which were placed in the sacred icon
     corner of the main room in the farmhouse. When a guest entered the house, he or she
     first made the sign of the cross in the direction of the icon corner and only then
     greeted the members of the household. Another word for human being or member of
     the community in ordinary conversation was "baptized soul" (*rissitty hengi*), "people
     of the cross" (*ristikansa*) or "baptized" (*rissitty*). Karelians also followed most of
     the fasts specified by the Orthodox church calendar.

18   The response of the elderly men here refers to an ancient myth of world creation known
     formerly among certain Finno-Ugrian peoples and recounted in Kalevala meter songs
     in Archangel Karelia as late as the 19th century (see Sarmela 1994:188–193).

19 Inha 1999/1911:401–402.
20 "Kirjeitä Karjalasta", in *Aamun Koitto*, 1907, no. 2: 17.
21 For an English translation of Agricola's list of deities, see *Books from Finland* 1988, vol. 1:3–8 (translator David Barrett).
22 See: Salmi. 1935. Martta Pelkonen 245. –Maria Iivanantytär Paretškoi, approx. 92 years.
23 See also: Salmi. 1935. Martta Pelkonen 299. –Anna Mikkilä, tailor's daughter; Salmi. 1935. Martta Pelkonen 372. –Outti Feudorantytär Torgouttšu, nee Lammas; Salmi? 1934–36. Martta Pelkonen 673. –Fodossu Stopanovna Homa; Salmi. 1934–36. Martta Pelkonen 681. –Sergei Plaketti.
24 See: Krohn 1915:47; Harva 1932:479–480; Lehmusto 1937:420, 423; Mansikka 1941:103; Pelkonen 1965:370; Virtaranta 1978:183; Pöllä 1995:292. See also: Suistamo.1936–8. Pauli Repo E 141, p. 15; Salmi. 1933. Martti Haavio 603; Sortavala. 1936–8. Niina Saarela E 141. –Maria Jyrkinen, 80 years; Ruskeala. 1936–8. Elsa Putto E 141; Suojärvi. 1936–8. N. Nehponen E 141; Salmi. 1936–8. Elias Bogdanov E 141. –Nasti Myllari, b. 1885; Salmi. 1936–8. Vasili Abramoff E 141; Vuokkiniemi. 1947. M.A. Junttila E 177:306. –Anna Vanhatalo, b. 1903; Salmi. 1936. Ulla Mannonen 226, 366. –Martta Kuha, 50 years; Salmi. 1958–9. Elsa Pukonen 247 (b. 1899). –Tatjana Suuronen nee Kirmonen, farm mistress, born 1908; Salmi. 1961. Elsa Jaatinen TK 26:183; Salmi. 1946. Otto Harju 4010. –Maria Kuosmanen, b. 1899; Rukajärvi or Repola. 1916 or 1922. I. Manninen 1954; Soutjärvi. 1943. S. Sääski 3483. –Paraskeeva Mironov, b. 1905; Tulomajärvi. 1943. Helmi Helminen 3451; Porajärvi. 1942. Helmi Helminen 1689, 2059; Tulemajärvi. 1932–38. Maija Juvas 63, 77, 79, 85–88. –Katri Markström; Salmi. 1932–38. Maija Juvas 172. –wife of Lutjonen.
25 E.g. Suojärvi. 1921–33. Martti Haavio 262. –Iivana Jänis, 65 years.
26 For examples from southern Italy, see Rivera 1988; di Tota 1981:328.
27 Ruskeala. 1937. Santeri Huovinen 105.
28 See also: Salmi. 1934–36. Martta Pelkonen 660. –Fodossu Stopanovna Homa; Salmi. 1935. Martta Pelkonen 362, 363; Salmi. 1936. Martta Pelkonen 188. –Marppu Miettinen, 68 years; Salmi. 1935. Martta Pelkonen 246. –Natalju Hilipäntytär Ryögy, widow, 61 years.
29 See Holmberg 1916:7–16; Manninen 1922:122; Haavio 1942:51; Kuusi 1955:240; Vilkuna 1956; Hautala 1960:13; Honko 1960:58, 88–89; Apo 1993a, 1995a, 1998.
30 The first Finnish folklore scholar in recent decades to explicitly bring the question of dynamistic forces back into the scholarly limelight was Satu Apo (1993, 1995, 1998).
31 Christfrid Ganander used the following Swedish terms to define the word *väki*: *styrka, kraft, magt, väldesaft, robur, succus* [=strength, force, might, powerful essence, vigour]" (Ganander 1787 III:228, in Siikala 1992:172–3).
32 See also Åstedt 1960; Utriainen 1992; Tarkka 1994; Apo 1998; Stark-Arola 2002.
33 SKVR I$_4$:24. Suopassalmi. 1889. Meriläinen 1283. –Simana Riikone, heard in his home district.
34 Kinnula. 1946. Otto Harju 3624. –Toivo Turpeinen, b. 1889.
35 Kajaani. 1915. Paulaharju 7658. –Kaisa Reeta Tornulainen.
36 Pistojärvi. 1889. Meriläinen II 1116. –Mihhei Wassiljef.
37 Lohtaja. 1936. K. Hakunti 74. –Sofia Nissilä, farm mistress, 83 years.
38 The two St. Georges were Great-martyr George the Victorious (April 23) and Hieromartyr George, Bishop of Armenia (September 30).
39 Although historians now agree that Valamo's founder Sergius was a Greek monk, in the tales he is, together with Herman, depicted as being alternately from St. Petersburg, Archangel Karelia, or simply 'Russian'.
40 The monastery of Valamo was founded by St. Sergius, a missionary from the West, along with Herman, a local pagan priest converted to Christianity. The exact date of the monastery's founding (and thus Sergius' and Herman's dates of death) is disputed, ranging from 960 to 1389 (see Kilpeläinen 2000: 112–119). The monastery of Solovki was founded later. According to the official history, a monk from Valamo named

Herman who sought desolate regions in the Russian Northwest reached the White Sea and decided to go to the island of Solovki. Another monk, Sabbatius, leaving his native monastery St. Cyril of White Lake, lived for a time at Valamo and subsequently left for the North, also arriving in Solovki. But it took the arrival of Zosima, a disciple of a Valamo saint, to make Solovki into a monastery, where Zosima became the first abbot. The monastery was known to Karelians as *Solovetski*, and was the most powerful monastery in Karelia, referred to by the laity as the "holy city". The sacred founders of Solovki and Valamo in the oral tales tend to be mythological, associated with supernatural power.

41 One of the great Karelian saints St. Alexander, spent his youth as a monk at Valamo monastery on Lake Ladoga, and then, having heard God's call, went inland to dwell in a cave in a remote wilderness area. He later moved to the River Svir to live as a recluse, where, according to the official biography, God appeared to him in the form of three angels and directed him to build a monastery. To the Karelian laity he was known as Oleksei Svirskii, an important holy hermit.

42 Originally a monk of Valamo, St. Arsenius of Konevits undertook a pilgrimage to Mt. Athos where the monks gifted him with the miracle-working icon of the Mother of God. Having returned to Valamo, he founded a monastery on a rock used by the local Karelian population as a sacred site for slaughtering horses as sacrifices to their gods. According to official legend, when St. Arsenius came to sanctify the place, demons fled from it in the form of black ravens. Karelians living in the area near Konevitsa monastery had their own versions of the legend, which they used to explain the place name of nearby Sortavala. See: Makslahti>Salmi. 1936. Ulla Mannonen 1134. –Martta Kuha, 54 years; Salmi. 1938. Mikko Mikkonen KT 131:190.–J.A. Mikkonen, elderly farm master; Sortavala. 1938. Juho Saikkonen KT 136:94; Sortavala. 1938. Juho Saikkonen 6; Joensuu. 1938. Maria Pitkänen PK 31:5643. –Heikki Koponen, b. 1892; Kangasniemi. 1894. Henrik Laitinen (vol. 2) 122.

43 While St. Nicholas (*Mikkula* or *Miikkula*) was not a monastery founder, he was the most popular saint in Orthodox Karelia, and was mentioned five times, three times in connection with Valamo, once for Solovki and once for Orusjärvi (Salmi. 1936. Martta Pelkonen 108; Salmi. 1957. Silja Rummukainen a)12, 16; Salmi. 1879. T. Schwindt VK 89:56). The picture received of him is that of a vague, mythical, 'background' divinity: he is the saint to whom even the founders of Solovki prayed for assistance (Salmi. 1935–40. Martta Pelkonen 448). There are no stories of his life or deeds connected to monasteries except for two brief references to him as a holy hermit who lived at Valamo, and in one case, who left imprints of his shoulders and feet in the rock on the island (Salmi. 1957. Silja Rummukainen a)12, 16). In nearby Olonets, a legend was recorded in which St. Nicholas saved a child lost at sea: the mother had dedicated the child to Valamo monastery, but on the boat trip the child had fallen overboard during a storm. Upon reaching the monastery, the mother went directly to St. Nicholas' icon, crying and praying, at which point the child, alive and well, miraculously appeared sitting on the altar. Even today, the narrator claimed, there is an icon commemorating the event in which a child is sitting on the altar with St. Miikkula standing nearby (Olonets. 1938. N. Leppänen 301). This legend finds its counterpart in a story from present-day Greece where anthropologist Jill Dubisch heard it while researching pilgrimage to the Church of the Annunciation on the Cycladic island of Tinos, home of a miracle-working icon of the Madonna:

"In the summer of 1988...I heard the following story while I was standing with a group of pilgrims just outside the church. A child who had been 'vowed' to the [Madonna] had fallen overboard from a ship on its way to Tinos. The ship had not turned around but had sailed on. However, the [Madonna] was watching over the child, and it was picked up by another ship which was passing by and brought to the church. When the grieving parents arrived, they found the child waiting for them beside the icon" (Dubisch 1990:126).

These two tales suggest an Orthodox-wide legend type whose motifs struck a chord with pilgrims: popular divinities provided protection not only at the sacred center but during the journey itself.

44 There is some dispute over the dates of St. Adrian of Andrusov's death, with some sources giving it as 1549, and other sources claiming it to be sometime during the end of the 1500s and beginning of the 1600s.

45 The "sea wind" was also the westerly wind, since the "sea" (Lake Ladoga) was located to the west of Olonets Karelia.

46 Tulomajärvi. 1943. Helmi Helminen 2372. –Anni Jogorov, b. 1894.

47 SKVR VII$_4$:3084. Salmi. 1884. –Vassilei Ivanov, over 50 years.

48 Suistamo. 1935. Eino Toiviainen KRK 154:193. –Julia Särkkälä.

49 Tulomajärvi. 1943. Helmi Helminen 2312. –Anni Jogorov, b. 1894.

50 Suistamo. 1935. Eino Toiviainen KRK 154:193. –Julia Särkkälä.

51 Tulomajärvi. 1943. Helmi Helminen 2312. –Solomanida Petrov, b. 1862.

52 Tulomajärvi. 1943. Helmi Helminen 2314. –Solomanida Petrov, b. 1862.

53 Suistamo. 1935. Eino Toiviainen KRK 154:193. –Julia Särkkälä.

54 Tulomajärvi. 1944. Helmi Helminen 2335. –Solomanida Petrov.

55 Kontokki. 1936. Vasili Jyrinoja E 132, pages 10–11.

56 See: Suistamo. 1884. Krohn 5507; Suojärvi. 1933. M. Haavio 392. –Marppa Tšutšunen, 68 years.

57 SKVR I$_4$:1981. Kiimasjärvi. 1889. –Arhippa Innine, heard from the elders in his home district; Tulomajärvi. 1943. Helmi Helminen 2252. –Olga Fomin, b. 1905.

58 See: Suistamo. 1884. Krohn 5506; Suistamo. 1884. Krohn 5609; Tulomajärvi. 1943. Helmi Helminen 2254. –Olga Fomin, b. 1905; Tulomajärvi. 1943. Helmi Helminen 2256. –Jevdokia Kunsin, b. 1860.

59 See: Suistamo. 1884. Krohn 5508; Border and Ladoga Karelia. 1916 or 1922. I. Manninen 1781–1783, 1785.

60 Sortavala archipelago, 1934. M. Haavio 936. –Riikonen's daughter, heard from Ilja's wife Anni, in Vasko village.

61 SKVR I$_4$:1981. Kiimasjärvi. 1889. –Arhippa Innine, heard from the elders in his home district.

62 For example Nolan and Nolan 1989; Bax 1990; Dubisch 1990; Eade and Sallnow 1991; Morinis 1992; Boissevain 1992; Gothóni 1994.

63 E.g. Eade and Sallnow 1991; Morinis 1992; Bowman 1991.

64 Valamo may have been founded as early as 12th century (Kirkinen 1981:275–276), while Konevitsa monastery was founded in 1393 and Solovki monastery in 1429 (Father Ambrosius 1981: 320–321).

65 See Tilvis 1989:60; Kilpeläinen 2000. According to one informant, trips to Solovki monastery departing from Soutjärvi, Olonets Karelia, consisted of 10–15 boats containing at least three persons each (Soutjärvi. 1943. Sirkka Valjakka. –Juho Kämlakov, Vasilista Mägisoff (b. 1852), Juho Spirikov (b. 1885), and Nastassa Iarloff (b. 1882)).

66 See Kirkkinen 1970; Tilvis 1989; Kilpeläinen 1995, 2000; Hirvonen et. al. 1994.

67 Kilpeläinen 1995, 2000.

68 E.g. Raivo 1994.

69 Kilpeläinen 1995, 2000.

70 An exception is Laitila (1995, 1998).

71 Sortavala. 1935–36. Juho Hyvärinen KRK 141:379; Sortavala. 1937. Juho Hyvärinen 1122.

72 See note 42.

73 See: Salmi. 1936. Pekka Pohjanvalo 108. –Nasti Kotirinne, 30 years; Salmi. 1937. Ulla Mannonen 4716.

74 See: Virtaranta 1964:181–182; Salmi. 1935–1940. Martta Pelkonen 448. –Miikkul Izrikki, 69 years; Suistamo. 1939. J. Hautala 969. –Ivan Tajakka, 70 years; Porajärvi. 1936. L. Laiho 4022. –Maksima Jevlona, b. 1863.

75 Impilahti. 1936. Juho Kuronen KT 129:45.

76 Salmi. 1935–40. M. Pelkonen 269.

77 Suistamo. 1961. Siiri Oulasmaa a)6216. –Ivan Ladovaara (Plattonen), 78 years; Impilahti. 1939. Johannes Jokio KT 236:38. –Antti Kammonen, b. 1860; Salmi. 1935–36. Pekka Pohjanvalo KRK 151:143. –Miina Ahokas, 65 years; Liperi. 1935–36. L. Lappalainen KRK 161:78; Suistamo. 1945. Frans Kärki 2415. –Mikko Issakainen, 81 years; Suistamo. 1936. Martta Kähmi 16. –Heard from her parents; Sortavala. 1935. Juho Hyvärinen KRK 141:203. –Jaakko Kuivalainen, 55 years; Tohmajärvi. 1937. Esteri Vatanen 98; Sotkamo. 1888. H. Meriläinen 5. – Esias Kalliokoski; Kuhmalahti. 1935. Kustaa Lahtinen KRK 31:27; Kiimasjärvi. 1903. R. Engelberg 1159. –Matti Jaukkonen; Salmi. 1934. Martti Haavio 1700. –Nastja Rantsi, 49 years; Sortavala. 1936. Selma Saikkonen KT 137:120. –Lauri Saikkonen, farmer, 62 years; Porajärvi. 1936. L. Laiho 4022. –Maksima Jevlona, b. 1863.

78 The practice of promising and bringing wool, butter, money, livestock and tapers to Christian saints at local village chapels in return for healing and protection was referred to as *jeäksintä* or *jiäksintä* in the following accounts: Salmi. 1936. Martta Pelkonen 188. –Marppu Miettinen, 68 years; Salmi. 1935. Martta Pelkonen 362. – Outti or Oudottu Feudorantytär Torgouttšu, nee Lammas; Salmi. 1909. U. Holmberg 545; Salmi. 1935. Martta Pelkonen 362. –Outti or Oudottu Feudorantytär Torgouttšu, nee Lammas; Salmi. 1937. Ulla Mannonen 4982. –Martta Kuha, 54 years; Tulomajärvi. 1944. Helmi Helminen 3421. –Houri Gregoljanov, 71 years; Salmi. 1932. Martta Pelkonen. KKTK–KKA. entry: *jiäksie*.

79 Salmi. 1935. Martta Pelkonen 244. –Maria Iivanantytär Paretškoi, approx. 92 years; Salmi. 1935. Martta Pelkonen 246, 248. –Natalju Hilipäntytär Ryogy, 61 years (here the collector notes: "The informant uses the term *voznesennu* as if the name for the festival was also the name of a saint.")

80 Salmi. 1934–36. Martta Pelkonen 798; Impilahti. 1935–36. Eino Toiviainen KRK 154:234. –Antti Kammanen, 75 years.

81 Salmi. 1935. Martta Pelkonen 362. –Outti or Oudottu Feudorantytär Torgouttšu, nee Lammas.

82 Suojärvi. 1941. Viktor Hankka 88.

83 According to the Orthodox legend of the Intercession, a vision of the Virgin Mary was seen by two devout men who were praying in the chapel of Blachernae on the eve of an attack by the Saracens on the city of Constantinople in 903 A.D. In this vision, Mary spread her cloak, housed in the chapel as a relic, over the large number of persons praying together for the salvation of Constantinople. The city's residents took heart and the Saracens were defeated (KP I:97–98; see also Timonen 1994:302–303).

84 Suistamo. 1909. U. Holmberg 588–9; also Suistamo. 1909. U. Holmberg 584.

85 Salmi. 1935. Martta Pelkonen 391.

86 Boyer 1998, 2000, 2002; Pyysiäinen 2002.

87 *Sviizu* was not a saint but the folk name for the holy day which commemorated the finding and raising of the cross, Sept. 14.

88 See also: SKVR II:931,934; Suojärvi. 1931. Nasti Lesonen 258. –Outotja V. Murto; Vitele. 1953. Jalo Kalima KT 265:5; Tulemajärvi>Salmi. 1932–38. Maija Juvas 265. –Katri Markström, 56 years.

89 Soutjärvi. 1962. J. Perttola 42. –Anna Klopova, b. 1874.

90 See: SKVR I$_4$:1315–1323.

91 The term *jumala* as used in the Orthodox Karelian folk religious ritual descriptions most often meant "God", "saint", or "holy icon". An alternative meaning was "ruler of the weather and natural phenomenon", particularly the supernatural agent responsible for lightning and thunder (see meanings 1., 2. and 3. under the entry *jumala* in the KKS volume A-J, p. 522).

92 KKS p. 394. See also: Salmi. 1934. A. V. Rantasalo 268. –Irinja Murto, 57 years.

93 KKS p. 394; Tulomajärvi. 1944. Helmi Helminen 2361. –Jevdokia Kohlojev, b. 1874.

94 Both Hannu Kilpeläinen (2000) and Riitta Tilvis (1989:28–38) see *jeäksinta* as a practice oriented solely toward sacred *pilgrimage* goals rather than a concept indigenous to the broader field of pre-Christian rituals oriented toward the

supernatural, and seek to explain the concept of *jeäksintä* as arising from the official, institutionalized Orthodox tradition: from Scripture, officially transmitted legends of holy persons, and other religious literature. The material examined in the present study, however, offers no evidence of a direct connection between folk usage of the term *jeäksintä* and Christian tales of holy persons making promises.

95 See also: Salmi. 1934–36. Martta Pelkonen 660. –Fodossu Stopanovna Homa; Salmi. 1935. Martta Pelkonen 362, 363; Salmi. 1936. Martta Pelkonen 188. –Marppu Miettinen, 68 years; Salmi. 1935. Martta Pelkonen 246. –Natalju Hilipäntytär Ryögy, widow, 61 years.

96 Four examples from Archangel Karelia, see KKS p. 496 under *jeäksitteä*.

97 One example from Archangel Karelia, see KKS p. 496 under *jeäksintähine*.

98 For more on the importance of food and drink in summoning the dead and erasing boundaries between the living and the dead in Orthodox Karelian rituals, see Utriainen 1998b:301.

99 For more on the classification of rituals into rites of passage, crisis rites and calendrical rites, see Honko (1979).

100 The way in which boundaries between the human sphere and forest sphere were represented was much more complex than what is presented here (see Tarkka 1994). What is presented here is a view of these boundaries solely from the perspective of ritual communication and exchange with sacred agents occupying the "other side".

101 By sacred center I do not mean an *axis mundi* or a repetition of a cosmogony as in Mircea Eliade's formulation (1963, 1991) of the sacred center, in which heaven and earth intersect and there is the possibility of breaking through to a transcendant realm. However, Eliade's characterization of the road to the sacred center as a "difficult road" (1991:18) does hold true for pilgrimage to monasteries in Orthodox Karelia: the sacred goal was usually a great distance from the pilgrims' homes, and pilgrimage custom usually demanded that the journey to the monastery be made on foot (Tilvis 1989:98–99; Kilpeläinen 2000:245, also: Suistamo. 1959. Siiri Oulasmaa E 246: 213–214, – Parakeeva Makkonen).

102 Strong similarities can be seen between these Karelian practices and those of Belorussians and Western Russian groups, which also were known to have taken offerings of food to the graves on the same holy days as Karelians: *radonica*, Whitsuntide, and "memorial Saturday" (Mansikka 1923:174–184).

103 See also: Salmi. 1946. Otto Harju 4010. –Maria Kuosmanen, b. 1899; Suistamo. 1958. Eino Hakala KT 290:265. –Anna Misukka, nee Kuuranen, b. 1890; Tulomajärvi. 1944. Helmi Helminen 2378. –Paraskeeva Bukkijev, b. 1874.

104 In Lutheran Finland, *proškenja* rites seem to have been entirely absent and the only ritual mode used to cure *nenä*-type illnesses were the aggressive *manaus-synty* incantation rites performed by a *tietäjä*. Although a discussion of why *proškenja* rites were used in Orthodox Karelia but not in Finland is beyond the scope of this book, a key factor may be the influence of the Orthodox Church and its emphasis on confession of sin. Clearly, the topic calls for further study.

105 Kontokki. 1936. Vasili Jyrinoja E 132, pp. 8–10.

106 See: Venehjärvi. 1917. Samuli Paulaharju 7399. –Ontippa of Suolahti farm, 73 years.

107 KKS p. 458; also: Vuokkiniemi. 1971. Sakari Vuoristo KT 457:26. –Olona Marttini, 88 years; 1909. P. Lesojeff VK 53:6. –Tatjana; Jyvöälahti. 1894. K. Karjalainen 229; Porajärvi. 1942. Helmi Helminen 1466. –Ivan Hermonen, 75 years; Salmi. 1938. Leo Jyrälä KT 127:36. –Pelagea Jesoi, workman's wife, b. 1882; Suistamo. 1884. Kaarle Krohn 5504; Salmi. 1933. Martti Haavio 500. –Jelena Kuha, 63 years; SKVR I$_4$:1040. Kivijärvi. 1908. –Asjon Kusma's daughter Tatjana; Salmi. 1935. Maija Juvas 267. –Katri Markström b. 1879, in Tulomajärvi.

Only in the Ladoga Karelian parish of Salmi was the *proškenja* ritual performed without bowing deeply, as it was considered by some to be sinful to bow to nature spirits (see: Salmi. 1936. Martta Pelkonen 161. –Marppu Miettinen ("Zakim Marppu"), 68 years; SKVR VII$_4$:3095. 1884. Salmi. –Stopa Jakoljov, over 60 years; Salmi. 1884. Kaarle Krohn 7844).

108 For a discussion of these mythical images, see Siikala 1992:153–166, 172–177, 187–205.

109 According to Pentikäinen (1971:237): "Usually the patient him/herself suspected the source of the contagion. He/she had for example drunk water, lain somewhere, thought or envisioned something, and in his/her mind had already asked the question: had it come from that?"

110 *Nenä* was not the only explanatory model available to explain mysterious illnesses. Marina Takalo, for example, defined four general categories of illness in her community of Oulanka, Archangel Karelia as follows: 1) *tartunainen*, or infection by earth, water, sauna, fire, a category which included, but was not limited to *nenä* illnesses; 2) illnesses caused by human agents, including curses, eyeings (evil eye), witches' arrows, etc.; 3) *vammat* or injuries caused by concrete objects (knife, axe, etc.); and 4) *Jumalantaudit* considered to be sent by God and beyond the powers of humans to cure (Pentikäinen 1971:234–235). The actual list of emically recognized illness types in Orthodox Karelia runs into the hundreds, as evidenced by the Ethnomedical Index of the Finnish Literature Society Folklore Archives.

111 There also existed other types of ritual divination: for example, divination using playing cards was also known. According to a professional female healer from Salmi, the 8 of clubs (*ristu kaheksniekku*) indicated wind-*nenä*, the nine of spades (*pada yhdeksäniekku*) revealed forest-*nenä*, the 10 of clubs (*ristu kymmenniekku*) indicated water-*nenä*, and the ace of spades (*padatuuzu*) revealed cemetery-*nenä*. If the cards indicated cemetery-*nenä*, then the diviner had to go further to determine from the cards whether the dead person in question was male or female, 'black-blooded', 'white-blooded' or 'cross-blooded'. (Salmi. 1936. Martta Pelkonen 162, 163, 164, 196. –professional healer Natalia Timofjouna Mironov, b. 1845).

112 See also: SKVR VII$_4$:1598. Suistamo. 1898. –Maksima's wife Okuliina, 43 years; Salmi. 1934. A.V. Rantasalo 253. –Okuliina Murto, 83 years.

113 See also: Salmi. 1935. Martta Pelkonen 275. –Maria Iivanantytär Paretškoi, approx. 92 years.

114 See also: Salmi. 1938. Heikki Lehmusto 11. –Matjoi Eronen, b. 1883.

115 The same was apparently also true for Eastern Finland. See: Orivesi. 1953. Hugo Hörtsänä 356. –Miina Vintter, widow; Orivesi. 1953(1941). Hugo Hörtsänä 204. – Emilia Lauttanen.

116 See also: Vuokkiniemi. 1894. K. Karjalainen 1690; SKVR II:867. Vonkerinsaari. 1884. –Luka Ondriane, 39 years; Pirttilahti. 1889. H. Meriläinen II 872. –Nikolai Kallio, 61 years; SKVR I$_4$:541. Jyskyjärvi. 1889; Himola. 1884. Krohn 6698.

117 Porajärvi. 1942. Helmi Helminen 1473. –Anni Patrikainen, 62 years.

118 The Karelian term here is *buabo*, meaning both 'grandmother' and more generally 'old woman'.

119 Sortavala. 1941. J. Hyvärinen 2353. –Maria Jokitalo, b. 1888.

120 As one informant from Finnish Lapland explained:
"The earth infects when one lies down in the meadow, it infects so badly that one's face is covered with scabs. Nukuli-Jussa looked at it and spoke. Then he took [the patient] to the sheep pen and there spun a piece of earth using a knife, spit on it and used it to wipe the scabs and said:

Maa puhas, jumalan luoma,	Pure earth, God's creation,
Älä vihaa lastas,	Don't hate your child,
Saat sä sen sittenkin,	You will receive him then
Kun kuolee.	When he dies.

He did this three times and then [the patient] recovered."
(SKVR XII$_2$:5804. Kittilä. 1920. – Juhan Erkki Kauppi, old man of the farm, 76 years).

121 See also: SKVR VII$_5$:5063. Suistamo. 1900. –Iivana Härkönen, 75 years, heard from his wife Palaga Saharjevna and her grandfather Ondrei Lytsy; SKVR VII$_5$:5064. Suistamo. 1906. – Konstantin Kuokka; SKVR VII$_5$:5065. Suistamo. 1884–5. –Helena Levantjovna, widow, 65 years; SKVR VII$_5$:5074. Ilomantsi. 1885. –wife of Räty;

SKVR VII$_5$:5075. Ilomantsi. 1885. –Juhana Puhakka; SKVR I$_4$:1972. Latvajärvi. 1886. –Miihkali Arhippaini; SKVR I$_4$:1973. Vuonninen. 1911. –Anni Lehtonen.

122 See also: SKVR VII$_4$:1984. Salmi. 1884. –Stepana Jaakonpoika, over 60 years; Salmi. 1921–1933. M. Haavio b)502. –Ofimja Kima, approx. 60 years; Tulomajärvi. 1944. Helmi Helminen 2335. –Solomanida Petrov; Salmi. 1936. Martta Pelkonen 161. – professional healer Natalia Mironov, b. 1845; Tulomajärvi. 1944. Helmi Helminen 2345. –Olga Fomin, b. 1905.

123 St. Blaise was a popular saint in Ladoga and Olonets, seen chiefly as the guardian of cattle and sheep. His official saint's day was February 11, but he was also honored on another day of the year as well, which, according to locality, could occur between July 20th and August 8th. These two days on which St. Blaise was honored were referred to as "Winter-Blaise" and "Summer-Blaise".

124 Kitee. 1894. O.A.F. Lönnbohm 1390.

125 Tohmajärvi. 1891. J.H. Hakulinen 246.

126 Porajärvi. 1943. Helmi Helminen 1482. –Ivan Hermonen, 75 years.

127 See also: Tulomajärvi. 1944. H. Helminen 2293. –Solomanida Petrov. b. 1862; Porajärvi. 1943. Helmi Helminen 2076. –Anni Patrikainen, 62 years.

128 The term *kalma* here refers to anything physically associated with death or the dead: cemetery soil, human bones, etc.

129 The same informant also stated that illness from the sauna or sauna steam could infect "especially if one thought about it" (Tulomajärvi. 1944. Helmi Helminen 2293. –Solomanida Petrov, b. 1862).

130 The Karelian term here, *kalman väki*, can refer either to 1) the actual cemetery dead, 2) the 'dead' supernatural beings often believed to reside in the cemetery *en masse*, or to 3) the impersonal, dynamistic force associated with cemeteries and the dead. The first meaning is more likely in this context.

131 See: Kivijärvi. 1911. I. Marttini b) 1042. –Maura Marttini.

132 Kuusamo. 1938. Maija Juvas 490.

133 Kuusamo. 1938. Maija Juvas 488.

134 See: Kuusamo. 1938. Maija Juvas 488.

135 Kangasniemi. 1935. Oskari Kuitunen b) 2650b). –Vilppu Laitinen, crofter, 68 years; see also Karttula. 1937. Juho Oksman 1433. –Taavit Tolonen, b. 1877, carpenter; Vuonninen. 1933. Samuli Paulaharju 22417. –Anni Lehtonen, b. 1868.

136 SKVR XII$_2$: 5443. Pohjois-Pohjanmaa. 1880.

137 Lapinjärvi. 1929. Maija Juvas (SS).

138 Porajärvi. 1943. H. Helminen 1486. –Ivan Hermonen, 75 years.

139 Koivisto. 1935. Erkki Kansanen 155. –Gunilla Hoikkala.

140 Lapinjärvi. 1929. Maija Juvas (SS).

141 Haukivuori. 1937. Oskari Kuitunen b) 3264. –Ruusa Laitinen, farm mistress, 55 years.

142 The idea that *nenä* illness was closely linked to the patient's inner perception of his/ her own bodily integrity is supported by the fact that while supernatural illnesses coming from outside sources such as witches' shot or magical arrows affected both humans *and* cattle, *nenä* illness affected only humans, and never livestock. It would make no sense for livestock to suffer from *nenä* illness, if a primary function of this particular interpretation of physical suffering was to maintain important cultural categories and boundaries in the perception of the sufferers themselves.

143 Sortavala. 1937. J. Hyvärinen 1247. –Maria Pärnänen, b. 1880; Aunus, Mägrätjärvi. 1942. Lauri Laiho 6596. –Juho Nikivoroff, 48 years.

144 See also SKVR I$_4$:1361. Akonlahti. 1839; SKVR I$_4$:1368. Akonlahti. 1894. –Teppana Hämäläini (Stahvei Bogdanoff); SKVR I$_4$:1412. Ponkalahti. 1877. –Huotari Lukkani; SKVR I$_4$:1362. Akonlahti? 1839; SKVR I$_4$:1393. Kivijärvi. 1911. –Sisso's wife; SKVR I$_4$:1391. Kivijärvi. 1913. –Sisso's wife, heard from Hoto Livojärvi, who was born circa 1730; SKVR I$_4$:1421. Uhut. 1834.

145 Vuokkiniemi. 1917. Paulaharju 7400; Salmi. 1934. M. Haavio 1656, 1657. –Natalia Rantsi, 49 years; Salmi. 1934. M. Haavio 1045, 1047. –Varvara Pulliainen, 74 years;

Salmi. 1934. M. Haavio 1057. –Lammas household; Salmi. 1934. M. Haavio 1063.
–Yrjö Meriö, teacher; Aunus. 1932–38. Maija Juvas 321; Korpiselkä. 1931–37. V.
Koljonen 136. –Nasti Vornanen; Aunus. 1932. M. Haavio 201; Sortavala. 1936. M.
Moilanen 814. –J. Avoketo; Aunus, Mägrätjärvi. 1942. Lauri Laiho 6596. –Juho
Nikivoroff, 48 years; Aunus. 1932. M. Haavio 163.

146 See Soutjärvi. 1943. Sylvi Sääski 3254. –Anton Osipahne, b. 1883.
147 Jyvöälähti. 1894. K. Karjalainen 239. See also: SKVR I₄:1470, 1474; Soutjärvi. 1943.
Sylvi Sääski 3256. –Maria Karkkine, b. 1878; Soutjärvi. 1943. Sylvi Sääski 3254. –
Anton Osipahne, b. 1883.
148 SKVR I₄:1470. 1911. Kivijärvi. –Iivana Juako's widow.
149 Also: Salmi. 1938. Heikki Lehmusto 61. –Nastja Mikkonen, farm mistress, b. 1870;
SKVR I₄:1466. Kenttijärvi. 1887. –Simo Karppane.
150 SKVR VII₅:3966. Ruskeala. 1894.
151 SKVR I₄:1466, 1473; Jyvöälahti. 1894. K. Karjalainen 239; see also Haavio 1949:158.
152 Salmi. 1934. Martti Haavio 1070. –elderly wife of Jehor Lammas.
153 See also: Salmi. 1961. Nasti Lempinen TK 57:111.
154 See: Ailio 1897:57; Jääskeläinen 1912:157; also: Salmi (Mantsisaari). 1950. Leena
Malinen E 193:86–88. –farm mistress Jumpponen, b. 1885.
155 See: Haavio 1949:155; also: Salmi (Lunkula). 1950. Leena Malinen E 193:120. –
Mitrei Löksö, b. 1870; Salmi (Mantsinsaari). 1933. Haavio 615. –Matrona Ondrevna,
80 years, and Jelena Kuha, 63 years; Salmi (Mantsinsaari). 1933. Haavio 627. –Old
Man Bolodin, approx. 80 years.
156 Ailio 1897:56–57; Mantsinsaari. 1933. Haavio 615. –Matrona Ondrevna, 80 years,
and Jelena Kuha, 63 years.
157 Salmi. 1932. Martta Pelkonen. KKTK–KKA, entry: *jiäksie.*
158 This taboo against contact with the earth and nature during the winter months was
also known in Estonian folk belief (Hiiemäe 1996:2), where the taboo was in force
until St. George's Day. In South Estonia in particular, it was believed that walking
barefoot or sitting on the ground before St. George's Day would result in illness
deriving from the earth or ground itself (RKM II 66, 515 (3) –Häädemeeste 1957;
RKM II 226, 410/1 (32). –Häädemeeste. O. Kõiva 1967).
159 Vieljärvi. 1947. A. Railonsala 4601. –Anni Agafonov.
160 Vieljärvi. 1947. A. Railonsala 3600. –Juho Rinneniemi.
161 See, for example, Vuokkiniemi. 1932. Samuli Paulaharju 18856. –Anni Lehtonen, b.
1868.
162 See: Vuokkiniemi (Kivijärvi). 1911. I. Marttini 1289; Vieljärvi. 1947. A. Railonsala
4601. –Anni Agofonov; Vieljärvi. 1947. A. Railonsala 3600. –Juho Rinneniemi;
Suistamo. 1959. Siiri Oulasmaa E 246:301. – Paraskeeva Makkonen.
163 See also: Vieljärvi. 1943. Maila Saarto 656.
164 See also: SKVR I₄: 1360–1362, 1366, 1368, 1373, 1384, 1391, 1393, 1405, 1412,
1421, 1424; SKVR VII₅: 3849, 3856.
165 The fact that the custom of referring to the bear using euphemisms is a longstanding
one can be seen from the fact that the bear's names in modern usage, *karhu* and
kontio, probably themselves originated as euphemisms, referring to the bear's rough
or *karhea* fur (see *karhu*, SSA, vol.1 , pp. 312) and its scrambling, lumbering gait (<
kontata, 'to crawl, be on all fours'; see *kontio*, SSA vol. 1, p. 398).
166 See also: Porajärvi. 1942. Helmi Helminen 1345; Tulomajärvi. 1944. Helmi Helminen
4137; Tulomajärvi. 1943. Helmi Helminen 3435.
167 Suistamo. 1939. Jouko Hautala 1179.
168 Venehjärvi. 1894. K. Karjalainen 250.
169 The theme of making peace is also commonly encountered in *proškenja* riutals. For
example: "I come to make amends, to greet you, to build peace, let me live in peace,
release me this day, this minute..."(Suistamo. 1884. Krohn 5537. –Irini Paramoona,
70 years).
170 Also: SKVR I₄:1399. Latvajärvi. 1872. –Miihkali Arhippaini; SKVR I₄:1441. Koljola.
1894. –Teppana Martiskaini; SKVR I₄:1362. Akonlahti? 1839; SKVR I₄:1366.

Akonlahti. 1877. –Prokko Iivanaini; SKVR I$_4$:1405. Vuokkiniemi. 1872. –Petri Teppini; SKVR I$_4$:1383. Kostamus. 1911; SKVR I$_4$: 1376a). Hietajärvi. 1910–11. – Miina Huovinen.

171 SKVR I$_4$:1428. Uhut. 1872. –Iivana Kusmin; SKVR I$_4$:1375. Hietajärvi. 1894; SKVR I$_4$:1424. Uhut. 1836.
The same sort of temporary truce can be seen in ritual communication with the forest carried out by hunters at the beginning of each hunting season (Tarkka 1994:61). In the Kalevala meter incantations addressed to the forest at this time, the hunter asks the bear to 'shake hands' on the pact and emphasizes that this sort of peace is exceptional – fighting and quarrelling being the general state of affairs between human and bear (ibid).

172 See also: Salmi. 1935. Martta Pelkonen 427. –Johor Lammas the elder or his wife Anni Spiridonantytär Lammas.

173 Porajärvi. 1943. Helmi Helminen 2076. –Anni Patrikainen, 62 years; see also SKVR I$_4$:1041. Kivijärvi. 1911. –wife of Kirilä-Hilippä; heard in Tollonjoki.

174 SKVR II:933.Ylälehenjoki. 1901. –Oksenja Kushmishna, 75 years; SKVR VII$_4$:3112. Soanlahti. 1884. –woman; SKVR VII$_4$:3116. Suojärvi. 1924; Salmi. 1940. Martta Pelkonen 322. –Palagu Juakoljouna Mikkonen, approx. 79 years; SKVR VII$_4$:2979. Suojärvi. 1920. –Grišan Vassa; Salmi. 1934. M. Haavio 1032. –Ustenja Plaketti, 74 years; Salmi. 1934–36. Martta Pelkonen 767.

175 *Ohto* was one of many names for the bear.

176 See also SKVR II: 974. Tulemajärvi. 1845.

177 Salmi. 1921–1933. M. Haavio b)502. –Ofimja Kima, approx. 60 years; SKVR VII$_4$:2497. Suojärvi. 1884; SKVR VII$_4$:1984. Salmi. 1884. –Stepana Jaakonpoika, over 60 years.

178 Salmi. 1935. Eino Toiviainen KRK 154:133. –Vasili Veledejeff, 72 years.

179 Tulomajärvi. 1944. Helmi Helminen 2378. –Paraskeeva Bukkijev, b. 1874.

180 Suojärvi. 1921–33. Martti Haavio 262. –Iivana Jänis, 65 years; Salmi. 1934. Martti Haavio 1068. –Elderly mistress of Rantsi farm, 70 years; Salmi. 1935. Mikko Mikkonen KRK 145:8; Salmi. 1884. Krohn 5849. –Olona Jakoljovna; Vitele. 1932. M. Haavio b) 133. –Ontrei Djelgoine, 76 years.

181 SKVR VII$_4$: 2480, 3095. Salmi. 1884. –Stopan Jakoljov, over 60 years.

182 As one informant explained: "...I have heard that people first asked the willows to be herders (*pajut paimeniksi*), the alders to be the cows' protectors (*lepät lehmän kaitsijaksi*), and if none of them wanted to watch over the cattle, then the old man of the forest himself (*metsän ukko*) was asked to fill this position, or his wife or his daughter. But if none of these wished to do this work, then God himself was asked to be the cowherd..." (Suistamo. 1957. Eino Toiviainen KJ 39:16660. –Raija Jänönen and Pauli Repo). See also: SKVR VII$_5$:3800. Suistamo. 1908. –Elessei Valokainen; SKVR VII$_5$:3817. Suojärvi. 1924; SKVR VII$_5$:3801. Suistamo. 1898. –Muaria Johorjouna, Juri's Muaria, approx. 60 years; SKVR VII$_5$:3795. Salmi. 1916; SKVR VII$_5$:3793. Salmi. 1884. –Vasslei Ivanov, over 50 years; Soutjärvi. 1962. J. Perttola 417. –Anna Klopova, b. 1874.

183 See also Ilomäki (1989:84); Pentikäinen (1971:219); Suistamo. 1933. Martti Haavio 635. –Maloi Karppanen, nee Soframoff, 80 years; SKVR VII$_5$:3790. Sortavala. 1886; SKVR I$_4$:1613. Uhut. –Outi Mihheynä; SKVR I$_4$:1611. Vuonninen. 1911. –Anni Lehtonen; SKVR I$_4$:1414a. Vuonninen. 1910. –Mikko Kossinen; SKVR I$_4$:1415. Vuonninen. 1911.–Anni Lehtonen; SKVR VII$_5$:3850. Ilomantsi. 1845; SKVR I$_4$:1394. –Kivijärvi. 1911. Iivana Juakko's widow.

184 See also SKVR I$_4$:1371. Akonlahti. 1911. –Huotari's wife; SKVR I$_4$:1387. Kivijärvi. 1893. –Iro Marttini.

185 See also SKVR I$_4$:1405. Vuokkiniemi. 1872. –Petri Teppini; SKVR I$_4$:1373. Kuivajärvi. 1894. –Maria Olekseintytär Huotarini, wife of Iivana Huovinen, born Akonlahti. Heard mostly from her mother; SKVR I$_4$:1360. Akonlahti. 1832; SKVR II$_5$: 3856. Ilomantsi. 1885. –Heikki Sorjonen; SKVR VII$_5$: 3849. Ilomantsi. 1846; SKVR I$_4$:1424. Uhut. 1836.

186 See also SKVR II:974. Tulemajärvi. 1845; SKVR VII$_5$:3858. Ilomantsi. 1909. –Outi Riihponi; Suistamo. 1935. Eino Toiviainen KRK 154:54. –Siiri Hentunen, heard from her parents; SKVR VII$_5$:3812. Korpiselkä. 1884. –Mikki Iivananpoika Shemeikka; SKVR VII$_5$:3792. Salmi. 1884; SKVR VII$_5$:3859. Ilomantsi. 1913. – Irina Ahponen; SKVR VII$_5$:3805, 3806. Suistamo. 1884. –Feodor Tsannikka, 63 years; Suistamo. 1935. Eino Toiviainen KRK 154:74. –Mirjami Lytsy, heard from her parents.

187 See also: SKVR I$_4$:1366. Akonlahti. 1877. –Iivanaini Prokko; SKVR I$_4$:1365. Akonlahti. 1871. –Simana Omenaini; SKVR I$_4$:1403. Vuokkiniemi. 1837; SKVR I$_4$:1361. Akonlahti. 1839. SKVR I$_4$:1430. Uhtua. 1872. –Vasilei Hanninen.

188 *Pohjola*, the mythical land of the North, was a strange and dangerous realm ruled by a female, the domain of the total 'Other' (see Siikala 1986; Tarkka 1990). By addressing the mistress of *Pohjola* as if she were the forest mistress, the 'otherness' of the forest here is strongly emphasized.

189 See also: SKVR I$_4$:1361. Akonlahti. 1839; SKVR I$_4$:1368. Akonlahti. 1894. –Teppana Hämäläini (Stahvei Bogdanoff); SKVR I$_4$:1412. Ponkalahti. 1877. –Huotari Lukkani; SKVR I$_4$:1362. Akonlahti? 1839; SKVR I$_4$:1393. Kivijärvi. 1911. –Sisso's wife; SKVR I$_4$:1391. Kivijärvi. 1913. –Sisso's wife, heard from Hoto Livojärvi, who was born circa 1730; SKVR I$_4$:1421. Uhut. 1834; SKVR VII$_5$: 3794. Salmi. 1879; SKVR II:981. Porajärvi. 1909. –Ofana; Sortavala. 1936. Toini Moilanen 945. –Antti Kolmonen, 52 years; Salmi. 1937–39. Eino Toiviainen 366. –Niilo Palvo; Säämäjärvi. 1928–29. E.V. Ahtia. KKTK–KKA; Paatene. 1936. Yrjö Mikkulainen KRK 249:10; Vieljärvi. 1943. Maila Saarto 784. –Mikko Sidarov, 70 years; Vieljärvi. 1943. Maila Saarto 600. –Darja Aksentjova, 33 years; Vieljärvi. 1943. Maila Saarto 599. –Maria Markovja Puorojeva, 65 years; Porajärvi. 1943. Helmi Helminen 1894. –Maria Simanainen, 67 years; Tulomajärvi. 1944. Helmi Helminen 3255. –Okulin Sidorov, 73 years; Tulomajärvi. 1944. Helmi Helminen 3256. –Solomanida Petrov, b. 1862; Tulemajärvi>Salmi. 1932–38. Maija Juvas 255. –Katri Markström, 56 years; Selki. 1938. Niilo Leppänen PK 49:8816. –worker, b. 1896; Tulemajärvi>Salmi. 1934. Martti Haavio 1126. –Okulina Jyssiva, 75 years; Porajärvi. 1959 (1909). Väino Salminen 3136. –Ofana (Ondrejev) Tarasov; Njekkula. 1943. Helmi Helminen 1793. –Juho Nikiforof, b. 1897; Tulomajärvi. 1944. Helmi Helminen 3257. –Nikolai Sykköjev, b. 1873; Tulomajärvi. 1944. Helmi Helminen 3259. –Olga Ukkojev, 60 years; Tulomajärvi. 1944. Helmi Helminen 3258. –Marfa Jogorov, 70 years; Porajärvi. 1944. Väinö Kaukonen 1955. –Maikki Mikittäinen, 47 years; Vitele>Salmi. 1935. Osmo Niemi 117. –Irinja Resanova, 54 years; Vieljärvi. 1943. Maila Saarto 657. – Aleksandra Ignatjova, 66 years; Vieljärvi. 1943. Maila Saarto 565. –Sandra Dubitski, 82 years; Porajärvi. 1944. Väinö Kaukonen 1918. –Anni Padrukainen, 73 years; Porajärvi. 1944. Väinö Kaukonen 1946. –Fedo Ahtoinen, 68 years; Salmi. 1934. Martti Haavio 1120. –Feodor Judin, 81 years; Salmi. 1934. Martti Haavio 1122. – Petter Putro's widow; Salmi. 1934. Martti Haavio 1121. –Houri, wife of Arhippa, approx. 75 years; Salmi. 1934. Martti Haavio 1130. –elderly master of Hatsinen farm, approx. 80 years; Salmi. 1934. Martti Haavio 1123. –Mari Palitskoi, farm mistress, 83 years; Salmi. 1934. Martti Haavio 1124. –Jelena Kovero, widow of Stepan Kovero, approx. 70 years; Salmi. 1934. Martti Haavio 1125. –Vasilij Kovero, approx. 70 years; Salmi. 1934. Martti Haavio 1129. –Varvara Pulliainen, 74 years; Salmi. 1934. Martti Haavio 1131 –wife of Teppana Tiainen; Salmi. 1934. Martti Haavio 1133. –elderly wife of Rantsi, approx. 70 years; Salmi. 1934. Martti Haavio 1134. –Muhi's widow, approx. 70 years; Salmi. 1934. Martti Haavio 1135. – Mari Judina, Sašan Mari, 71 years; Salmi. 1934. Martti Haavio 1136. –Oksenja Petrovna Karhu, 81 years; Salmi. 1934. Martti Haavio 1137. –Oudi Sotikov, 84 years; Salmi. 1934. Martti Haavio 1138. –Anna, wife of Jehor Lammas, 73 years; Salmi. 1934. Martti Haavio 1139. –Anni Kuokkanen, 74 years; Suistamo. 1935. Martti Haavio 1721. –Aksenja Mäkiselkä, 58 years; Salmi. 1934. Martti Haavio 1527. –Ustenja Plaketti, 74 years; Ladoga Karelia. 1934. Martti Haavio 1302; Suojärvi. 1933. Martti Haavio b) 662. –Ogoi Meäränen, 80 years; Suistamo. 1935. Niina Saarela KRK

153:86. –Marja Jyrkinen, 53 years; Salmi. 1957. Lyyli Niiranen KJ 36:15668. –Olga Niiranen, b. 1895; Salmi. 1952. Helvi Kuusamo 58. –Palaga Pajula, 57 years.

St. George's role in this respect is also familiar from the Estonian tradition: "St. George was transformed into a ruler of wolves, who bridled his subjects on St. George's Day forbidding them to kill domestic animals from that day onwards" (Hiiemäe 1996:5).

190 See also SKVR I$_4$:1419. Lonkka. 1839; SKVR I$_4$:1386. Kivijärvi. 1892; SKVR I$_4$:1408. Venehjärvi. 1872; SKVR I$_4$:1413. Vuonninen. 1872. –Ohvo Homani; SKVR I$_4$:1409. Venehjärvi. 1872. –Hökkä-Petri.

191 According to Holmberg (later Harva, 1923), ants were the concrete manifestation of the forest spirit. Many rituals connected to the forest spirit feature visits and offerings to anthills.

192 According to Mall Hiiemäe (1996:5), St. George's role as a forest spirit can also be found from Estonian and Russian folk traditions: "St. George as a herdsman of wolves has developed into quite a clear-cut image of a guardian spirit. Both Estonian and Russian incantations appeal to a forest spirit called St. George, pleading him to change into the guardian of cattle".

193 Tulemajärvi > Salmi. 1932–38. Maija Juvas 257. –Katri Märkström, 56 years.

194 When St. Alexander of Svir left Valamo and went to the Svir region for solitude, he founded a new monastery. According to the official version of this story, this came about through a noble prince, Andrew Zavalishin who, while hunting in the forest, discovered St. Alexander and was so moved by his life of holiness that he became his disciple, and later a monk at Valamo with the name of Adrian. St. Adrian eventually founded his own monastery, known as Andrusov, located on a peninsula in Lake Ladoga. There is some dispute over the dates of his death, with some sources giving it as 1549, and other sources claiming it to be sometime during the end of the 1500s and beginning of the 1600s. In addition to founding this small monastery, Adrian of Andrusov (referred to by informants variously as *Ondrei Ondrayski / Antrei Antonski*, etc.) was known by the Karelian rural populace as a holy hermit who lived an ascetic life in the wilderness.

195 See also SKVR II:931. Vitele. 1921. –Ondrei Jelkoinen, 77 years; Vitele. 1953. Jalo Kalima KT 265:5.

196 According to Orthodox legend, Basilissa was a young female martyr whose miraculous emergence, unscathed, from fire and the den of wild beasts led to the governor of Nicomedeia being converted to Christianity at the beginning of the 4th century A.D. (KP I: 15–16). See also: Salmi. 1935. A.V. Rantasalo 448. –Irinja Murto, 59 years.

197 Probably a name derived from or referring to the Orthodox saint Onufrious the Great, who in the 4th or 5th century A.D. lived for 60 years in the Egyptian desert wilderness as a holy hermit (KP II:893–897). As a folk saint, *Onufri* or *Onofrii* was generally considered the saint responsible for watching over the turnip crop, and on whose festival day the turnips were planted. See: Aunus. 1942. Lauri Laiho 6595. –Juho Nikivoroff, 48 years; Jänkäjärvi. 1944. Väinö Kaukonen 1901. –Hilippä Lesonen, 57 years.

198 See also: Archangel Karelia. 1931. Iivari Ievala 374. –Anni Kiriloff, 54 years; Tulomajärvi. 1944. Helmi Helminen 2339. –Matrona Agejev, b. 1871; Salmi. 1934. Martti Haavio 1023. –Varvoi Pulliainen 74 years.

According to Talve (1990:195), the term *suku* in Finland historically referred to kinship descent reckoned through the father's line, while the term *heimo* referred to kinship descent reckoned through the mother's line.

199 Suistamo. 1920. Väinö Salminen 2604; Korpiselkä. 1924. E. Vartiainen n.2. –Nasto Vornanen.

200 See: Tulomajärvi. 1944. Helmi Helminen 2338. –Anni Jogorov, b. 1894; Tulomajärvi. 1944. Helmi Helminen 2339. –Matrona Agejev, b. 1871; Tulomajärvi. 1944. Helmi Helminen 2341. –Maria Onofrejov, 46 years; Salmi. 1934. Martti Haavio 1068. – elderly wife of Rantsi, approx. 70 years; Suistamo. 1939. Jouko Hautala 1063. –

Sandra Lösönen, 78 years; Vuonninen. 1932. Samuli Paulaharju 18786. –Anni Lehtonen, b. 1868.

201 See, for example: Haavio 1937; Lehmusto 1937; Harva 1932; Harva 1948:503; Sarmela 1994: 56–57.

202 Suistamo. 1936–38. Martta Kähmi E 141:115; Suistamo. 1936–38. Pauli Repo E 141.

203 Suistamo. 1936–8. Martta Kähmi E 141:115; See also: Suistamo. 1936–8. Simo Oinola E 141; Suistamo. 1936–8. Pauli Repo E 141.

204 Tulemajärvi. 1932–38. Maija Juvas 83, 85. –Katri Markström; Salmi. 1932–38. Maija Juvas 172. –wife of Lutjonen; Tulemajärvi. 1932–38. Maija Juvas 191. –Okuliina Jyšševa.

205 Haavio 1934:86; Suojärvi. 1936–8. N. Nehponen E 141. –Paraskeeva Lällö, 70 years; Suistamo. 1936–8. Pauli Repo E 141:12; Tulomajärvi. 1944. Helmi Helminen 3451. –Jevdokia Kunsin, b. 1860; Tulemajärvi. 1932–38. Maija Juvas 85. –Katri Markström.

206 Salmi. 1932–38. Maija Juvas 172. –wife of Lutjonen.

207 Salmi. 1932–38. Maija Juvas 212. –Mari Tšubar.

208 Sortavala. 1936–8. Niina Saarela E 141. –Maria Jyrkinen, 80 years.

209 See also: Lehmusto 1937:423.

210 Tulomajärvi. 1943. Helmi Helminen 3872. –Jevdokia Kohlojev, b. 1874.

211 See also: Tulemajärvi. 1932–38. Maija Juvas 248. –Katri Markström.

212 See also: Tulemajärvi. 1932–38. Maija Juvas 100, 101. –Katri Markström.

213 The top of the oven was the place of honor in the one-room farmhouse, where the most respected person in the household (usually the old farm master, or a bride before her weddding day) slept, since it was the warmest place in the farmhouse.

214 Tulomajärvi. 1944. Helmi Helminen 3852. –Semoi Tupitšin, b. 1892.

215 See also: Tulemajärvi. 1932–38. Maija Juvas 85. –Katri Markström.

216 Tulomajärvi. 1944. Helmi Helminen 3852. –Semoi Tupitšin, b. 1892. According to folk informants from Ladoga and Olonets Karelia, "only three or four families from the vast parish of Suistamo were able to hold *piirut* feasts. *Piirut* were held only once every decade in the history of the parish." (Suistamo. 1936–38. Pauli Repo E 141, p. 15); "Not everyone could hold *muštaallisia*, these were feasts which were twice as large as *lounaalliset*" (Kolatselkä. 1944. Helmi Helminen 3853. –Akim Lomojev, b. 1874).

217 See also Tulomajärvi. 1944. Helmi Helminen 3821. –Jevdokia Kohlejev, b. 1874.

218 Tulemajärvi. 1932–1938. M. Juvas 77. –Katri Märkström.

219 See: Suistamo. 1947. U.T. Sirelius E 178, p. 59; Suistamo. 1947. U.T. Sirelius E 178, p. 55–56. –Matjoi Plattonen; Tulomajärvi. 1944. H. Helminen 2301. –Olga Fomin, b. 1905.

220 Suistamo. 1947. U.T. Sirelius E 178, pp. 55–56. –Matjoi Plattonen.

221 Korpiselkä. 1933. Vilho Koljonen 46. Parentheses in original.

222 Tulomajärvi. 1944. H. Helminen 2301. –Olga Fomin, b. 1905.

223 See Harva 1932:476; Harva 1948:343; Honko 1960:58; Heikkinen 1998: 39. See also: Salmi. 1937. Viivi Räbinä KT 136:32; Suistamo. 1937. Martta Kähmi 342; Säämäjärvi. 1928–9. E.V. Ahtia. KKTK–KKA.

224 Tulomajärvi. 1944. Helmi Helminen 2308. –Solomanida Petrov, b. 1862.

225 Vuonninen. 1911. Paulaharju 4360. –Anni Lehtonen. See also SKVR I$_4$:1053.

226 Pentikäinen 1971:237. –Marina Takalo, b. 1890.

227 SKVR I$_4$:1030. Kontokki. Nasto Lesojeff 70. –Miihkali Puavila's wife.

228 Vuonninen. 1911. Paulaharju 4360. –Anni Lehtonen. See also SKVR I$_4$:1053.

229 Pistojärvi. 1930. Iivari Ievala 160. –Iro Trohkimaini, b. 1870.

230 See: SKVR I$_4$:1017, 1060, 2431; SKVR VII$_4$:3118; Suojärvi. 1931. Nasti Lesonen b)257. –Outotja Murto, 75 years; Suojärvi. 1884. Krohn 6093; Vuonninen. 1916. Paulaharju 6079. –Anni Lehtonen; Kivijärvi. 1911. Olona Marttini 24. –Wife of Sisso; Porajärvi. 1942. H. Helminen 1466. –Ivan Hermonen, 75 years; Pistojärvi. 1938. Maija Juvas 541. –Varvana Koljonen, 82 years; Uhtua. 1930. Iivari Ievala 133. – Olga Mitroffanoff, b. 1872.

231 Suojärvi. 1892. A.A. Branders, *Tietoja Suojärven pitäjästä*, pp. 75–76. See also Genetz 1870:94.
232 Soutjärvi. 1962. J. Perttola 56. –Anna Klopova, b. 1874.
233 According to some informants, forest-*nenä* occurs when "a pain has escaped from the forest" (Vuokkiniemi. 1900. Iivana Marttini 200. –Muarie Remsujeff, 40 years; Vuokkiniemi. 1900. Iivana Marttini 373. –wife of Sisso, 65 years).
234 Common names for *nenä*-illnesses included *nakkautuminen* and *heittäytyminen*, both of which derive from Finnish/Karelian verb forms meaning 'to throw oneself, fling oneself' (see e.g. Virtaranta 1958:126; Kontokki. 1936. Vasili Jyrinoja E 132, pp. 8–10).
235 See Honko 1962:89, 110–113; Pentikäinen 1969:96; Kemppinen 1967.
236 Morinis 1992: 6, emphasis mine.
237 Kuhmalahti. 1935. Kustaa Lahtinen KRK 31:27; Kiimasjärvi. 1903. R. Engelberg 1159. – Matti Jaukkonen.
238 Vieljärvi. 1947. Artturi Railonsala 3397.
239 See: Sortavala. 1935. J. Hyvärinen KRK 141:205; Jaakkima. 1879. T. Schwindt VK 89:71; Porajärvi. 1884. Kaarle Krohn 6733; Salmi. 1936. Pekka Pohjanvalo 17; Vala mlk. 1959. Siiri Oulasmaa a)4550; Sortavala. 1938. Juho Saikkonen PK 30:5391.
Anti-clericalism is not an unusual feature of popular religious discourse: as anthropologists have documented for Catholic Europe (Behar 1990, Badone 1990, Riegelhaupt 1984, Freeman 1978, Cutiliero 1971), the primary complaints levelled against priests and other religious officials, namely greed, hypocrisy, and sexuality, can be found (and have been found throughout history) wherever the church exerts social, political or economic control and influence over people's lives. Sexual stereotypes of priests and monks may not be literal but they are nonetheless symbolic commentaries on their power, and the power of the institutions to which they belong (Badone 1990) . It is not difficult to imagine how a monastery like Valamo played a role as a major institutional power in the Ladoga coastal areas. The folk narratives do not give us the particulars of how this power operated or affected the lives of the people nearby, but it does express, in subtle ways, their attitudes toward it. Anti-clerical discourse can be seen as a type of societal control: "both societal control over the powerholders and the control that powerholders may be expected to exercise over themselves"(Brandes 1990:191).
240 Sortavala. 1936. Selma Saikkonen KT 137:120; Suistamo. 1961. Siiri Oulasmaa a)6212.
241 Sortavala. 1935. Juho Hyvärinen KRK 141:379; Salmi. 1936. Pekka Pohjanvalo 17.
242 See, for example: Salmi. 1935–40. M. Pelkonen 269.
243 Salmi. 1935–36. E. Laine KRK 144:239.
244 Sortavala. 1935. Juho Hyvärinen KRK 141:203; Sotkamo. 1888. H. Meriläinen 5.
245 Valamo. 1936. Pekka Pohjanvalo 133; Sortavala. 1936. Juho Hyvärinen 783; Sortavala. 1937. Juho Hyvärinen 1122.
246 Archangel Karelia. 1937. Ulla Mannonen 4798.
247 See: Tilvis 1989: 102–104; Kilpeläinen 2000:247; Salmi. 1957. Silja Rummukainen a)11; Impilahti. 1938. Mikko Jaakkola PK 29:5242. –Filip Pauloff, b. 1855; Sortavala. 1936. Juho Hyvärinen 783. –Matti Pulli, b. 1882; Salmi. 1935–40. Martta Pelkonen 266. – Tatjana 'Hötti', nee Jaronen, 69 years; Salmi. 1935–1940. Martta Pelkonen 374. –Outti or Oudottu Feudorantytär Torgouttšu, nee Lammas; Salmi. 1934. Martti Haavio 1700. –Nastja Rantsi, 49 years; Salmi. 1936. Pekka Pohjanvalo 108. –Nasti Kotirinne, 30 years; Sortavala mlk. 1959. Siiri Oulasmaa a) 4550. –Anna Votkin, nee Kalevalainen, 68 years; Suistamo. 1961. Siiri Oulasmaa a) 6216. –Ivan Ladovaara (Plattonen), 78 years; Makslahti. 1936. Ulla Mannonen 1139. –Martta Kuha, 54 years; Säämäjärvi. 1928–29. E.V. Ahtia, KKTK–KKA, entry *obrazu*.
248 Suistamo. 1959. Siiri Oulasmaa E 246:213–214.–Paraskeeva Makkonen.
249 See also: Salmi. 1961. Lydia Suvioja TK 98:6.
250 Vuokkiniemi. 1911. I. Marttini b) 1193. –Ontro Marttini, 90 years.
251 Hannu Kilpeläinen (2000:249–250) has pointed out that sending a family member

or child on a *jeäksintä* vow to perform unpaid labour and live at the monastery may
have been part of an economic survival strategy for the poorest members of the
population or during times of famine: the volunteer was fed and clothed by the
monastery (which was obligated to taken in those who came to work off a sacred
vow) and even returned home at the end of the agricultural season bearing foods
given by the monastery to tide the family over for the winter: cabbages, carrots,
beets, berries and apples.

252 For example, Riitta Tilvis (1989:65) tells how the parents of one of her informants
had turned their prayers to Ss. Sergius and Herman, the founders of Valamo monastery,
when their son fell ill, and promised to send the boy for a year to Valamo.

253 See: Salmi. 1935–40. M. Pelkonen 268; Kiimasjärvi. 1903. R. Engelberg 1159.

254 Soutjärvi. 1943. Sirkka Valjakka 689. –Juho Kämlakov, Vasilista Mägisoff (b. 1852),
Juho Spirikov (b. 1885), and Nastassa Iarloff (b. 1882).

255 Säämäjärvi. E.V. Ahtia 1924–32 (entry: *jeäksimöz*). KKTK–KKA.

256 Tulemajärvi. 1942. Helmi Helminen. –Solomanida Petrov, b. 1862. KKTK–KKA.

257 "Marina Takalo's father Iivana Nikitin visited Solovki monastery on the White Sea
in 1917, after having promised to make the pilgrimage if he won the dispute in Taavo
village concerning his inheritance and the court case associated with it, which dealt
with the ownership of the Taavo fields" (Pentikäinen 1971:154–155).

258 As in the following example:
"Our mother went to school at Orusjärvi monastery. Mama was a quick learner. She
told us that it was the kind of place where the people walked on dry land to the
monastery, but every now and then the water rose. There were two nice boys there
fulfilling a vow because of their sins, one had gotten a girl pregnant but had not
married her. Many people went there because of their own sins."
(Priazha. SKSÄ 121. 1992).

259 Suistamo. 1945. Frans Kärki 2415.

260 Kuhmalahti. 1935. Kustaa Lahtinen KRK 31:27.

261 Impilahti. 1935–36. Eino Toiviainen 234.

262 This tale resembles the New Testament account of St. Peter walking on the water
(Matt. 14:29–31): Peter got out of the boat, and he walked on the water and came
toward Jesus, but looking at the wind he was afraid and began to sink. 'Lord, save
me!'. Instantly Jesus reached out and took hold of him, saying, 'You of little faith!
Why did you doubt?'

263 For other mentions of restrictions against women, see: Impilahti. 1935–6. Eino
Toiviainen KRK 154:234. –Antti Kammanen, 75 years; Salmi. 1935–40. Martta
Pelkonen 269; Salmi. 1957. Silja Rummukainen a)16. –Maria Titov, 50 years. For
other mentions of the cult surrounding Adrian of Andrusov, see: Salmi. 1936. Ulla
Mannonen 1135. – Martta Kuha, 54 years.

264 See also: Salmi. 1935. Juho Kylläinen KRK 127:57. –Serkei Skuukin, 60 years;
Impilahti. 1936. Juho Kuronen KT 129:45. –Klaudia Ruuskanen b. 1912, died 1929,
farm mistress Anni Ruuskanen b. 1897; Sortavala. 1938. J. Hyvärinen 1518. –Jaakko
Kiukkonen, farmer, b. 1878; Ruskeala. 1938. Anna Mustajärvi PK 29:5302. –Anna
Auvinen, b. 1870; Ruskeala>Impilahti. 1939. Eino Toiviainen 550. –Juho
Silvennoinen, 72 years; Salmi. 1879. T. Schwindt VK 89:56.

265 See also: Sortavala<Olonets. 1936. Juho Hyvärinen 167. –Mikko Samiloff, b. 1900
in Olonets.

266 Porajärvi. 1884. Kaarle Krohn 6733.

267 Salmi. 1935. Martta Pelkonen 414. –Anni Spiridonantytär Lammas, nee Herranen.

268 Porajärvi. 1884. Krohn 6734.

269 Porajärvi. 1884. Krohn 6733. –Luka Ondriainen.

270 Oulu. 1930. Samuli Paulaharju 13732. –Anni Lehtonen, approx. 50 years.

271 Salmi. 1972. Martta Pelkonen 804. –Malanju Saveljov.

272 For a nearly identical narrative by a different informant concerning the chapel at
Palojärvi, see Tilvis 1989:52.

273 Salmi. 1935. Martta Pelkonen 362. –Outti or Oudottu Feudorantytär Torgouttšu,

nee Lammas.
274 Salmi. 1934–36. Martta Pelkonen 661. –Fodossu Stopanova Homa.
275 See also: Salmi. Pekka Pohjanvalo KRK 151:320. –Alexandra Präysy, 60 years; Sortavala. 1938. Juho Saikkonen 6; Makslahti. 1936. Ulla Mannonen 1134. – Martta Kuha, 54 years.
276 See also: Kenttijärvi. 1889–1894. Meriläinen II 443.
277 For example Porajärvi. 1942. Helmi Helminen 1466. –Ivan Hermonen 75 years.
278 Porajärvi. 1936. Lauri Laiho 4033. –Maksima Jevlona, b. 1863.
279 SKVR VII$_4$:1984. Salmi. 1884. –Stepana Jaakonpoika, over 60 years; Impilahti. 1933. A.V. Rantasalo 131. –Marfa Ardjeff, 58 years; Salmi. 1934. Martti Haavio 1068. –Elderly mistress of Rantsi farm, nee Kostiainen, approx. 70 years; Tulemajärvi. 1943. Helmi Helminen 2345a. –Olga Fomin, b. 1905.

Abbreviations for archival source materials

E = Kansantieteellisiä kuvauksia (Ethnographic descriptions). 1889-present. Helsinki: Finnish Literature Society.

KKTK-KKA = Kotimaisten Kielten Tutkimuskeskus, Karjalan Kielen Arkisto (Karelian Lexical Archives of the Research Institute for the Languages of Finland).

KRK = Kalevalan riemuvuoden kilpakeräys (Collection contest in honor of the100th anniversary of the Kalevala). 1935-6. Helsinki: Finnish Literature Society.

KT = Kansantieto-lehti kysely (Answers to the questionnaire from the journal 'Folk Knowledge'). 1936-present. Helsinki: Finnish Literature Society.

PK = Paikallistarinain kilpakeräys (Collection contest of local tales). 1937. Helsinki: Finnish Literature Society.

SKVR = Suomen Kansan Vanhat Runot (Ancient Poems of the Finnish People). 1908-1948. Helsinki: Finnish Literature Society.

TK = Tarinakilpailu (Tale competition). 1961. Helsinki: Finnish Literature Society.

VK =Vähäisiä keräelmiä (Minor collections). 1900-1930s. Helsinki: Finnish Literature Society.

Literature Cited

Ailio, Julius. 1897. "Uhritavoista Mantsin- ja Lunkulansaarella Salmissa", in *Virittäjä* 4:54–57.

Antes, Peter. 1994. "Etiche Religiose a Contatto", lecture paper given at the 1st Summer School on Religions in Europe, Castello Abbazia di Badia a Passignano, August-September.

Anttonen, Pertti. 2000. "Cultural Homogeneity and the National Unification of a Political Community", in Anttonen, Pertti (ed.), *Folklore, Heritage Politics, and Ethnic Diverity: A Festschrift for Barbro Klein*. Botkyrka: Multicultural Centre, pp. 253–278.

Anttonen, Pertti & Matti Kuusi. 1999. *Kalevala-lipas*. Helsinki: Finnish Literature Society.

Anttonen, Veikko. 1996. *Ihmisen ja maan rajat: 'pyhä' kulttuurisena kategoriana*. Helsinki: Finnish Literature Society.

____. 2000. "The sacred", in Braun, Willi & Russell T. McCutcheon (eds), *Guide to the Study of Religion*. London & New Yorl: Cassell, pp. 271–282.

Apo, Satu. 1989. "Nainen ja kuolema. Karjalaiset itkuvirret", in Nevala, Marja-Liisa (ed), *"Sain roolin johon en mahdu" : suomalaisen naiskirjallisuuden linjoja*. Helsinki: Otava, pp. 28–38.

——.1998. "'Ex cunno come the folk and force: concepts of women's dynamistic power in Finnish-Karelian tradition", in Apo, Satu, Aili Nenola and Laura Stark-Arola (eds.), *Gender and Folklore: Perspectives on Finnish and Karelian Culture*. Studia Fennica Folkloristica 4. Helsinki: Finnish Literature Society, pp. 63–91.

Asplund, Anneli. 1994. "Mother and daughter – in the footsteps of the itinerant singers", in Siikala, Anna-Leena and Sinikka Vakimo (eds), *Songs Beyond the Kalevala: Transformations of Oral Poetry*, Studia Fennica Folkloristica 2. Helsinki: Finnish Literature Society, pp. 343–364.

Badone, Ellen. 1990. "Introduction", in Badone, Ellen (ed), *Religious Orthodoxy and Popular Faith in European Society*. Princeton, NJ: Princeton University Press, pp. 3–23.

Barrett, Justin L. 1998. "Cognitive constraints on Hindu concepts of the divine". *Journal for the Scientific Study of Religion* 37: 608–619.

____. 1999. "Theological correctness", *Method & Theory in the Study of Religion* 11 (1999): 325–339.

____. 2000. "Exploring the natural foundations of religion". *Trends in Cognitive Science* 4(1): 29–34.

Bax, Mart. 1990. "The Madonna of Medjugorje: religious rivalry and the formation of a devotional movement in Yugoslavia", in *Anthropological Quarterly* 63(2): 63–75.

Behar, Ruth. 1990. "The struggle for the church: popular anticlericalism and religiosity in post-Franco Spain", in Badone, Ellen (ed), *Religious Orthodoxy and Popular Faith in European Society*. Princeton, NJ: Princeton University Press, pp. 76–112.

Bell, Catherine. 1992. *Ritual Theory, Ritual Practice*. New York and Oxford: Oxford University Press.

Benthall, Jonathan and Ted Polhemus (eds). 1975. *The Body as a Medium of Expression*. New York: Dutton.

Berking, Helmuth. 1999. *The Sociology of Giving*. London : Sage.

Binde, Per. 1999. *Bodies of Vital Matter: Notions of Life Force and Transcendance in Traditional Southern Italy*. Göteborg: Acta Universitatis Gothoburgensis.

Boissevain, Jeremy. 1992. "Introduction", in Boissevain, Jeremy (ed) *Revitalizing European Rituals*. London and New York: Routledge, pp. 1–19.

Bowman, Glenn. 1991. "Christian Ideology and the image of a holy land: the place of Jerusalem pilgrimage in the various Christianities", in in Eade, John and Michael Sallnow (eds), *Contesting the Sacred: the Anthropology of Christian Pilgrimage*. London and New York: Routledge, pp. 98–121.

Boyer, Pascal. 1996. "What makes anthropomorphism natural: Intuitive ontology and cultural representations". *Journal of the Royal Anthropological Institute* (n.s.) 2: 1–15.

——.1998. "Cognitive tracks of cultural inheritance: How evolved intuitive ontology governs cultural transmission", *American Anthropologist* 100: 876–889.

——.2000. "Functional origins of religious concepts: Conceptual and strategic selection in evolved minds [Malinowski Lecture 1999]", *Journal of the Royal Anthropological Institute* 6: 195–214.

——. Forthcoming. "Why do gods and spirits matter at all?", in Pyysiäinen, Ilkka and Veikko Anttonen (eds.), *Current Approaches in the Cognitive Science of Religion*. London: Continuum.

Brandes, Stanley.1990. "Conclusion: reflections on the study of religious orthodoxy and popular faith in Europe", in Badone, Ellen (ed), *Religious Orthodoxy and Popular Faith in European Society*. Princeton, NJ: Princeton University Press, pp. 185–200.

Brettell, Caroline B. 1990. "The priest and his people: the contractual basis for religious practice in rural Portugal", in Badone, Ellen (ed), *Religious Orthodoxy and Popular Faith in European Society*. Princeton, NJ: Princeton University Press, pp. 55–75.

Christian, William A. Jr. 1981. *Local Religion in Sixteenth-Century Spain*. Princeton, N.J.: Princeton University Press.

Connerton, Paul. 1989. *How Societies Remember*. Cambridge: Cambridge University Press.

Cutiliero, José. 1971. *A Portuguese Rural Society*. Oxford: Clarendon Press.

De Certeau, Michel. 1984. *The Practice of Everyday Life*. Translated by Steven Rendall. Berkeley: University of California Press.

Di Tota, Mia. 1981. "Saint cults and political alignments in Southern Italy", in *Dialectal Anthropology* 5:317–329.

Douglas, Mary. 1966. *Purity and Danger. An analysis of concepts of pollution and taboo*. London: Routledge and Kegan Paul.

——. 1975. *Implicit Meanings. Essays in anthropology*. London and Boston: Routledge and Kegan Paul.

Durkheim, Emile. 1965 (1912). *The Elementary Forms of the Religious Life*. New York: Free Press.

Durkheim, Emile, and Marcel Mauss. 1963/1903. *Primitive Classification*. (Transl. by Rodney Needham) Chicago: University of Chicago Press.

Eade, John. 1991. "Order and power at Lourdes: lay helpers and the organization of a pilgrimage shrine", in Eade, John and Michael Sallnow (eds), *Contesting the Sacred: the*

Anthropology of Christian Pilgrimage. London and New York: Routledge, pp. 51–76.

Eade, John and Michael Sallnow. 1991. "Introduction", in Eade, John and Michael Sallnow (eds), *Contesting the Sacred: the Anthropology of Christian Pilgrimage.* London and New York: Routledge, pp. 1–29.

Eliade, Mircea. 1963. "Sacred places: temple, place, 'centre of the world'", in Eliade, Mircea (ed.) *Patterns in Comparative Religion.* New York: World Publishing Company.

——.1991. *The Myth of the Eternal Return or Cosmos and History* (Transl. from the French by Willard R. Trask). Princeton, N.J.: Princeton University Press.

Falk, Pasi. 1994. *The Consuming Body.* London: Sage.

Father Ambrosius. 1981. "Luostarilaitos Karjalassa", in *Karjala I: Portti Itään ja Länteen.* Hämeenlinna: Arvi A. Karisto Oy, pp. 315–334.

Firth, Raymond. 1946. *Malay Fishermen: Their Peasant Economy.* London: Routledge and Kegan Paul.

——. 1951. *The Elements of Social Organization.* London: Watts.

Foster, George M. 1965. "Peasant Society and the Image of Limited Good", in *American Anthropologist* 67: 293–315.

Freeman, Susan Tax. 1978. "Faith and fashion in Spanish religion: notes in the observation of observance", in *Peasant Studies* 7(2):101–123.

Geertz, Clifford. 1973. *The Interpretation of Cultures : Selected Essays.* New York: Basic Books.

Genetz, Arvid. 1870. "Kuvaelmia kansan elämästä Salmin kihlakunnassa", in *Koitar*, pp. 84–109.

Godelier, Maurice. 1999. *The Enigma of the Gift.* Chicago: University of Chicago Press.

Gothóni, René. 1994. *Tales and Truth : Pilgrimage on Mount Athos.* Helsinki: Helsinki University Press.

Grimes, Ronald L. 1985. *Research in Ritual Studies.* Metuchen, N.J.: Scarecrow Press and the American Theological Library Association.

Guthrie, Stuart E. 1993. *Faces in the Clouds: A New Theory of Religion.* New York: Oxford University Press.

——. 1996. "Religion: What is it?" *Journal for the Scientific Study of Religion* 35: 412–419.

Haavio, Martti. 1936. "Calawan poian paasi", *Virittaja*, pp. 267–284.

——.1934. "Piirut. Suvun vainajien juhla", in *Kotiseutu*, pp. 85–91.

——.1937. "Lisätietoja piiruista", in *Virittäjä*, pp. 424–433.

——. 1943. *Viimeiset runolaulajat.* Porvoo & Helsinki: WSOY.

——. 1949. "Karjalainen hekatombi, Mantšinsaaren suuri uhrijuhla", in *Kotiseutu*, pp. 153–161.

Haraway, Donna. 1992. "The promises of monsters: a regenerative politics for inappropriate/d others", in Grossberg, Lawrence, C. Nelson and P. Treichler (eds), *Cultural Studies.* Routledge: New York, pp. 295–337.

Harva (Holmberg), Uno. 1916. *Jumalauskon alkuperä.* Helsinki: Otava.

——.1923. "Metsän peitossa", in *Kalevalaseuran Vuosikirja* 3, pp. 16–60.

——.1932. "Karjalaista kansanuskoa ja palvontaa", in Härkönen, Iivo (ed.), *Karjalan Kirja.* Porvoo: WSOY, pp. 469–482.

——. 1948. *Suomalaisten muinaisusko.* Porvoo. WSOY.

Hautala, Jouko. 1960. "Sanan mahti" in Hautala, Jouko (ed), *Jumin keko: tutkielmia kansanrunoustieteen alalta.* Helsinki: Finnish Literature Society, pp. 7–42.

Heikkinen, Kaija. 1998. "The role of own and 'other's' everyday in the construction of identity: the case of Finnish-Karelian families", in Apo, Satu, Aili Nenola and Laura Stark-Arola (eds.), *Gender and Folklore: Perspectives on Finnish and Karelian Culture.* Studia Fennica Folkloristica 4. Helsinki: Finnish Literature Society, pp. 278–291.

Hiiemäe, Mall. 1996. "Some possible origins of St. George's Day customs and beliefs", in *Folklore*, vol. 1:9–25.

Hirvonen, Sari, Hannu Kilpeläinen, Leena Mäkelä (eds). 1994. *Te menitte asumaan meren saareen...:tutkimuksia Valamon luostarista.* Heinävesi: Valamon luostarin kirjasto.

Holmberg: See Harva.

Honko, Lauri. 1959. *Krankheitsprojektile. Untersuchung über eine urtumliche Krankheitserklärung.* FFC 178. Helsinki: Academia Scientiarum Fennica.

———. 1960. "Varhaiskantaiset taudinselitykset ja parantamisnäytelmä", in Hautala, Jouko (ed), *Jumin keko: tutkielmia kansanrunoustieteen alalta.* Helsinki: Finnish Literature Society, pp. 43–111.

____. 1962. *Geisterglaube in Ingermanland.* FFC 185. Helsinki: Academia Scientiarum Fennica.

———. 1974. "Balto-Finnic lament poetry", in Leino, Pentti (ed.), *Finnish Folkloristics.* Helsinki: Finnish Literature Society, pp. 9–61.

———. 1979. "Theories concerning the ritual process: an orientation", in Honko, Lauri (ed.), *Science of Religion: Studies in Methodology.* The Hague, Paris, New York: Mouton Publishers, pp. 369–389.

Hämynen, Tapio. 1998. "Karjalan yhteiskunta ja talous 1800-luvun lopulta toiseen maailmansotaan", in Nevalainen, Pekka and Hannes Sihvo (eds.), *Karjala: Historia, Kansa, Kulttuuri.* Helsinki: Finnish Literature Society, pp. 153–206.

Ilomäki, Henni. 1989. "Charms as linguistic expressions of dichotomized nature and culture", in Hoppál, Mihály and Juha Pentikäinen (eds), *Uralic Mythology and Folklore.* Budapest: Ethnographic Institute of the Hungarian Academy of Sciences & Helsinki: Finnish Literature Society, pp. 77–87.

Jetsu, Laura. 1999. "Signs of Christianity in rituals of death and funerals in Russian Karelia", in Valk, Ülo (ed.) *Studies of Folklore and Popular Religion*, vol. 2. Tartu: Department of Estonian and Comparative Folklore, University of Tartu, pp. 131–143.

Järvinen, Irma-Riitta (ed.). 1981. *Legendat. Kansankertomuksia Suomesta ja Karjalasta.* Helsinki: Finnish Literature Society.

———. 1989. "World view in Finnish-Karelien sacred legends", in Hoppál, Mihály and Juha Pentikäinen (eds), *Uralic Mythology and Folklore.* Budapest: Ethnographic Institute of the Hungarian Academy of Sciences & Helsinki: Finnish Literature Society, pp. 89–96.

———. 1993. "Sacred legends and the supranormal tradition in Greek Orthodox Karelia", in *ARV, Nordic Yearbook of Folklore*, pp. 37–42.

———. 1996. "Communication between the living and the dead through rituals and dreams in Aunus Karelia", in *Folklore and the Encounters of Traditions: Finnish-Hungarian Symposium on Folklore and the Encounters of Traditions.* Jyväskylä: University of Jyväskyla, pp. 41–48.

———. 1998. "Wives, husbands and dreams: family relations in Olonets Karelian narratives", in Apo, Satu, Aili Nenola & Laura Stark-Arola (eds.), *Gender and Folklore: Perspectives on Finnish and Karelian Culture.* Helsinki: Finnish Literature Society, pp. 305–316.

———. 1999. "Cemetery sacrilege and folk conceptions of God and punishment in Russian Karelia", in Valk, Ülo (ed.) *Studies of Folklore and Popular Religion*, vol. 2. Tartu: Department of Estonian and Comparative Folklore, University of Tartu, pp. 121–130.

Järvinen, Irma-Riitta and Senni Timonen. 1992. "Memorial rituals and dreams in a Karelian village", in *Byzantium and the North*, VI:56–59.

Jääskeläinen, Viljo. 1912. "Bokin päivillä Salmin Lunkulassa", in *Kotiseutu*, pp. 156–158.

Jääskinen, Aune. 1981. "Karjalan ikoneista", in *Karjala I: Portti Itään ja Länteen.* Hämeenlinna: Arvi A. Karisto Oy, pp. 307–314.

Kemppinen, Iivar. 1967. *Haudantakainen elämä: karjalaisen muinaisuskon vertailevan uskontotieteen valossa.* Helsinki: Karjalan Tutkimusseura.

Kieckhefer, Richard. 1989. *Magic in the Middle Ages.* Cambridge: Cambridge University Press.

Kilpeläinen, Hannu. 1995. "Pilgrimage in Karelia: the case of Valamo in the 1930s", in *Byzantium and the North: Acta Byzantina Fennica*, pp. 96–122.

____.2000. *Valamo – karjalaisten luostari? Luostarin ja yhteiskunnan interaktio maailmansotien välisenä aikana.* Helsinki: Finnish Literature Society.

Kirkinen, Heikki. 1970/1963. *Karjala Idän Kulttuuripiirissä.* Helsinki: Kirjayhtymä.

———. 1981. "Kalevalainen Karjala ja kristinusko", in *Karjala I: Portti Itään ja Länteen.*

Hämeenlinna: Arvi A. Karisto Oy, pp. 259–280.

Kirkinen, Heikki, Nevalainen, Pekka and Sihvo, Hannes. 1995. *Karjalan kansan historia.* Porvoo-Helsinki-Juva: Werner Söderström.

KKS = *Karjalan kielen sanakirja (Dictionary of the Karelian Language).* 1968—. Helsinki: Lexica Societatis Fenno-Ugricae XVI₁–.

Knuuttila, Seppo. 1986. "Runonlaulaja estradilla", in *Kirjokannesta kipinä,* Yearbook of the Kalevala Society 66: 118–124. Helsinki: Finnish Literature Society.

Kohonen, Niilo (ed). 1983. *Valamo and its Message.* Helsinki: Valamo-Seura ry.

Konkka, Unelma. 1985. *Ikuinen ikävä : karjalaiset riitti-itkut.* Helsinki: Finnish Literature Society.

KP I = *Kirkkovuoden pyhät I.* 1979. Joensuu: Ortodoksinen Kirjallisuuden Julkaisuneuvosto.

KP II = *Kirkkovuoden pyhät II.* 1979. Joensuu: Ortodoksinen Kirjallisuuden Julkaisuneuvosto.

Krohn, Julius. 1894. *Suomen suvun pakanallinen jumalanpalvelus. Neljä lukua suomen suvun pakanallista jumaluus-oppia.* FLS Editions 83. Helsinki: Finnish Literature Society.

Krohn, Kaarle. 1915. *Suomalaisten runojen uskonto.* Helsinki: Finnish Literature Society.

——. 1917. *Suomalaiset syntyloitsut: vertaileva tutkimus.* Helsinki: Finnish Literature Society.

Kuusi, Matti. 1955. "Pohjoispohjalaista taikuutta kahden vuosisadan takaa", in *Kalevalaseuran Vuosikirja* 35: 221–246.

Köngäs-Maranda, Elli. 1967. "The cattle of the forest and the harvest of water: the cosmology of Finnish magic", in Helm, June (ed), *Essays on the Verbal and Visual Arts. Proceedings of the 1966 Annual Spring Meeting of the American Ethnological Society.* Seattle & London: American Ethnological Society and University of Washington Press, pp. 84–94.

Lainio, Eino and Niilo Kohonen (eds). 1983. *Valamo and Its Message.* Helsinki: Valamo Seura ry.

Laitila, Teuvo. 1995. "Kilvoittelu ja vaihto ihmisen eettisinä suhteina luontoon karjalaisen perinteen valossa", *Ortodoksia* 44:85–98.

——.1998. "Kansanomainen ja kirkollinen ortodoksisuus Raja-Karjalassa", in Nevalainen, Pekka and Hannes Sihvo (eds), *Karjala: historia, kansa, kulttuuri.* Helsinki: Finnish Literature Society, pp. 383–415.

Lakoff, George, and Mark Johnson. 1980. *Metaphors We Live By.* Chicago: University of Chicago Press.

Lavonen, Nina and Aleksandra Stepanova. 1999. "Kansanusko ja ortodoksisuus Karjalan tasavallassa", in Laitila, Teuvo and Tuija Saarinen (eds.) *Uskonto ja identiteetti. Suomalais-ugrilaisten kokemuksia ja vaiheita Venäjällä ja Neuvostoliitossa.* Helsinki: Finnish Literature Society, pp. 29–41.

Lawson, E.T. and R.N. McCauley. 1990. *Rethinking Religion: Connecting Cognition and Culture.* Cambridge: Cambridge University Press.

Lehmusto, Heikki. 1937. "Muistajaiset", in *Virittäjä,* pp. 417–423.

Leino, Pentti. 1986. *Language and Metre: Metrics and the Metrical System of Finnish* (translated by Andrew Chesterman). Helsinki: Finnish Literature Society.

Leskinen, Eino. 1934. "Lunkulan pässiuhri", in *Yearbook of the Kalevala Society,* vol. 14:86–91.

Lintinen, Jaakko. 1959. *Säikähtäminen.* Seminar thesis. S 84. Department of Folklore Studies, University of Helsinki.

Lock, Margaret. 1993. "Cultivating the body: anthropology and epistemologies of bodily practice and knowledge", in *Annual Reviews in Anthropology* 22: 133–155.

Lock, Margaret, and Scheper-Hughes, Nancy. 1987. "The mindful body: a prolegomenon to future work in medical anthropology", in *Medical Anthropology Quarterly* 1(1): 6–41.

Luhrmann, T. M. 1989. "The Magic of Secrecy", in *Ethos* 17:2:131–165.

Lukkarinen, J. 1918. *Vienan Karjalassa.* Hämeenlinna: Arvi A. Karisto Oy.

Lyotard, Jean-François. 1984. *The Postmodern Condition : A Report on Knowledge*. Manchester: Manchester University Press

Lönnrot, Elias. 1985. *Vaeltaja: muistelmia jalkamatkalta Hämeestä, Savosta ja Karjalasta 1828*. Helsinki: Finnish Literature Society.

Manninen, Ilmari. 1922. *Die Dämonistischen Krankheiten im Finnischen Volksaberglauben*. FFC 45. Helsinki: Academia Scientiarum Fennica.

Mansikka, V.J. 1923. "Eräs inkeriläis-itäkarjalainen vainajainjuhla", in *Suomi V;2, Juhlajulkaisu professori Kaarle Krohnin kuusikymmenvuotispäivänä toukok. 10:ntenä v. 1923*. Helsinki: Finnish Literature Society, pp. 171–184.

——.1924. "Itkujen Tuonela", in *Kieli ja kansatieteellisiä tutkielmia: juhlakirja prof. E.N. Setälän kuusikymmenvuotispäiväksi 27.2.1924*. Helsinki: Suomalais-ugrilaisen Seuran toimituksia 52, pp. 160–180.

——.1941. "Karjalais-Inkeriläisiä pyhimyksiä ja juhlapäiviä", in *Virittäjä* 1, pp. 97–105.

——.1943. "Keväänalkajaiset ja Yrjön päivä", in *Virittäjä*, pp. 166–198.

Mauss, Marcel. 1972/1904. *A General Theory of Magic* (translated by Robert Brain). London and Boston: Routledge and Kegan Paul.

——.1990/1950. *The Gift: The Form and Functions of Exchange in Archaic Societies*. London: Routledge.

Mayol, Pierre. 1998. "Propriety", in De Certeau, Michel, Luce Giard, and Pierre Mayol, *The Practice of Everyday Life, Volume 2: Living and Cooking*. Minneapolis & London: University of Minnesota Press, pp. 15–34.

Moreno, Isidoro. 1994. "Modernidad, Secularizacion y Perduracion de las Fiestas Religiosas Populares", lecture paper given at the 1st Summer School on Religions in Europe, Castello Abbazia di Badia a Passignano, August-September.

Morinis, Alan. 1992. "Introduction", in Morinis, Alan (ed), *Sacred Journeys: The Anthropology of Pilgrimage*. Westport: Greenwood Press, pp. 1–30.

Motz, Marilyn. 1998. "The practice of belief", in *Journal of American Folklore*, vol. 111 (441):339–355.

Nenola-Kallio. 1981. "Itämerensuomalaiset itkuvirret", in Asplund, Anneli and Matti Hako (eds), *Kansanmusiikki*. Helsinki: Finnish Literature Society, pp. 44–52.

Nesti, Arnaldo. 1994. "Il 'fatto religioso' nella fenomenologia contemporanea", lecture paper given at the 1st Summer School on Religions in Europe, Castello Abbazia di Badia a Passignano, August-September.

Nieminen, Markku. 1995. *Vienan runokylät kulttuuriopas*. Helsinki: Finnish Literature Society.

Nolan, Mary Lee and Sidney Nolan. 1992. *Christian Pilgrimage in Modern Western Europe*. (Studies in Religion). Chapel Hill: University of North Carolina Press.

O'Neil, Mary R. 1984. "Sacerdote ovvero strione: ecclesiastical and superstitious remedies in 16th century Italy", in Kaplan, Stephen L. (ed), *Understanding Popular Culture: Europe from the Middle Ages to the 19th Century*. Berlin: Mouton, pp. 53–84.

Otto, Rudolf. 1969. *The Idea of the Holy : an Inquiry into the Non-Rational Factor in the Idea of the Divine and its Relation to the Rational*. London: Oxford University Press.

Pardo, Italo. 1989. "Life, death and ambiguity in the social dynamics of Inner Naples", in *Man* 24(1):103–123.

Parkin, David. 1991. *Sacred Void: Spatial Images of Work and Ritual among the Giriama of Kenya*. Cambridge: Cambridge University Press.

Pelkonen, Lauri. 1965. "Kuolemaan liittyvät tavat ja uskomukset", in Pelkonen, Lauri (ed) *Suojärvi I*. Pieksämäki: Suosäätiö, pp. 367–373.

Pentikäinen, Juha. 1969. "The Dead without Status", in *Temenos* 4:92–102.

——. 1971. *Marina Takalon uskonto. Uskontoantropologinen tutkimus*. Helsinki: Finnish Literature Society.

Pentikäinen, Juha (ed.). 1999. *"Silent as waters we live": Old Believers in Russia and Abroad*. Helsinki : Finnish Literature Society.

Piela, Ulla. 2001. "Aikojen rajat Simana Sissosen parannusriitissä". In Eeva-Liisa Haanpää, Ulla-Maija Peltonen and Hilpi Saure (eds), *Ajan taju. Kirjoituksia kansanperinteestä ja kirjallisuudesta*. Helsinki: Finnish Literature Society, pp. 48–67.

Pyysiäinen, Ilkka. 2001. *How Religion Works: Towards a New Cognitive Science of Religion* (Cognition & Culture Book Series; 1.) Leiden: Brill.

Pöllä, Matti. *Vienan Karjalan etnisen koostumuksen muutokset 1600–1800 –luvulla.* Helsinki: Finnish Literature Society.

Raivo, Petri J. 1994. "Herran valitsemat paikat: Suomen Ortodoksisten luostarien maisemalliset mielikuvat pyhiinvaeltajien kokemina 1918–1939". In Hirvonen, Sari, Hannu Kilpeläinen and Leena Mäkela (eds.), *Te Menitte Asumaan Meren Saareen...*; Heinävesi: Valamon Luostarin Kirjaston Julkaisuja, pp. 61–76.

Riegelhaupt, Joyce. 1984. "Popular anti-clericalism and religiosity in pre-1974 Portugal", in Wolf, Eric (ed), *Religion, Power and Protest in Local Communities.* Berlin: Mouton, pp. 93–116.

Rivera, Annamaria. 1988. *Il Mago, Il Santo, la Morte, La Festa: Forme Religiose nella Cultura Popolare.* Bari: Dedalo.

Roper, Lyndal. 1994. *Oedipus and the Devil: Witchcraft, Sexuality and Religion in Early Modern Europe.* London and New York: Routledge.

Sarmela, Matti. 1969. *Reciprocity Systems of the Rural Society in the Finnish-Karelian Culture Area With Special Reference to the Social Intercourse of the Youth.* FFC 207. Helsinki: Academia Scientiarum Fennica.

——. 1981. "Karjalaisista tavoista", in *Karjala I: Portti Itään ja Länteen.* Hämeenlinna: Arvi A. Karisto Oy, pp. 223–255.

——. 1994. *Atlas of Finnish Ethnic Culture 2.* Helsinki: Finnish Literature Society.

Sauhke, Niilo. 1971. *Karjalan praasniekat.* Jyväskylä: Gummerus Oy.

Sault, Nicole. 1994. "Introduction: The Human Mirror", in Sault, Nicole (ed), *Many Mirrors: Body Image and Social Relations.* New Brunswick, NJ: Rutgers University Press.

Schneider, Jane. 1990. "Spirits and the spirit of capitalism", in Badone, Ellen (ed), *Religious Orthodoxy and Popular Faith in European Society.* Princeton, NJ: Princeton University Press, pp. 24–54.

Siikala, Anna-Leena. 1980. "Miina Huovinen: vienakarjalainen verbaaliekstaatikko", in Alver, Bente Gullveig, Bengt af Klintberg, Birgitte Rørbye and Anna-Leena Siikala (eds), *Parantamisen taitajat.* Helsinki: Kirjayhtymä, pp. 54–82.

——. 1986. "Myyttinen Pohjola", in Kuusi, Matti, Pekka Laaksonen and Hannes Sihvo (eds.), *Kirjokannesta kipinä: Kalevalan juhlavuoden satoa.* Kalevalan vuosikirja 66. Helsinki: Finnish Literature Society, pp. 82–88.

——. 1992. *Suomalainen samanismi.* Helsinki: Finnish Literature Society.

Sklar, Deidre. 1994. "Can bodylore be brought to its senses?", in *Journal of American Folklore* 107(423):9–22.

SSA=*Suomen Sanojen Alkuperä: Etymologinen Sanakirja (The Origin of Finnish Words: An Etymological Dictionary).* 1992. Helsinki: Finnish Literature Society and the Research Institute for the Languages of Finland.

Stark, Laura. 1994. "Popular religion in Southern Europe: a summary of recent anthropological research", in *Suomen Antropologi* 4. 19:34–50.

——. 1995. "Karelian Monasteries and Pilgrimage in Oral and Written Narrative. Institutional and 'Folk' Representations of the Sacred", in *Temenos* 31:181–214.

——. 1996. "The Folk Interpretation of Orthodox Religion in Karelia from an Anthropological Perspective", in Ülo Valk (ed.), *Studies in Folklore and Popular Religion,* Vol 1. Tartu: University of Tartu, pp. 143–157.

——. Forthcoming. "Narrative and the social dynamics of magical harm in late 19th-century and early 20th-century Finland". To be published in: *Popular Magic and Modern Europe*, Willem de Blécourt and Owen Davies (eds). London: Sutton Books.

Stark, Laura, Irma-Riitta Järvinen, Senni Timonen, and Terhi Utriainen. 1996. "Constructing the moral community: Women's use of dream narratives in a Russian Orthodox Karelian village", in Robert B. Pynsent (ed.), *The Literature of Nationalism.* London: Macmillan, pp. 247–274.

Stark-Arola, Laura. 1997. "Sacred persons and places of Karelian monasteries in oral and written descriptions". *Ortodoksia* 46:131–148.

———.1998a. *Magic, Body and Social order: the Construction of Gender Through Women's Private Rituals in Traditional Finland.* Studia Fennica Folkloristica 5. Helsinki: Finnish Literature Society.

———.1998b. "Lempi, tuli ja naisten väki – Dynamistisista suhteista suomalais-karjalaisessa taikuudessa ja kansanuskossa", in Pöysä, Jyrki ja Anna-Leena Siikala (eds.) *Amor, Genus ja Familia: Kirjoituksia kansanperinteestä.* Tietolipas 158. Helsinki: Finnish Literature Society, pp. 117–135.

———.1998c. "Sacred beings and 'mirror' communities: from bodily ailment to collective self-image in Orthodox Karelian folk ritual". *Temenos* 34:195:220.

———.1999a. "Sacred centers and preconceived journeys: insights into the cultural construction of religious experience in Orthodox Karelia", in Gábor Barna (ed.) *Religious Movements and Communities in the 19ᵗʰ–20ᵗʰ centuries. Acta Ethnographica Hungarica*, vol. 43:81–107.

———.1999b. "Christianity and the wilderness: syncretisms in Karelian magic as culture-specific strategies", in Ülo Valk (ed.), *Studies in Folklore and Popular Religion* vol 2. Tartu: University of Tartu, pp. 93–120.

———.2002. "The dynamistic body in traditional Finnish-Karelian thought". In Anna-Leena Siikala (ed.) *Myth and Mentality: Studies in Folklore and Popular Thought.* Helsinki: Finnish Literature Society, pp. 67–103.

Talve, Ilmar. 1990. *Suomen Kansakulttuuri.* Helsinki: Finnish Literature Society.

Tarkka, Lotte. 1994. "Metsolan merkki – metsän olento ja kuva vienalaisrunostossa", in Laaksonen, Pekka and Sirkka-Liisa Mettomäki (eds), *Metsä ja Metsänviljaa.* Yearbook of the Kalevala Society 73:56–102.

———.1998. "Sense of the forest: nature and gender in Karelian oral poetry", in Apo, Satu, Aili Nenola and Laura Stark-Arola (eds), *Gender and Folklore: Perspectives on Finnish and Karelian Culture.* Helsinki: Finnish Literature Society, pp. 92–142.

Taylor, Charles. 1989. *Sources of the Self: The Making of the Modern Identity.* Cambridge: Cambridge University Press.

Thomas, Keith. 1970. "The relevance of social anthropology to the historical study of English witchcraft", in Douglas, Mary (ed), *Witchcraft Confessions and Accusations.* London: Tavistock Publications, pp. 47–80.

Tiemersma, Douwe. 1989. *Body Schema and Body Image: An Interdisciplinary and Philosophical Study.* Amsterdam: Swets & Zeitlinger.

Tilvis, Riitta. 1989. *Jiäksiminen kriisiriittinä. Pyhän lupauksen antaminen ja toteuttaminen Salmin pitäjässä 1890–1939.* Department of Comparative Religion, unpublished pro-gradu thesis. University of Helsinki.

Timonen, Senni. 1987. "The cult of the Virgin Mary in Karelian popular tradition", in *Byzantium and the North: Acta Byzantina Fennica* 3:101–119.

———.1994. "The Mary of Women's Epic", in Siikala, Anna-Leena and Vakimo, Sinikka (eds), *Songs Beyond the Kalevala: Transformations of Oral Poetry.* Helsinki: Finnish Literature Society, pp. 301–329.

Turner, Victor W., and Edith Turner. 1978. *Image and Pilgrimage in Christian Culture: Anthropological Perspectives.* Lectures on the History of Religions, 11. New York: Columbia University Press.

Utriainen, Terhi. 1992. *Kuolema tekstinä. Kuoleman ja ihmisen väliset merkityssuhteet vienankarjalaisen Anni Lehtosen perinneteksteissä.* Unpublished licentiate thesis. University of Helsinki, Department of Comparative Religion.

———.1998a. "Feminine and masculine in the study of Balto-Finnic laments", in Apo, Satu, Aili Nenola & Laura Stark-Arola (eds), *Gender and Folklore: Perspectives on Finnish and Karelian Culture.* Helsinki: Finnish Literature Society, pp. 175–200.

———.1998b. "Occupying a space as eyes and body: comments on the diversity of fieldwork, postures of knowledge, and summer experiences in an elderly women's village in Olonets Karelia", in Apo, Satu, Aili Nenola and Laura Stark-Arola (eds), *Gender and Folklore: Perspectives on Finnish and Karelian Culture.* Helsinki: Finnish Literature Society, pp. 292–304.

Virtanen, E. A. 1942. "Jaakko Fellmann Vienan Karjalassa v. 1829", in *Suomalainen*

Suomi 7:388–394.

Virtanen, Leea. 1968. *Kalevalainen laulutapa Karjalassa.* Helsinki: Finnish Literature Society.

Virtaranta, Pertti. 1958. *Vienan kansa muistelee.* Porvoo: WSOY.

——. 1964. *Lyydiläisiä tekstejä.* Helsinki: Suomalais-ugrilainen seura.

——. 1978. *Vienan kyliä kiertämässä: Karjalaiskylien entistä elämää Venehjärvestä Kostamukseen.* Helsinki: Kirjayhtymä.

Voyé, Lillian. 1994. "La Religion en Postmodernité", lecture paper presented at the 1st Summer School on Religions in Europe, Castello Abbazia di Badia a Passignano, August-September.

Vuorela, Toivo. 1960. *Paha silmä suomalaisen perinteen valossa.* Helsinki. Finnish Literature Society.

Waronen, Matti. 1898. *Vainajainpalvelus muinaisilla suomalaisilla.* FLS Editions 87. Helsinki: Finnish Literature Society.

Åstedt, Kaarina. 1960. "Mytologisista *Nenä*-Yhdynnäisistä", in *Kalevalaseura Vuosikirja* 40, pp. 307–322.

Index

anger 15, 48, 52–53, 64, 70, 80, 86, 110, 177–179, 182–183

asceticism 170–171, 175

bear 41, 48–49, 60, 70, 76, 109, 111–113, 119–120, 122, 126, 128, 130, 132, 172, 177, 192, 197, n.165

binding, trussing up the forest 25, 43, 113–117, 185–186

body 7, 14–15, 26–27, 29, 48, 58, 61, 64, 76, 111, 150–152, 160, 167, 190, 196

boundaries, symbolic 21, 23, 30, 54, 65, 75–76, 91, 99–101, 105, 107–111, 123, 128, 133, 136–137, 144, 151–152, 157–158, 175, 177, 179–180, 183–184, 186, 188, 190, 192–193, 196–198, n.100, n.142

bread (used in divination or offering) 52, 66–67, 89, 90–94, 112, 125, 142–143

cattle 13, 18, 36, 40–41, 47, 53, 60, 62, 64, 66–70, 75–76, 95, 104, 111–124, 126–132, 136, 140, 145, 147, 150–152, 154, 159, 185–186, 190, n.123, n.142, n.182, n.192

cemetery 12–13, 40–41, 43, 45–46, 48–50, 53, 60, 66, 71, 77–80, 91, 96, 98, 102, 104–108, 110, 116, 139, 141–144, 147–149, 177, 180, 182–183, 188, 192–197, n.111, n.128, n.130

charcoal (used in divination) 89–94

church – see *tšasouna*

cognitive perspective on religion 7–8, 21–22, 29, 32, 35, 93, 99, 106, 183–186, 196

community of nature spirits 45–47, 52, 126–127, 133–137, 147–152, 183

competition with nature 147, 175–177, 195

cows – see cattle

culture 11, 13–14, 18–19, 29, 31–32, 36, 39, 54–55, 58, 62, 65, 71, 76–77, 89, 100–101, 105, 107, 110, 128–129, 133, 147–154

cult of traces 167–168, 187, n.13

dead, the 7, 12–13, 15–17, 21, 29, 33, 39–40, 42–47, 49–50, 55, 60–61, 69–72, 75–76, 79–80, 103, 110, 128, 136–153, 157–158, 177–179, 184–186, 192–193, 195, 198

divination 13, 17, 71, 77, 83–84, 88–99, 116, 148, 152, 187, n.111

dreams 13, 17, 61, 79–80, 94–99, 108, 115–116, 141–142, 146, 179

earth spirits 51, 53–54, 60, 68, 102, 115, 195

ethics 15, 23, 37, 40, 84, 126, 138, 175, 186, 197–198

exchange 11, 13–15, 20–21, 23, 30, 32–33, 39–42, 52, 58, 61, 66, 68, 75, 77, 79–80, 88, 111, 147, 149, 152, 157, 162, 175–177, 183, 193, 195, 197–198, n.16

fishing 18, 39, 66, 68, 75, 94, 136, 141

floating rock motif 59, 164

folk religion 18, 28–39, 52, 55, 61–66, 69–72, 124, 157, 178

forest 18, 33, 38, 46–49, 51, 53, 67, 69, 71, 75–78, 86, 91–92, 96, 98, 102–106, 108–117, 119–121, 123, 125, 128, 131, 133–134, 148, 150–154, 172, 177–179, 184–185, 192, 196–198

forest spirit 12–13, 35, 51, 53, 60, 66, 111–117, 121–133, 149, 184–185, 190

forest–cover 35, 60, 66–67, 76, 111, 113–117, 125–127, 132, 144, 150, 190

gestures, symbolic 15, 26, 41, 61, 185

gifts and offerings 15, 20–21, 33, 41–42, 53, 68, 78, 80, 84–88, 95, 97, 104, 121, 142, 145–146, 150, 177, 181, 185, 197–198

graveyard – see cemetery

growth 21–22, 57, 89, 111, 119, 123, 152–154, 190, 192

harmony with nature 127, 147, 177

healing 13, 49, 61, 63, 77, 81–83, 88, 94, 96–97, 109, 159–160, 162, 177–183, 191, 193, 198, n.78

holy days – see *jyrki, muistinsuovatta, pokrova, ruadintšat*, Whitsuntide

holy hermits 57, 59, 71, 126, 133, 168–171, 175–177, 189, 195, 197

holy icons 13, 15–16, 31, 36–37, 46–48, 60, 63, 77, 91, 95–96, 106, 117, 133, 148, 169, 178–181, 183, 188, 195–197

holy vow – see *jeäksintä*
hunting   18, 39–40, 49, 75, 136, 150, 196, n.5, n.171, n.194

icons – see holy icons
illness   13, 15–17, 35, 41–43, 47–49, 52, 60, 62, 64, 66, 68–70, 75–102, 107–111, 115–118, 132, 135, 148–149, 151–152, 159–164, 177–183, 192–193, 195, 198, n.110, n.129, n.142, n.158
impurity   21–23, 31, 70–71, 75, 153, 158, 180, 190, 192, 198

Jesus   50, 66, 71, 104, 126, 128, 130, 146, 158, 163, 167–168, 177, 184, 187–188, 199
jeäksintä   13, 41–42, 58, 61–62, 68–69, 71, 119, 139, 157–164, 180, 185, 193, n.251, n.258
jyrki   50, 63–64, 80, 111, 120, 129–130, 141, 186, 199, n.87, n.102

kalma   46, 48–49, 80, 84, 92, 104, 106, 116, 153, 192, n.128, n.130
kinship titles   31, 134

liminal   54, 123, 126, 186
limited good, image of   32, 40, 75, 145, 175–176, 193
luonto   42–43, 47, 82, 101, 108–111

manaus   81, 83, 86–88, n.104
memorial rites   142–146
miracles   41, 162, 172, n.42–n.43
miraculous healings   159
monastery   29, 41, 46–47, 50–51, 54–63, 68, 71–72, 131–132, 158–172, 175–184, 187–190, 193, 195–196, n.40–n.43, n.64–n.65, n.101, n.194, n.239, n.251–n.252, n.257–n.258
monastery founders   59, 71, 159, 165, 167–171, 176–177, 184, 188, 197
Monastery of the Holy Trinity   50, 54, 59, 132, 158–159, 163, 165, 187
morality – see ethics
muistinsuovatta   63–64, 79–80, 141–142, n.87, n.102

nature   18, 21, 47, 110, 119–120, 129, 136, 147–154, 175–176, 179, 192, n.158
nature spirit – see forest spirit, water spirit, earth spirits, wind spirits
nenä illness   64, 77–102, 108–110, 115, 117, 135, 147–148, 151–152, 177–

180, 188, 195–196, n.110, n.142
non–growth   123, 183

onni   32
open body image   99–101, 107
other world   19, 21, 26, 42–47, 52–53, 57, 65, 69, 71, 81, 86, 88, 106, 126, 133, 135, 137, 146–147, 150, 152, 186, 196–197

piirut   40, 139–140, 142–143, n.216
pilgrimage   7–8, 13, 15, 17, 39, 41–42, 54–62, 68, 71, 75, 119, 157–171, 179, 185, 187–188, 190, 193, 195, 197, n.42–n.43, n.94, n.101, n.257
pilgrims   54–60, 76, 157–160, 163–164, 167–171, 176, 185, 187–191, 196–198, n.43, n.101
Pohjola   45–46, 130, n.188
pokrova   63–65, 80, 94, 120–122, 141, 186, 199, n.87, n.102
pominominen   25, 66–69, 79–80, 138, 144
poverty   39, 136, 170–171, 175
praasniekka   32, 39, 55, 70, 117, 136, 199
prayer   15, 36–37, 39, 57, 66–67, 71, 81, 102–103, 125–126, 141, 146, n.252
pre–Christian   12–14, 28, 30, 34, 36–38, 42, 55, 68, 148, 182, 196–197, n.94
proškenja rite   13, 17, 43, 60, 77–88, 96–103, 106–108, 116, 126, 132, 134–135, 137, 147–150, 152, 160, 178, 184–185, 187–191, 195, n.104, n.108, n.169
purity   21–23, 31, 70–71, 75, 128, 153–154, 158–159, 164, 180, 184, 186, 190, 192–193, 197–198

reciprocity – see exchange
renunciation   171, 175
ritual communication   13–15, 26, 52, 55, 124, 126, 128, 133, 137–138, 150–152, 197, n.100, n.171
ritual, criteria for   24–25, 60–61, 81, 188
ritual specialist – see *tietäjä*
ruadintšat   63–64, 79–80, 141, n.87, n.102

sacred agents   21–22, 28, 30, 39–41, 45, 50–54, 61–66, 70, 75, 80, 98, 103, 111, 126–129, 133, 138, 140, 146–150, 177, 183–186, 193, 196–197, n.100
sacred boundaries   70–72, 75–76, 128, 154, 157, 175, 179, 184, 186, 188, 190, 192

sacred center 55–56, 58, 60, 70–72, 75–76, 154, 157–160, 164–166, 169–172, 177, 179–180, 184, 188, 190–192, 198, n.43, n.100
sacred, definition of 20–23, 27, 30–32, 150, n.101
sacred groves 39, 52, 183, 196
sacrificial festivals 12, 55, 61, 117–118
saints 12–13, 15, 29, 31, 33, 35, 40–42, 45–47, 50, 57–58, 60–61, 65–66, 68, 70–72, 75–76, 117–119, 124–133, 147, 157–158, 167, 171, 175–176, 178, 184, 186, 189, 193, 195–198, n.13, n.41, n.78
seasonal rites 16, 36, 66, 112, 119–124, 128, 131, 140–141, 186, 199, n.123
Solovki monastery 50, 160–165, 172, n.64–n.65, n.257
Ss. Sergius and Herman 50, 59, 60, 172, 187, n.252
SS. Zosimus and Sabbatius 50, n.40, 168
St. Adrian of Andrusov 50, 58, 66, 132, 167, n.44, n.194
St. Aleksander of Svir 50, 60, n.41
St. Alexis 171
St. Arsenius of Konevits 50, 58, 182, n.42
St. Blaise 50, 65, 104, 128–129, 131, 133, 176, n.123
St. George 16, 50, 62, 65–66, 68, 119, 126, 128–133, 146, 197, n.38, n.189, n.192
St. Nicholas 41, 50, 63, 65–66, 118, 121, 131, 166, 168, 176, 178, 180, 199, n.43
Stroitsa (monastery) – See Monastery of the Holy Trinity
Stroitsa (holy day) – See Whitsuntide
summer – see seasonal rites

supernatural motifs (linked to monasteries) 58, 167, 170, 182
supernatural punishment 40, 41, 49, 52–53, 79–81, 116, 164–167, 177–182
syncretism 14, 131, 133, 197, n.4
synty 81–83, 87–88, n.104

taboo 31, 45, 120, 122–123, 153, 177, 183, n.158
tietäjä 7, 19, 42–46, 65, 67, 77–79, 81–99, 108–109, 113, 115, 117, 137, 178, 181, 187, n.7, n.104
trees 13, 48–49, 52, 64, 78, 85, 95, 103, 114–117, 120, 123, 129, 137, 147–148
truce with wilderness 119–124, n.171
tšasouna 12–13, 15, 28, 31, 33–36, 38–39, 41–42, 46–47, 50, 54, 58, 61–63, 65, 68, 79–80, 95–96, 107, 117–119, 124, 143, 146, 148, 158–160, 163, 166, 177, 178–183, 189, 195–196, n.12, n.43, n.78, n.104, n.239

Valamo monastery 50, 55–56, 59–60, 158–160, 162–163, 171, 176–177, 187, 189–190, n.41, n.43, n.252
village chapel – see tšasouna
village festival – see praasniekka
water spirit 12–13, 39, 50, 60, 66, 68, 79, 98, 116, 126–127, 132, 135
Whitsuntide 63–64, 79–80, 120, 141, 199, n.87, n.102
wind spirits 13, 51
winter – see seasonal rites
Virgin Mary 16, 31–32, 46, 50, 52, 57, 63, 65, 126, 128, 130, 133, 163, 178, 180, 197, 199, n.83
wolf 118, 130
vow – see jeäksintä
väki–force 15, 42–50, 82, 87, 101–102, 107–108, 110, 120, 123, 125, 183, 192, n.31, n.130

www.ingramcontent.com/pod-product-compliance
Lightning Source LLC
Chambersburg PA
CBHW081738270326
41932CB00020B/3317